Such teaching as Mary Lutyens had came from governesses and a few years at Queen's College, Harley Street, London. But her real education began when, in 1923 at fourteen, her most unconventional mother took her to India and Australia and plunged her into a very different world. Her first novel was published, with great success, when she was twenty-four. She married conventionally, but without much happiness, and had a daughter. Later she added serial and short story writing to the novels she continued to produce and, in 1945, made a second marriage which has, together with her family, remained the central feature of her life.

Mary Lutyens has achieved a second career as a biographer, having published many works of non-fiction, all based on original sources. In 1967 she was made a Fellow of the Royal Society of Literature. She lives in London and has travelled extensively, most frequently to Venice, on which her husband, J.G. Links, wrote a well-known guide. Her most recent publication is *The Life and Death of Krishnamurti* (1990).

Also by Mary Lutyens

TO BE YOUNG

and published by Corgi Books

EDWIN LUTYENS

by his daughter

MARY LUTYENS

BLACK SWAN

EDWIN LUTYENS
A BLACK SWAN BOOK 0 552 99417 0

Originally published in Great Britain by John Murray (Publishers) Ltd

PRINTING HISTORY
John Murray edition published 1980
Black Swan edition with minor revisions published 1991

The cover shows a preliminary sketch design for the east front of the
Viceroy's House, New Delhi, dated September 1912. Artist unknown.
Reproduced by permission of the British Architectural Library, RIBA,
London.

This book is set in 11/13 Erhardt
by Falcon Typographic Art Ltd

Black Swan Books are published by Transworld Publishers Ltd.,
61-63 Uxbridge Road, Ealing, London W5 5SA, in Australia by
Transworld Publishers (Australia) Pty Ltd, 15-23 Helles Avenue,
Moorebank, NSW 2170, and in New Zealand by Transworld Publishers
(NZ) Ltd, Cnr Moselle and Waipareira Avenues, Henderson, Auckland.

Made and printed in Great Britain by
Cox & Wyman Ltd, Reading, Berks.

Contents

Preface

I have long wanted to write a memoir of my father but was hesitant because of my ignorance of the technicalities of architecture. Now, however, that his architecture has become the subject of so much expert study, I feel free to write an account of his personal life without making any attempt at a critical appraisal of his work.

Apart from my recollections, this book is based on my parents' letters to each other, some 2,500 of his and 2,000 of hers. My father was a wonderful letter-writer – or so it seems to me. A shy, inarticulate man, hiding his shyness behind a barrage of quips, jokes and witty drawings, it was only in his letters to my mother that he revealed the true sensitivity and seriousness of his nature.

Almost all my parents' letters are now in the Library of the Royal Institute of British Architects on indefinite loan from Lady Richard Percy (formerly the Hon. Mrs Clayre Ridley). They have been expertly catalogued by Mrs Angela Mace to whom I am profoundly grateful, and I should also like to thank David Dean, the Librarian, for his courtesy.

Most of my father's letters were available to Christopher Hussey for his definitive life of my father, published by *Country Life* in 1950, and I wish to acknowledge the immense help that book has been to me. Quotations from correspondence between my father and Herbert Baker come from this source and are published here with the permission of *Country Life*. Three other books I have drawn on are *A Blessed Girl* by my mother (Hart-Davis 1953), an exchange of letters between her and the Rev. Whitwell Elwin; her autobiography,

7

Candles in the Sun (Hart-Davis 1957) and my own account of my childhood and youth, *To Be Young* (Hart-Davis 1959).

I wish to thank Nigel Nicolson for his permission to quote Lady Sackville's letters and diaries and for so kindly lending me transcripts of the diaries and sketches by my father. My thanks are also due to the following for their help: Charles Lutyens, Mrs Margaret Richardson, Mrs Betty Massingham, the Rev. Herbert Ward, Mrs Susan Mary Alsop, Gavin Stamp, Richard Gilbert Scott, Sir Rupert Hart-Davis, Mrs Margaret Boyce, Mrs Margery Shoosmith and Nicholas Taylor.

I have retained my father's punctuation and spelling in his letters but have written out his abbreviations in full and altered his paragraphing since he was apt to make every sentence a new paragraph.

CHAPTER ONE

The Beginnings
1869–1887

Edwin Landseer Lutyens was born on 29 March 1869, at 16 Onslow Square, London, one of thirteen children – ten boys and three girls. He was the tenth child and ninth boy.

The Lutyens family can be traced back to Nicolaus Lütkens, a barber by profession, probably of Dutch origin, who, on 14 November 1706, became a citizen of the free city of Hamburg. On that same day in 1706 he married Catherine Segers. Their son, Barthold, was born in 1713. Barthold came to England in his twenties and in August 1740 married Ann, daughter of Clement Bohem, at St Antholin's church in the City. In December of that year he was naturalized a British subject, changing his name to Bartholomew Christopher Lutyens (the Lut rhymes with hut). He worked in a shipping company which traded with the East India Company.

The only son of Bartholomew and Ann, Nicholas (1742–95), became a successful West India merchant. In 1769 he married an heiress possessed of £2,000, Mary, daughter of Daniel Mesman, a silk weaver of Spital Square. As well as a house in London, Nicholas acquired a house at Broxbourne, Hertfordshire, from where he hunted regularly. They had fourteen children, four girls and ten boys. One boy and a girl died young.

Four of the sons entered the army. The youngest, Englebert (1784–1830), served throughout the Peninsular War in the XXth Regiment of Foot, becoming a Captain in 1813. In 1820 his regiment was stationed on St Helena and on 10 February that year he was appointed Orderly Officer and intermediary between Napoleon's Court at Longwood and the Military Governor, Sir Hudson Lowe, at Plantation House. Englebert resigned the appointment on 15 April 1821, as the result of an unfortunate incident: Napoleon wished to present to the library of Englebert's regiment his three-volume life of Marlborough by Coxe; he therefore sent the books to Englebert's apartment at Longwood so that he might take them to his regiment. The books had first to be shown to Sir Hudson Lowe who objected to the gift on the grounds that the first volume bore the inscription 'L'Empereur', though not in Napoleon's writing. Napoleon was forbidden to use the imperial title, so Englebert was ordered to give the books back. This he refused to do, considering it to be an unnecessary insult to the dying man. Sir Hudson Lowe sent them back himself.

As children we were told that Englebert was on duty the night after the post-mortem on Napoleon, guarding his remains, when waking from a doze he was just in time to stop a rat from making off with Napoleon's heart. We were as proud of this romantically intimate connection with the very heart of Napoleon as we were ashamed, being royalists, of our direct descent in the female line on our mother's side from Oliver Cromwell through his youngest daughter Frances. Alas, I was to discover that the story of Englebert's vigil was a myth. He had left Longwood and returned in disgrace to the military camp on the island three weeks before Napoleon's death on 5 May 1821, but at any rate one can be proud of him for refusing to give back the books. On 26 May Count Monthalon sent him a pair of pistols at the request of Napoleon with a message commending his conduct during the fourteen months he had been at Longwood, and Countess Bertrand sent him a coral brooch and a lock of Napoleon's hair.[1] The matter of the books was eventually brought before the Commander-in-Chief, the Duke of York, in England; Englebert was exonerated, promoted to the rank of Brevet Major and given £500 compensation. He never married. He died of a liver complaint on his way back from India where he had gone with his regiment.

Englebert's elder brother Charles, the second son of Nicholas and Ann Lutyens, born in 1773, was the grandfather of Edwin Lutyens. He had a very distinguished career as Deputy-Commissary-General of the Army. A great deal is known about his professional life from his military reminiscences which have been preserved in the family – a leather-bound folio volume of over two hundred closely written foolscap pages in his own hand. Stuck into the volume are twenty water-colour drawings illustrating incidents in his story by the artist A. Shaw who exhibited at the Royal Academy between 1829 and 1837. Although Charles was called General Lutyens he never made claim to any military rank. True, he wore uniform and was empowered to give orders to officers, but he was never a combatant officer, the Commissariat in those days coming under the Treasury. He was Commissariat Officer in the field throughout Sir John Moore's 1808–9 campaign in the Peninsular War, serving under Sir David Baird for whom he had a profound admiration. He suffered all the horrors of the famous retreat on Corunna, and on 16 January 1809, at the Battle of Corunna, he saw Sir John Moore killed by a cannon ball and his body

[1] These family relics have disappeared. A photograph of the pistols appears in a book published in 1915, *Letters of Captain Englebert Lutyens*, edited by Sir Lees Knowles. The original letters are in the British Library (Additional MSS 20211). After Napoleon's death his copy of Coxe's life of Marlborough went to the XXth Regiment of Foot (afterwards the Royal Fusiliers).

carried away in an army blanket. In the same battle he also saw Sir David Baird's arm shot off at the socket. He mentions a Captain Lutyens saving the life of a Spanish boy during the retreat. This must have been his brother Englebert because the boy was sent back to England with Englebert's regiment. All this is told in the second half of Charles's detailed reminiscences, probably a unique record of the part played by the Commissariat in the Peninsular War.

The first half of the memoir records Charles's experiences in Copenhagen when he was sent there to settle the Danish claim for compensation for the damage done by the British Army in the bombardment of that city. In 1808 the British had asked neutral Denmark to surrender their fleet for fear it should fall into the hands of the French. When the Danes refused, the British bombarded Copenhagen, destroying a great part of it. Charles had nothing but sympathy for the Danes, yet so unpopular were the British that when he arrived in Copenhagen to pay the compensation he was nearly murdered and narrowly avoided being put in prison. His wife, Charlotte, who had gone with him, *was* imprisoned with their children and only managed to escape through the intervention of her father, the Hanoverian General de Wangenheim.

A large portrait of de Wangenheim was in due course inherited by my father and hung in our hall. It shows a stout, happy-looking gentleman in a white wig and scarlet coat with ruffles, holding his cocked hat while standing on a hill and pointing to a burning city in the distance. It was known in the family as a portrait of 'one of our ancestors watching the burning of Sodom and Gomorrah'. I believed this for years. As a matter of fact de Wangenheim was not an ancestor of ours. Charles had two sons and a daughter by Charlotte but they all died unmarried in their twenties. The younger son, Augustus, an officer in the Hanoverian Guard Hussars, while on holiday in Greece in 1828, joined in a skirmish with the Greek patriots against the Turks on the island of Scio (Chios) and was killed.

Charlotte, whom Charles had married in Hamelin in 1795, died in 1813. Four years later Charles married a Miss Mary Jones of Broxbourne, twenty years his junior, who died eighteen months later in childbirth. The baby also died. Charles's third marriage was in May 1824 to Frances Jane Fludger of Pangbourne about whom nothing is known except her rather handsome appearance from a portrait. They had two sons and two daughters. Although vigorously condemning venality in his reminiscences and no doubt honest by the standards of his day, Charles must have made a considerable fortune out of his profession or else acquired wealth with one of his wives, for after his retirement he was able to live in great style at Southcote House,[1] a fifteenth-century moated manor with forty bedrooms, situated in the valley of the Kennet, three and a half miles from the centre of Reading. He won a reputation for open hospitality and as a fearless rider to hounds. His reminiscences show him to have been a man of deep compassion, especially when describing the retreat on Corunna. He died at Southcote House in December 1848, aged seventy-five.

Charles's elder son by Frances Fludger, Charles Henry Augustus, was Edwin Lutyens's father. He was born at Southcote House on 15 January 1829, and educated at a private day school in Hammersmith which necessitated a daily double journey by coach. It was natural for him to take up an army career. The intention was that he should go to Woolwich

[1] Southcote Manor, as it was afterwards called, fell into decay and was demolished in 1926. A block of flats has been built on the site but the empty, grass-grown moat is still there. The house was originally a monastery and later a stronghold of the Roundheads.

and join the Royal Artillery but when it was found that there was no vacancy his father bought for him in 1848, shortly before his own death, a commission in the XXth Regiment of Foot, the regiment in which Englebert had served. The regiment was immediately sent to Canada. On arrival in Montreal the officers discovered that the military pack of hounds which the garrison had owned since 1826 had been advertised to be sold in New York. They at once lodged an objection and took over the hounds, horses, cottage, kennel buildings and a field. The name of Charles Lutyens is recorded in the Club House of the Montreal Hunt as being Master from 1851–2. Like many artillery officers and engineers in those days Charles had been trained in draughtsmanship but he showed unusual talent as can be seen by his water-colour drawings of Niagara Falls and other places in Canada. Several of his pictures still hang in the Club House at Montreal.

On 24 November 1852, when Charles was twenty-three, he married in Montreal a nineteen-year-old Irish girl, Mary Theresa Gallwey, an orphan who was staying with her brother, Thomas Gallwey of the Royal Engineers, Governor of Montreal.[1] Mary's family came from Killarney. Her father, John Gallwey, a major in the Royal Irish Constabulary, had in 1819 married an Irish beauty, known as 'Biddy the Beautiful', the daughter of a man with the felicitous name of Neptune Blood. Biddy had died in 1836 at the age of only thirty-six. John Gallwey had married again in 1840 and died four years later.

A first cousin of Mary's, Peter Gallwey, was a distinguished Jesuit priest who founded the College of St Francis Xavier in Liverpool. Mary had been brought up in a convent and being of a saintly disposition had made up her mind to

[1] Thomas Gallwey (1821–1906) became a Lieutenant-General. He was Governor and Commander-in-Chief in Bermuda from 1882–8, and created a KCMG in 1889.

become a nun when an incident occurred which destroyed her faith in the Roman Catholic Church. The cause of her disillusionment, as told to us by my father – and I have never heard it contradicted – was that the girls in the convent were encouraged to write notes to the Virgin Mary and leave them on the altar of the chapel, where, they were assured, the Virgin herself came to collect them. One day Mary discovered that the notes were really taken away by the nuns. As a result of this she left the convent and became a devout Evangelical Protestant, much to the disappointment of Father Peter Gallwey.

Since Mary was, from all accounts, beautiful and must have been much in demand in Montreal where there were as yet comparatively few women, one can assume that Charles had great charm as well as good looks. He was very tall with the exceptionally long legs characteristic of the Lutyens side of the family. It seems too that although a very junior officer he must have been considered eligible, for no objection was made to the marriage by Thomas Gallwey.

At the end of 1852 the Lutyenses returned to England with his regiment. Two years later the regiment was ordered to the Crimea, but to Charles's great disappointment he was somehow delayed in Malta and did not reach the Crimea until September 1855 when the war was over. He remained there for some months with the army of occupation – months in which he made dozens of drawings of Sebastopol and the country round about it.

On his return to England in 1856 Charles was one of the first officers to pass through the newly founded Army School of Musketry at Hythe and later at Aldershot. Up till 1857 musketry practice was carried out in full dress. A story was related of Charles, in his regimental magazine after his death, that one day while he was carrying out his duties as an instructor, dressed up in scarlet tunic, shako and sword, the local hunt happened to pass by. Unable to resist the temptation he sprang on to his horse and joined in the chase.

In 1857 Charles invented a reflecting instrument for judging distances for long-range artillery. It was called a stadiometer and was used throughout the service for nearly forty years. In this same year, 1857, realising that he loved painting more than soldiering, he retired from the army with the rank of Captain in order to take up painting professionally in London. At first he had a house at 6 Palace Gate Terrace; then in 1864 he bought 16 Onslow Square which was his London home for the next forty years. On settling in London he went to study with Sir Edwin Landseer who became a close friend. Charles helped Landseer in the design for the Trafalgar Square lions, commissioned in 1859, though not put in place for eight years. The two artists worked on the lions in the studio of the successful sculptor, Baron Carlo Marochetti. Lutyens painted some animal pictures for Marochetti in 1869 for which he received £225 altogether. He obtained through Landseer commissions to paint the horses of Landseer's rich clients, including the Prince of Wales and the Duke of Westminster. He painted a dozen or more Derby winners. He would make a model of the animal in clay, from this a drawing and finally his oil painting.

From 1862 to 1903 Charles exhibited every year at the Royal Academy and was hung on the line. He never became an Academician, however. He was at the height of his artistic career in the seventies. According to his little red sales book he earned £525 in 1862, rising to £1,723 in 1873. By 1879 his earnings had dropped to £625. His last recorded sale was in 1903, a year in which he earned only £430. The price of his pictures varied between £20 and £30. He must also have had quite a large private income to start with, but this, as well as his earnings, seems to have dwindled, for by the Nineties he had become very poor.

Charles Lutyens claimed in later life to have rediscovered

16

what he called 'the Venetian secret' – an ancient formula for obtaining a particularly luminous shade of red used by the great Venetian masters. He offered to share this secret with members of the Academy and was bitterly hurt when they did not want to hear about it. He published a novel in 1893 entitled *The Venetian Secret* which does little to explain it. He told the secret to his son Frederick, who was also an artist, and at Frederick's death in 1924 the secret was lost. There is a dark, deep luminosity about some of the backgrounds of Charles's pictures that may well have been the result of 'the secret'. He continued to paint until his death in 1915 at the age of eighty-six. By that time he was almost blind and had to ask his daughter to pick out the colours for him. (There was an exhibition of his work at Eastbourne and Winchester in 1971.)

While still keeping on his house in Onslow Square, Charles bought a house on the Common at Thursley in Surrey in 1876. Called The Cottage it was in fact the largest house in the village (now called Street House). It had to be large in order to accommodate his huge family. Mary Lutyens produced fourteen children between 1853 and 1876. There was another addition to the family in 1880 when the first wife of the eldest son, Charles Benjamin, died in an accident leaving a baby daughter. Mary Lutyens immediately adopted this baby whose father was in Ceylon where he had started a coffee plantation. One year the whole of the coffee crop had to be dug up as a result of beetle in its roots. Charles Benjamin was obliged to borrow money from his father to replant the estate with tea. In return he made over half the estate to his father. Eventually this proved to be a very good investment but not until many years after his father's death. When Charles's only unmarried daughter died in 1926 she left me and my sister Elisabeth £1,000 each, derived from the tea: it soon went the way of the coffee.

17

Charles Benjamin married again and had four sons and a daughter.

The second son of Charles and Mary, John, became a Colonel in the Indian Army. He was a great friend of Rudyard Kipling who made him the human hero in the racing story, *The Maltese Cat*, owner of the equine hero. John married but had no children. The third son, Henry Lionel, died at six years old. Judging by a bronze of him by Marochetti he was an exceptionally beautiful little boy. My father told us that his mother often spoke of him, that he was called Daisy and that he had converted a Jew to Christianity before his death. True, he had called himself Daisy so perhaps the conversion story is also true.

The next son was still-born so he does not count. The fourth was Frederick (Fred), the sharer of 'the Venetian secret'. A professional artist, his pictures were at times indistinguishable from his father's. He used to hunt three times a week at Thursley from London. He published a sporting romance, *Mr Spinks and his Hounds*, jointly illustrated by himself and his father. He had four sons. Of Charles's fifth son, Graeme, there is no record, so presumably he died young. The sixth, Francis Augustus (Frank), married but had no children. He published a book called *Through the Post* and a volume of light verse, *Fables by Fal* (his initials), amusingly illustrated by himself with drawings of animals. The seventh son, Lionel, was an estate agent. He had two sons and a daughter; the eighth, Arthur, went to the Malay States as a coffee planter; he had two sons.

At last in 1868, after all these boys, came a girl, Mary, always called Molly. That she was beautiful is shown by a full-length portrait of her by her father as a young woman; she remained very good looking all her life. She married a rich man, Major George Wemyss. Adoring children, it was sad that she had none of her own. Under her married name she published two children's books and half a dozen delightful novels. The tenth child was Edwin Landseer, never called anything but Ned. Then came another daughter, Aileen (pronounced Eileen). She never married and remained at The Cottage taking care of her father after her mother's death in 1906.

William (Bill or Willie) was the twelfth child and youngest boy. He was a great runner; at Cambridge he won the mile against Oxford four years running, and in July 1898 he set up a new British record for the 1,000 yards which he held for thirty-one years. It was said of him after his death in 1950 that he was the greatest miler England had ever known. On leaving Cambridge he took Holy Orders, and in 1916, as a Cowley Father, he joined the Oratory of the Good Shepherd at Cambridge. He had a spiritual flock of Cambridge ladies who were deeply shocked when he married at the age of seventy. He was a very jolly character and a great joker with a distinct physical resemblance to his brother Ned. He told me that he had first been attracted to his wife because she was the life and soul of the party at a funeral. This remark is worthy of Ned who said to his youngest sister Margaret on her wedding day (she did not marry until her late fifties), 'Well, Margy, I expected to come to your funeral but never to your wedding.' This sister, the baby of the family, was in her early life a professional pianist and piano teacher. The Lutyens clan has now so multiplied that it is difficult to keep track of all the cousins.

We never knew any of my father's many brothers except Bill whom I, at any rate, knew well. He officiated at my first wedding and christened my daughter. He was the only one to survive Father. At intervals Father would put on a top hat and morning coat in the morning and our nannie would tell us that he had gone to the funeral of one of his brothers.

* * *

19

When Ned was born in 1869 Edwin Landseer had wanted to adopt him – at least that is what we were told – but his mother would not have parted with him to anyone, least of all to Landseer of whose morals she disapproved. For many years Landseer had been the acknowledged lover of Georgiana, Duchess of Bedford, by whom he was said to have had several children – a liaison which had kept him from marrying. He was, however, allowed to be the child's godfather, and Ned was given his name. We children always regretted our grandmother's decision over the adoption, believing that if it had been allowed some of the £200,000 that Landseer left would have come to us. But Ned would probably have fared very badly; Landseer was already an alcoholic by 1869 and died four years later.

We were brought up to believe that as a result of rheumatic fever as a small boy Ned was considered too delicate to go to school and shared his sisters' governesses (there was a resident French governess at one time) and was given some extra schooling in the holidays by his brother Fred who was nine years older. All the other boys went to public schools and most of them to Cambridge. In later years Ned several times expressed regrets to his wife that he had not been better educated and wished that he had had 'a wider range giving greater power of sympathy'. He also wished that his own son had gone to a public school, not so much that he might have had a better education as that he might have got to know his peers and feel at ease with them, an advantage which he himself felt the lack of; he had often offended male clients, he said, by not knowing how to talk to them. Yet he told his children that he owed his success to never having been to school or university. Books certainly meant very little to him. Osbert Sitwell quotes him as saying, 'Any talent I may have was due to a long illness as a boy, which afforded me time to think, and to subsequent ill-health, because I was not allowed to play games, and so had to teach myself, for my

20

enjoyment, to use my eyes instead of my feet. My brothers hadn't the same advantage.'[1]

I now find from a letter, written in August 1911, that he did go to school. This letter was written after seeing the rather bad school reports of his two eldest children, then aged thirteen and ten: 'I boil up with resentment at the cruelty of all modern systems of education – It makes me realise how I loathed the 2 years I was at school and the dullness of them and the blind apathetic – injustice – and the dead levels (for the masters' conveniences – then I was at *very* bad schools) of the layered classes – and the pupils are mere salmon as they are in a Canadian river that are caught to be canned for the catchers benefit.' I have no idea when these two years of schooling took place, but I feel sure it was only day schools he went to in London. It is certain that he never went to a public school.

Ned's sister, Molly, only a year older than Ned, has described their childhood in two little books, *All About All of Us* and *Things We Thought of*, published by Constable in 1911. We used to love them as children and I still read them with delight. The first book is very thinly disguised as fiction and is the only record in existence of Ned's childhood. Ned is called Peter in this book and the other children are also given pseudonyms except for Fred and Aileen who appear under their own names. The devoted nannie, who came to the Lutyenses in 1854 and stayed until her death nearly sixty years later, also appears under her real name of Priscilla. On the cover of *All About All of Us* is a coloured reproduction of Aileen on the family donkey from a portrait by her father, and on the cover of *Things We Thought of* is a coloured reproduction of Molly on a horse, also from a portrait by Charles.

Molly tells her story in the first person, purporting to be nine years old. According to her they spent half their time

[1] *The Scarlet Tree*, p. 266 (1946).

21

in London and half in the country. 'Mother took the Cottage [at Thursley] as a surprise for us,' she wrote. 'I knew but the others didn't. She calls it the Cottage, only it's really a house. She loves it and sits on the lawn and sighs and says, "How delicious".' This tells us that it was Mrs Lutyens's idea to have a country house and that it was acquired in the Seventies when Charles Lutyens's career was at its peak. (Postal guides confirm this.) It had a large garden with a sloping lawn, a vegetable garden and fruit trees. Peter (Ned) 'built lovely railways in the garden'. When Molly tumbled into Waterloo Station and squashed the signal-box flat, Ned was not cross, but to make up she played 'mad bulls' with him, a game he loved. From the little village store, the only shop in Thursley, they bought sherbet for a penny which foamed in their mouths; then they roared and butted each other and stamped on the ground. At the beginning of all competitive games they would promise 'Bar prayers'. We too as children used to promise not to pray to win, so our father must have passed this on to us.

'Peter was old for his age [eight] because he had been ill.' He bought a fishing rod at that time out of his own money which was 'longer than the dining-room table'. His love of fishing remained with him, the only sport he ever indulged in. He also made boats from scooped-out pieces of wood which kept upright in the water. The family had two ponies, a donkey cart and a coachman. Ned was a very nervous rider (the family love of horses and hunting was not passed on to him). He often had 'nervous fits'; once when he found a spider in the bread at tea he 'had nervous fits for the rest of the evening, shaking his hands about and declaring that he could not walk upstairs'. On the other hand he was brave about putting the worm on the hook when fishing. Once, when their mother had neuralgia, Ned bought a bottle of scent from the village store and took it into her saying, 'Why should lovely woman suffer? I have brought you some eau de clore'. He poured it all over her head and 'she said it made her feel better though it did not smell very nice'. One day he walked all the way into Godalming to buy Nannie a vase. It had 'A present for a good boy' inscribed on it because he could not find one for 'a good woman'. 'Nannie said she would think of it as a present *from* a good boy which pleased him very much.'

In London Molly and Ned went collecting once for a children's Charity Home called the Bird's Nest. Molly did not manage to collect a penny whereas Ned came home with his tin full, so even at that age he must have had a winning way with him. It was in London that Ned got lost one day. 'Nannie ran all up Queen's Gate and all down Exhibition Road looking for him and he was holding her hand all the time. He *was* tired. Nannie had thought he was one of the others.'

Unfortunately Molly gives only very few glimpses of their mother. 'Aileen thinks Mother's hair is black but it isn't really.' 'Mother is lovely. She has a green dress with lace on it . . . "Listen, my darlings! When you see Mother talking to a visitor, you must sit quiet, like good little children, until he has gone." "But he wouldn't ever go if we sat quiet," Aileen said, and it's quite true. Mother's visitors don't ever want to go till we come. We must have our mother to ourselves sometimes.' When their mother wanted to hug the small children, which she often did, she would kneel down to open her arms to them so as to be on their level. Only once do we see her rather stern: the day the new pony arrived 'she said, "Charles!" in her clergyman's voice'.

Every morning the children would sit on their mother's bed and she would read them 'a chapter', presumably from the Bible. Sundays seem to have been rather a trial; there was Sunday School in London as well as church and they were not allowed to ride the rocking horse downstairs as on week days.

Molly reveals more about their father. He used to tell them lovely stories about animals. He bought the old pony who could go no faster than a walk in the pony cart because it was so thin and the gypsies had been unkind to it. One day Aileen and Bill, playing where they had been told not to play, knocked a large hole in one of his pictures. They hid behind the piano until eventually Bill confessed 'and Father only kissed them and said "Darlings, I know you will never do it again," and they didn't.' Molly describes another occasion when the older boys were 'seriously naughty'. 'They had been shooting with a bow and arrow which was very disobedient, and they had shot a hole through a picture, and they might have shot each other. So at bedtime father went upstairs with a whip, and he found the three boys kneeling down by the bed in their nighties, saying their prayers. Then father was moved with compassion and he didn't whip them, but he went out and bought them a piece of sugar-cane and some beautiful peaches. And the boys were very sorry they had been naughty. That was the only time father was going to punish them seriously.'

* * *

Apart from a deep affection for Molly and, to a lesser extent, Aileen, Ned seems to have cared very little for his siblings. During his childhood his father was often away staying in grand houses painting horses. In later years, with his soldierly bearing and long white beard, Captain Lutyens became a patriarchal figure in Thursley. A neighbour described how in middle-age 'he used to stalk into Thursley Church with his family, and while they knelt in prayer he stood erect and "smelt" his top hat – he was very Protestant. When a visiting parson once said something he disliked he marched down the aisle and banged the church door behind him. He had an old white pony on which he rode about, sometimes to Meets, though he had to ride very short to keep his feet off the ground'. It was also said of him that he learnt to play the fiddle in order to employ a destitute Belgian violin teacher.

It is probable that Charles Lutyens did not at first fully appreciate his nervous, delicate son who was frightened of horses, nor does Ned seem to have been particularly fond of his father. The boy's delicacy accentuated his bond with his mother. While inheriting his father's long legs, it was from his mother that he derived his Irish colouring, his very blue eyes and almost black curly hair. His mother remained throughout his life his ideal of womanhood. When he told his wife-to-be that he was the only child of a widow, he no doubt wished it were true. Although he believed himself to be her favourite he could not have received from her all the attention he craved. He used to tell us after her death that he was bound to go to heaven because she was sure to be there, being a saint, and it would not be heaven for her without him. He felt no need, however, to emulate her piety; he reacted against the religious observances of his youth; in all the years I knew him he never went to church, even on Christmas Day, except for weddings, funerals and christenings, or unless it was a church of his own designing.

One of the things Ned greatly admired about his mother was her nails which, he said, fitted over her fingers like the skin of an almond. His own nails fitted like almond skins, but since he never cleaned them there was a permanent black ridge under them compounded of lead pencil, tobacco and newsprint. When he filled in a crossword clue wrongly (he was to become a *Times* crossword addict) he would use his fingers to smudge out the soft-pencilled letters.

I can believe that my father was a very happy child, especially in the term time in the country when his boisterous brothers were at school. (He told us how once one of his brothers threatened to unscrew his navel with a screwdriver so that his legs would drop off.) I have enough of him in me to know the joy of wandering by myself as a child through woods and along lanes for hours on end 'imagining' and never being bored. His imaginings would, of course, have been very different from mine but the mood of creation would, I think, have been the same except that quite early on he felt the need to give outward expression to his imaginings. His gift for drawing was as natural to him as perfect pitch is to some people. He would begin his enchanting sketches – always witty, sometimes rude in a schoolboyish way – anywhere on the page and one could see from his smile that he was clearly seeing them on the blank paper. At first the isolated lines gave one no idea of what the finished picture was to be. He often started with two or three ovals side by side which might turn into anything.

As a boy Ned roamed the Surrey countryside looking at old buildings or watching new ones going up. On wet days he would spend his time at Tickner's, the village carpenter's shop, or he would go to the local builder's yard at Godalming where he was always welcome to stand and watch what was going on. He was intensely inquisitive about the few things that really interested him, and he had a remarkably quick eye and a phenomenal memory for detail. From old Tickner he learnt the ways of wood and how to recognise when the oak was ready for felling by the taste of the acorn.

It has been said of him that he was 'a natural mathematician'; this seems to imply that he never had to learn mathematics any more than he had to learn to draw, but I think he must have learnt a good deal from Fred or from those two years at school, for he was familiar with the differential calculus, which surely has to be taught? It would be more accurate to say that he had a natural *gift* for mathematics. He must also have learnt some Latin since he frequently uses Latin tags in his letters.

A Thursley neighbour, Randolph Caldecott, whose illustrations for children's books with their farms and cottages and country inns were still extremely popular throughout my childhood, is said to have inspired Ned to turn his creative gift to architecture. I believe it is far more likely that he *had* to become an architect – one cannot think of any other art at which he would have excelled. It was the natural outcome of his talents for mathematics, drawing and observation, combined with his extraordinary visual memory. These gifts he may have inherited. That he also had a creative imagination of genius is one of those genetic freaks that cannot be analysed or explained. Fortunately for him he had no great versatility, the curse of so many artists, and no real interests outside his creative work.

Ned in the course of his wanderings was able to observe every detail of the building process from digging the foundations, putting in the drains, tiling the roof and putting up the chimney stacks. For this reason he always got on wonderfully well in his practice with the men who were actually carrying out his designs. Knowing that he loved and thoroughly understood their different crafts, they gave of their best to him. There is in his houses this atmosphere of love for the materials with which they are constructed. In his country houses he always used the local brick or stone. He believed that houses and villages should disappear into their backgrounds, unless, of course, they had to be built on the top of a hill, or, as grand mansions, at the end of an avenue. But Surrey cottages were his first love, cottages that nestled and fitted the lives of those who lived in them and fitted also the English climate and landscape. His windows were small, with small leaded panes, because he believed that a house was for protection. A large window gave the occupier a sense of insecurity; an enemy might creep up and look in and take him unawares. He detested 'picture windows' as much as steel window frames; and it is noteworthy that the first thing the owner of a picture window does is to get it covered by a blind or net curtain. In London he loved Portland stone and the

27

beautiful soft soot-shadows thrown on it after many years by the prevailing wind.

Ned as a boy devised his own means of teaching himself perspective and accuracy. He would carry about with him in his wanderings a small pane of clear glass and several pieces of soap sharpened to fine points. Looking through the glass at some detail of a building he wanted to learn about he would trace it with the soap. The glass, cleaned with a damp rag, could be used for innumerable sketches. It was his form of *camera obscura*. The only drawback to this method was that he left behind so few sketch-books; indeed, only five small sketch-books of his have so far come to light.

* * *

By the age of fifteen it had become obvious to Ned's father as well as to Ned himself what his profession was to be. Early the following year, 1885, before his sixteenth birthday in March, he was sent to the South Kensington School of Art (now the Royal College of Art) to study architecture. His first letter to his mother after starting at the school was ten pages long, written from Onslow Square. It is undated except for 'Tuesday', begins 'My darling Mother' and ends 'Your very loving son, E. L. Lutyens'. It contains one most revealing passage:

> Read the following extract to father it is from the Surrey Archeological Society's paper. Speaking of Sutton Place, Guildford, 'The whole house is built of brick and terra cotta no stone whatever being used in its construction or ornamentation.' When I came home from my first excursion to Sutton I told father it was built of terra cotta and brick which he flatly contradicted and said that it was impossible terra cotta being used for building purposes then, and that it was fine sandstone. Not that I bring any accusation against father but only to show him,

28

what a small amount of confidence I have, in the little that I know, to allow myself to be convicted [convinced?] of a thing which I knew was wrong and that it only shows how necessary it is for me to concentrate my whole attention, energy and time in possessing that confidence and also obtain that great amount of knowledge required to help make a 'successful architect', and an architect without that success (not financial necessarily) is, well I can't describe it.

The letter ends in bathos: 'Does Arthur come up next Sunday we shall have to share our top hat again. My billycock handed down from Frank [six years older] has a hole in the top, it was there when I had it.' All Ned's clothes were passed down from one or other of his brothers. The legs of the trousers, he told us, used simply to be cut off at the bottom so that the fork came somewhere near his knees.

An undated, unpunctuated letter to his sister Molly which, from other references, can be placed in the early part of 1886 is the only written record by Ned of his progress at the Art School: 'I have to pass examination in Perspective in about fortnight's time ought to pass easily does not matter if I don't.' But there exists in the Drawings Collection of the Royal Institute of British Architects a portfolio containing drawings of his work while at the School. Of particular interest is a drawing of the elevation of a country house which won him at eighteen the National Bronze Medal.

He did not finish the course. He believed after two years that he had learnt all it had to teach him.[1] Some time in 1887, after his eighteenth birthday, he became a paying apprentice in the office of Ernest George, one of the most

---

[1] It might be thought that these were the two years he had so 'loathed' at school if he had not added in his letter of 1911 that he had been at '*very* bad schools'.

popular architects of the day. Ned was no admirer of Ernest George; his heroes at that time were Norman Shaw, Philip Webb and William Morris. The senior assistant in George's office was Herbert Baker, seven years older than Ned. Baker had been captain of cricket and football at his public school, Tonbridge; he revered the public school ethic of team spirit, was a Christian idealist and a great reader of poetry. He always carried a volume of Wordsworth in his pocket. In spite of the difference in age, upbringing and temperament he and Ned became friends. In the autumn of 1888 they went on a walking tour together in Wales which was a great success.

Baker records in his memoirs that Lutyens did little work in the office; he watched and criticised the work of the others and joked his way through the six months he remained there. 'He puzzled us at first, but we soon found that he seemed to know by intuition some great truths of our art which were not to be learned there.'[1]

Ernest George was a great believer in sketch-books which Ned despised, relying on his wonderfully retentive memory. Years later he would recall 'a distinguished architect who took each year a three weeks holiday abroad and returned with overflowing sketch books. When called on for a project he would look through these and choose some picturesque turret or gable from Holland, France or Spain and round it weave his new design.'

While he was in Ernest George's office Ned worked at night on his own designs in his bedroom at Onslow Square which, he said, he had 'fitted up with Dutch shutters and an over-sized and overhanging fireplace'. He was now itching to set up in practice on his own. He would not have to wait long.

[1] *Architecture and Personalities*, p. 15 (1944).

CHAPTER TWO

Webbs, Jekylls and Emily
1888–1897

A strong and beneficial influence on Ned Lutyens at this time was Barbara Webb, a Surrey neighbour, wife of Robert Webb, Lord of the Manor of Milford, Witley and Thursley, who lived in the beautiful little pink Georgian manor-house at Milford, now a hotel-restaurant, between Godalming and Milford. Barbara was a much younger sister of Sir Alfred Lyall who had been Foreign Secretary to the Government of India from 1878–81 when Lord Lytton was Viceroy. She had stayed with her brother in India from 1879 before she married and had made great friends with the Lyttons, a friendship which was kept up after their return from India. From a photograph I have of her when she first went to India, aged thirty-four (she married late), she can be described as *jolie laide*. She evidently possessed great charm since Lord Lytton, a connoisseur of women, became very devoted to her. She was one of the few women in India who was lively and amusing without being fast.

Having no children of her own, Barbara Webb took a special interest in Ned who was twenty-four years younger than her. She was probably the first person to recognise his genius; she encouraged his ambition and understood that his flippant manner was a mask to hide his lack of confidence in the presence of strangers. She gave him a standing invitation to Milford, both because she enjoyed his company and because she felt that he should meet as many people as possible in order to overcome his shyness. She had a very wide circle of friends. He, on his side, gradually transferred to her some of the worship he felt for his mother. He called her his 'blessed Barbara', his 'Baa Lamb', and devised a symbol when writing to her of a woolly lamb with a halo. It is quite possible that he was a little in love with her.

Ned's visits to Milford House were his first introduction to the ways of a conservative country gentleman of means, for although his own father was a gentleman he was also a Bohemian and an eccentric. Moreover, by the time Ned entered Ernest George's office, Charles Lutyens's income from horse-portraiture had fallen off; he had begun to go blind and had difficulty in keeping up his two establishments. He began to practise strange economies, using newspapers for the table cloths and mending his own boots. Meat was banished from the house and the family were not allowed to use more than one plate for all courses. Moreover, he had odd habits such as soaking roast potatoes in tea to soften them. The house became very untidy. When visitors came, the clutter was kicked under the flounced cover of the sofa. These signs of poverty and disorder disturbed Ned profoundly. His aesthetic sense as well as his sense of order – he had a very tidy mind – was outraged. When he had a home of his own he never allowed a loose cover on a sofa or arm-chair. All his life he was terrified of ending up in the same circumstances as his father. The contrast between the orderliness of Milford House and the chaos of The Cottage at Thursley was such that he visited the Webbs as often as possible when he was in the country.

It may have been through either Barbara Webb or his own family that Ned obtained his first important commission. In the spring of 1889, when he was barely twenty, he was asked by a friend of both, Mr Arthur Chapman, to build a nine-bedroom house for him at Crooksbury near Farnham. Charles Lutyens had painted a portrait of Mr Chapman's wife, Agnes, a sister of Harry Mangles of Littleworth, the well known rhododendron grower. Arthur Chapman had been a partner for many years in the export-import house of Pigott, Chapman & Co in Calcutta. He had just retired and wanted to settle in the country near his brother-in-law. By the time Ned received the commission from him he knew him well enough to be dining with him and his wife every Friday in London.

On the strength of the signing of the Crooksbury contract and a legacy of £100 from Sir Edwin Landseer's sister, who had inherited the bulk of her brother's fortune, Ned decided to waste no more of his father's money. While continuing to sleep at Onslow Square he took two white-panelled rooms for an office at No 6 Gray's Inn Square and put up his name on a brass plate outside the street door. He started with only one very old assistant called Barlow who had been a builder. Ned was so nervous while Crooksbury was being built that he owned afterwards that he had only dared visit the site after the workmen had gone home.

Lutyens's practice gradually grew. During the next few years he went to no parties and saw no one in London apart from family and clients, and often worked until two o'clock in the morning. He made a habit of designing something every day whether it was ever to be used or not. There are no records of those years except for what he himself recalled. In an address to the Cambridge Architectural Society in 1932 he told of one experience at this time – what he called 'a great personal adventure':

Staying at a house I met my hostess's father who, as a sapper in India, was told off to build barracks. His design, probably like those pre-Mutiny buildings of which

33

we should be proud, had been turned down, and a typed set of plans of bungalow style sent to him to erect. These he had criticised as being ungentlemanlike, refused to build them, and resigned.

When I met him he was 80 years old and blind. At dinner he told me that since he had been blind he had designed two buildings, a Cathedral and an Opera House. I asked him what they were like. He said he could not see to draw and had found no one who would draw them for him. I volunteered my services.

His lady wife, overhearing our conversation, shook her head, tapping her forehead with her forefinger. I said 'May I draw?' and directly after dinner the table was cleared and, with plenty of squared paper, we began. He warned me that the Opera House was eliptical and the Cathedral rectangular. I have always regretted that I chose the rectangular building as being the easier to draw. I began to his dictation. He dictated rather quicker than I could draw. I made some mistakes, but my dictator being blind seemed to make my errors of small account, and on I went.

It was nearer two than one o'clock when his old wife came down in her dressing gown, to scold us as naughty children who ought to be in bed. Looking over my shoulder at my rough plan, section and elevation, she said, 'Oh! but it is *beautiful*!' and the old man's blind face lit up as though all sorrows were of the past.

Lutyens was to recommend to his students in later years that they should try dictating a design in figures from memory: 'It entails much thought and accurate statement of fact and there is no danger of being run away with crosscountry by a soft-nosed pencil.'

*   *   *

In the same year as Ned received the Crooksbury commission, 1889, he met the woman who, of all others, was to have most influence on his career – Miss Gertrude Jekyll. They were introduced by Harry Mangles, Mrs Chapman's brother, for whom Ned was building a gardener's cottage. Gertrude Jekyll had been born in 1843, so she was twenty-six years older than Ned. She was living at this time with her widowed mother and her younger brother, Colonel Herbert Jekyll, and his wife at Munstead, near Godalming, a large comfortable house built by her father in the late Seventies; but she was looking forward to building a house of her own for which she had already planned and partly planted the garden.

Colonel Jekyll had in 1881 married Agnes, the youngest daughter of the nine children of William Graham, for many years MP for Glasgow, a most generous patron of the Pre-Raphaelites. He was also a collector of Italian primitives. Agnes Jekyll was a very cultivated woman, widely read; she had travelled much with her father, had a host of friends and a house in London as well as Munstead. She had inherited part of her father's collection, including some superb Burne-Jones tapestries. She had a great gift for making a home, and served the most delicious imaginative food. She published many articles on cookery and one book, *Kitchen Essays*. In 1918 she was made a Dame.

Ned came to know Herbert and Aggie Jekyll well through Gertrude, and spent many happy week-ends with them. Aggie Jekyll was my godmother and since I stayed several times at Munstead House I can understand why my father enjoyed going there so much. It was the apogee of opulent comfort and order without grandeur, smelling of pot-pourri, furniture polish and wood smoke. As well as the perfect food there were always the latest books laid out on a long stool in front of the fireplace. The lavatory bowls were of flowered blue china with wide mahogany surrounds; the Bromo paper, on

35

a large porcelain plate, was splayed into a fan (this was done by twisting it with the heel of the hand); the brass jugs for the hot water shone like gold. There seemed to be dozens of servants, yet the atmosphere was informal, homely; one felt at ease; it was almost impossible to be shy when staying there. Lady Jekyll (Herbert was knighted in 1901), as I remember her, was very plump, with beautifully dressed white hair and a soft pink face.

Although Ned became very fond of Aggie and Herbert Jekyll, Gertrude was the real draw for him at Munstead. This extraordinary woman was described in her youth as 'a young lady of singular and remarkable accomplishments – carving, modelling, house-painting, carpentry, smith's work, repoussé work, gilding, wood-inlaying, embroidery, gardening, and all manner of herb and flower knowledge'.[1] She was also a water-colour artist, a good writer and an excellent photographer, illustrating all her books with her own photographs. She had been at the Kensington School of Art, had travelled in Italy and Greece, and been a friend of Hercules Brabazon and Ruskin. She had always been short-sighted but by the time Ned got to know her, her eyesight had so deteriorated that she had been obliged to give up painting, her greatest love. Gardening and garden design then became her passion. She was still able to make very beautiful pictures out of shells (we had two of them at home), and she could still write and take photographs.

Miss Jekyll was short and stumpy. Ned called her Bumps, 'the mother of all the bulbs', and we always knew her as Aunt Bumps. With her small steel-rimmed spectacles and thin grey hair screwed back into a tight bun she looked intimidating. I was always in great awe of her. William Nicholson's portrait of her at the National Portrait Gallery, painted in 1920, is a breathing likeness.

[1] *Our River* by G. D. Leslie (1888).

Miss Jekyll and Ned drove round the Surrey countryside together in her pony cart looking at old houses, farms and cottages and discussing their methods of construction. Miss Jekyll knew very little about architecture and Ned even less about gardening. His houses needed gardens and her revolutionary ideas of garden planting and design needed houses. Each found in the other the perfect complement. It was the beginning of a collaboration that was to last almost to her death in 1932. Soon after they met he began building for her a cottage on Munstead land which she called The Hut. In 1896 he was to design for her the house she had always dreamed of having – Munstead Wood. It was close to The Hut. The garden, which became so famous, was almost mature by the time she moved into the house. Partly formal, partly wild, it merged almost imperceptibly into the wood through a woodland path. One of Lutyens's three surviving sketch-books contains pen-and-ink and wash drawings for Munstead Wood, what he called Bumpstead. He took no commission on this house.

I lived at Munstead Wood for several weeks in the autumn and winter of 1933, almost a year after Aunt Bumps's death. I had been very ill and Lady Jekyll had lent me the house in which to recuperate. None of Miss Jekyll's things had as yet been touched; her clothes were still hanging in her bedroom cupboard, her gardening boots and tools were by the back door. What impressed me most was the meticulous neatness of her work-room; the small drawers in one chest held all the necessities for her shell pictures – the shells and pieces of coral carefully graded as to size and colour. Her presence filled the house which still seemed to give off the scent of new wood. Although a small house, the wide first floor gallery, in which stood glass-fronted cupboards containing her blue and white china, gave it a sense of great spaciousness. This gallery, sixty feet long and ten feet wide with windows along one side, had been achieved by building it out to form a loggia below. The sad thing about staying there was the realisation of the ephemeral nature of a garden; it had already lost its contours and felt neglected – and no wonder, for it had needed eleven gardeners, as well as Miss Jekyll herself, to keep it up whereas now there was only one.

At the beginning of the Jekyll-Lutyens association the patronage was nearly all on her side. She introduced him to the people who consulted her about their gardens so that he might design the architectural features. Then, as his success grew, he brought her in to make the gardens for nearly all the houses he built or enlarged.

Through the Jekylls Ned made many friends, most of whom became his clients. One of the most valued was Aggie Jekyll's sister Frances who in 1888 had married Jack Horner of Mells Manor in Somerset, a woman of even greater talent, culture and charm than Aggie. She had been a pupil of Ruskin's and was a leading member of the Souls. Then there was Princess Louise, Marchioness of Lorne (afterwards Duchess of Argyll), for whom Miss Jekyll had designed textiles. The Princess commissioned Ned in 1896 to build an additional wing to the Ferry Inn at Roseneath and make alterations to Roseneath Castle, Dumbartonshire, one of the Argyll properties where the Lornes lived. Princess Louise told Ned that she liked him because he was not a courtier. But the friend Ned met through Gertrude Jekyll who was to be of almost as much help to him as Miss Jekyll herself was Edward Hudson. Hudson, who had made his money out of printing, founded in 1897 *Country Life* to which Miss Jekyll contributed anonymous Gardening Notes. From the first, every number of this weekly magazine contained an illustrated article on some new or old country house. Practically all Lutyens's best work from the time of his first meeting with Hudson in 1900 became the subject of the main article with its beautiful photography. The first article to appear was on Crooksbury in September 1900, by which time the house had been enlarged. Lawrence Weaver, the first architectural editor of *Country Life*, published a collection of these articles on Lutyens's work in a folio volume in 1913. Hudson's personal devotion to Lutyens became as great as his admiration for his work.

*   *   *

It was Barbara Webb, however, who introduced Ned to Lady Emily Lytton in the spring of 1896. Mrs Webb still kept her large circle of friends although she was already suffering from the cancer which was to kill her the following year, and she liked sometimes to take Ned with her when she went out. On this occasion he had gone with her to one of the weekly musical parties given by Monsieur and Madame Jacques Blumenthal at 43 Hyde Park Gate. The Blumenthals' parties were fashionable and always very well attended. They were friends of the Jekylls as well as of Princess Louise.

Emily Lytton was there that evening with her eldest sister Betty, married to Gerald Balfour, a younger brother of Arthur Balfour. Betty and Emily were the daughters of Robert, first Earl of Lytton, who had been Viceroy of India from 1876–80; he had died in 1891 while Ambassador in Paris. Always bad at managing his finances, it was found on his death that due to a dishonest man of affairs his widow had been left very badly off. The ancestral home, Knebworth House, Hertfordshire, had to be let and Lady Lytton moved to a small house in the same county called The Danes. Her elder son, Victor, was at Eton when his father died. In order to send him to Cambridge and his younger brother, Neville, to Eton, Lady Lytton had become a lady-in-waiting to Queen Victoria in 1895 at a salary of £500 a year. When it had been suggested to Emily that she might help the family by becoming a maid-of-honour at £300 a year she had indignantly turned down the idea, declaring herself to be a republican. The middle sister, Constance, who never married and was later to become a militant suffragette, was making pin-money out of journalism. Lady Lytton had left it to Betty Balfour to bring Emily out, and although Emily adored Betty, as did everyone who knew her, she suffered very much in her shyness from having her conversation at dinner parties overheard by Betty and criticised.

Emily was not yet twenty-two and Ned was twenty-seven when they met in 1896. She was already beginning to feel on the shelf. A dangerous romance with Wilfrid Scawen Blunt, the poet, thirty-four years older than her, with whom she had been infatuated, had recently come to an end after three years, leaving her with a feeling of emptiness which she had tried to fill by taking up social work at a girls' club in Bethnal Green. She was tall, fair, pretty and blue-eyed, but gauche and over-plump. Intensely shy, Blunt's attentions had given her a certain amount of self-confidence. For many years she had poured out her heart to an old clergyman, Whitwell Elwin, the incumbent of Booton in Norfolk, who had been editor of the *Quarterly Review*. From a book of these letters which she published when she was eighty we know of her intimate feelings from the age of thirteen until her marriage. Two years before she met Ned she had confessed to Elwin that there was a blank in her life which would never be filled until she married – that she had 'a longing for a complete and soul-satisfying love'.

Emily had no interest in music, so one can believe Ned when he told her afterwards that he had first noticed her across the room because she looked so bored, cross and miserable. There and then he resolved to make her happy. He asked Barbara Webb who she was, and Mrs Webb, knowing all the Lyttons well from Indian days, introduced them. The only thing Emily remembered of this first meeting was that on telling him that she was going on to a ball he had asked her, 'Do you dance till you are dishevelled? I do.' She did not even catch his unusual name which sounded to her something like luncheon or luggage.

They met several times at dances that summer. She found him 'an amusing but somewhat eccentric young man and a good dancer'. He talked a great deal about his mother and it was then that she gained the impression that he was the only child of a widow. It was the first time Ned had been really in love. He wrote to her during their engagement that she was the only woman he had ever loved, but in a subsequent letter he mentioned the 'three romances' he had told her about, adding that now she knew of them she knew everything about him.

Ned confessed his feelings for Emily to Mrs Webb who promised to ask him to Milford if Emily ever came to stay there. Emily did go for a long visit in September; Mrs Webb kept her promise and asked Ned for the weekend although she must have known that his falling more deeply in love with Emily could only cause him unhappiness since he would never be allowed to marry her. When he arrived on Sunday morning, 20 September, Emily had gone off on her bicycle to meet Gerald Duckworth (founder of the publishing firm and Virginia Woolf's half-brother) in whom she was much more interested than she was in Ned and who she hoped was interested in her. Gerald met her on the road and took her to Hindhead to spend the day at the house of his step-father, Leslie Stephen, where she found the whole family. 'Stella [Duckworth] looked lovely,' Emily wrote to her mother, 'and the two daughters [Vanessa and Virginia] promise to be very pretty later on. Is Mr Leslie Stephen an idiot? He is quite deaf, which made me horribly shy and he never said a word at lunch, but groaned and grunted and heavily sighed.'

Emily returned to Milford rather disappointed, although she

had had 'a perfectly heavenly day'. If Gerald Duckworth had proposed there seems little doubt but that she would have accepted him. But 'Mr Lutyens' was there when she got back and determined to make up for all the time he had lost of her company during the day. After dinner he proposed that they should bicycle together to see a house at Thursley he was rebuilding for Robert Webb, Warren Lodge, about five miles away. There was a full moon; they broke into the house through a window and wandered all over it. The next morning Ned took her to call on Miss Jekyll who was now installed in The Hut while Munstead Wood was being built. 'She is a most enchanting person and lives in the most fascinating cottage you ever saw,' Emily told her mother. 'Mr Lutyens calls her Bumps, which is a very good name. She is very fat and stumpy, dresses like a man, little tiny eyes, very nearly blind. There is a huge old-fashioned fireplace, with chimney-corner seats and big blazing logs.'

When it rained in the afternoon Ned and Emily decided that they would go and have 'a surprise dinner with Bumps'. They spent the afternoon buying mutton chops, eggs, sponge cake, macaroons, almonds and bulls-eyes, and turned up about six. Getting out of the carriage, Emily dropped all the eggs and smashed them. She was very clumsy and apt to drop things. Nevertheless, they 'reeled into the house shrieking with laughter'. Bumps was delighted to see them and they set to work to cook the chops and make tipsy cake. They then sat down to the best dinner Emily had ever had. It is surprising that she managed to cook a chop, never having cooked anything in her life before, but perhaps it was Ned who did it. After dinner they sat in the big inglenook and drank tumblers of hot elderberry wine made by Bumps. 'It was altogether the most heavenly evening you can imagine.' Gerald Duckworth was evidently quite forgotten.

Ned returned to London next morning to work but was back again on Thursday. While he was away Barbara Webb gave Emily some advice about not encouraging him too much, for he was inclined to be 'bumptious'. After his return he and Emily made some more delightful expeditions together, including another evening with Bumps and a visit to Guildford where he bought a red lacquer cabinet which he said would 'look nice in our home'. Emily thought he was probably joking. It was during this visit that he spoke about designing a casket for her to contain all manner of small treasures. On 29 September he was writing to her from London to say that the casket was rapidly taking shape in his mind; he hoped it would be ready in time for her birthday on 26 December. The bottom compartment would 'receive a roll of plans for a house such as we talked of. These plans are in the shape of EL'. He meant her to understand that the plans were to be for their own home, her initials being the same as his, but again she was not sure how far he was joking, though she believed he did care for her.

Emily stayed at Milford House for a month and Ned seems to have gone there again more than once. It was hardly fair of Barbara Webb to have encouraged him when she had warned Emily not to do so. Emily's impression that he cared for her was confirmed in a letter he wrote to her on 17 October after his final visit. His frivolous manner had not prepared her for the seriousness of its tone. He had had to go to Frome in Somerset on a job and wrote in the train on his way back to Paddington that evening:

My dear Lady Emily

It is with your little pencil that I write – I felt wretched in the train, leaving you this morning and now how I regret – Bumps or no Bumps – that I did not have the courage to play truant to my work and stay by you – but then I should have broken away and you might have hated me.

I would have told you how I loved you – Would you have

43

laughed? Except my love, I have nothing to offer you. I am poor – unknown – and little altogether—

My life's work would be yours – and I shall now work the more earnestly so that I may, in time, become more worthy of your dear self – all that I have is at your feet – I love you ever so – I dare not ask anything of you – the little hope I have in me is so large a stake to lose – that the very thought of it makes me feel ill and sick—

One word from you would turn my world, to one great sphere of happiness and I would become a man – give me some chance to prove it. Before I realised your name I loved you and being with you at Milford House has only made it grow the more, so that my whole horizon is filled with and by you—

I am in a coupé at the end of the train – the receding landscape through the window – draws, with quick perspective – my very hope – even as I write. Everyone must love you so that I can only be one amongst many others – I could write miles to you but I dare not persecute you and after all I cannot say more than, that I love you. I love you—

Yours
Ned Lutyens

Emily's reply from Milford House is dated 19 October:

Dear Mr Lutyens

Your letter touched me very much. Why did you think I should laugh? At present I can only thank you for what you say to me. My mind is too uncertain for me to say more one way or another, and I can only ask you to wait and give me time to think it over. But whatever I settle I hope that you will believe that my interest in your work is very real and deep. Bumps is quite right in what she says. I do not want to be a frivolous influence in your life, but the reverse, and your work is always what will interest me most. No one will be more pleased than I am to hear that you are getting on and making a name for yourself, as I am quite sure you will in time.

Does my letter sound horrid? I hope not, but it would not be fair if I said more, when I know so little at present what I feel.

We saw Bumps yesterday, who was charming to me. I do love her. When we come back from Paris perhaps you will come to the Danes for a day or two and we will talk about it.

Yours very sincerely
Emily Lytton

Ned replied that same evening from Gray's Inn Square:

Dear Lady Emily,

I felt so unworthy, in all respects, that laughter would have brought me no surprise – it is no frivolous influence that you have on me. Your influence is great and I know full well, how good. If I frivol with you, it is with the happiness of being with and near you.

That you should be kind is all I could expect from what I know to be you, only I have so little to offer you – a small white house and my poor life – I always see you in that wee white house, with a red cabinet. It is not size that helps in life – so long as all one would have is there. A band outside is playing the Washington Post. It makes me ache. How I would give – that I might have your love. Your 'one way or another' gives me a little gleam of hope. May I hold to this? It is enough for me to work for – for I have no heart to press you – to do aught but what you would – and I will wait only don't let it be long. If you marry let it be some good man who would worship you as I do and would. I dare not say all I feel – it all seems

45

so selfish – even the good you bring to the surface and make in me.

Bumps is lovable – only don't let her abuse me. She knows nothing of how much you are to me and if she did even Bumps would see that you could make me man! and give my work the serious touch it wants. Help me. Without you all seems dreariness – a hearth without a fire.

I should have pleasure in coming to the Danes but I have so little to say – though to me everything. I can only ask God to bless you and give you of the best. Here I shudder, knowing how small a manner of thing I am.

I cannot write – I feel flat and the world about me flatter still. I stand as on some drear hill alone, a desert round me. The lovely valley seems to rise and give me warmth – and you – then I wax strong and great and worthy of you. Nothing there is between us and all seems beautiful. Then I realise to wake and I turn cold and bleak and though the valley is still beautiful it is far distant and I alone.

It is so hard to be righteously unselfish when I want so much although I cannot say how well I wish you. What can I do?

Yours sincerely
Ned Lutyens

Emily had now returned to the Danes from where she wrote on 23 October:

Dear Mr Lutyens,

I have been thinking a great deal about your letter, and have told my mother about it, and I feel that I ought to tell you at once that it is hopeless for you to think of me any more. You probably do not know that I have no money of my own, and you tell me that you have nothing but your love to offer. Under these circumstances you will feel yourself that it is hopeless to consider the matter any further. If I saw any hope I would give it you, but there is none. Mother says that she would rather we did not meet, or write or see each other again. It may seem hard but it is better so. You will feel this too. We have had some happy times together which we shall both like to remember.

I want to say something to you for the future if I only knew how. It is this. You have said that I could make you man, and give your work the serious touch it wants. I may not help you in the way you want, but I should like to tell you how much I trust and believe in your power to become a distinguished man some day. I feel so sure you will if you only try your best, and put your whole life in your work. You have it in you to do great things, I am sure of it, and if you will only believe in yourself as I believe in you. And when I hear that you are getting on and making your name known, I shall feel so proud to think you cared for me, and that I have been something in your life. I will pray God to bless you and give you strength to prove before all the world that I was right to put my faith in you.

All that I write seems so cold and horrid, but you will know I do not mean it so. I suffer in the thought that I have brought you only pain, but you will know how much against my will it was, and forgive me. I shall hear of you sometimes from Mrs Webb, great things I hope and believe. She will help you I know.

Will you send me the casket still? I should like to have it, only perhaps it would be better not. Do as you think best. I should like to hear from you just once again to know that you understand what I have said so badly, and that you will take comfort and courage, and go forth like a knight of old (as you said) and conquer a name and

47

fortune for yourself. I ask it of you though perhaps I have no right.

Goodbye, and may God bless you always. It is the prayer of

Yours? (I cannot write sincerely)
Emily Lytton

Lady Lytton herself wrote to 'Mr Lutyens' by the same post, pointing out that he was entirely unknown to her – they had not even been introduced – and that Emily had nothing but a small allowance she gave her, and even after her, Lady Lytton's, death Emily would have 'only a small sum of settled capital which her father left her' (this was £5,000), so she begged him not to seek out Emily any more and to try to overcome his kindly feelings towards her.

Ned answered both these letters on 25 October while staying at Munstead House. To Lady Lytton he wrote, thanking her for her kindness; she could have written in no other way but he could not alter his love for Lady Emily. He should have remembered that he had nothing to offer except the income he made of about £1,000 a year and the possibility of a life insurance. To Emily he wrote in deep pain:

Dear Lady Emily,

I received your kind letter here last night. It already seems years ago. I understand too well, and thank you for all you are to me. It never for one moment occurred to me whether you had money or not – I should have remembered only that I had none but what I can make and save but I forgot everything but that you existed.

I will try if only for your sake to obey Lady Lytton loyally. It is hard. I can't write. If only like that knight of old I could have seen some hope – some Grail – how I would fight.

I want no name, no fortune, for myself, but I will since

48

you have asked it of me and my prayer will be that I may win some deserved happiness.

I do not know if Lady Lytton would like me to send that casket. I cannot keep it even if I would nor could I destroy it. It belongs to the past and is no longer mine. I would take it as another kindness from your hands to accept it. Bless you for thinking of it.

May you never have the sorrow that is mine and may God keep and bless you. You must not suffer for me: that you should suffer makes it worse. I cannot bear that thought. There are things in this world which are inevitable and by these things man may prove himself man.

I will trust in the God you pray to.

Oh to know you could have loved me so as to have remained

Yours ever
Ned Lutyens

Emily could not bear to leave it like that. The written word always meant more to her than the spoken, and by this time she had fallen in love with him from his letters. Inarticulate in speech, he was able to express the truth of himself in words. She took two days to think over his letter and then wrote:

Dear Mr Lutyens,

Would it comfort and help you and give you the gleam of hope you need to know I could have loved you, oh so well! which means I suppose that I love you now. If it is wrong of me to have told you, God must forgive me. I could not bear that you should suffer all alone, and I thought it might make you happy to know that I too cared, and that I felt your pain not only out of kindness. I had not the strength to resist the happiness of making you happy.

I trust you not to ask more of me but on the contrary

to help me to be good and obedient to Mother's wishes, though it is very very hard. The present must remain as it is, the future is in better hands than ours, and God is kind.

I dare not tie myself or you. We may both wish to change. If you could love someone instead of me, someone who could bring you more than I can you would know that I should be the first to rejoice at what could bring you joy, and you would feel the same for me I know.

But should all be as it is now, come to me when you feel that you are man sufficient, and that like that knight of old you have proved your knighthood. For the present I trust you to be patient, and to keep as a secret in your heart, the secret of mine. No one must ever guess.

I should so love that casket. If you would send it, I will explain to Mother that it was promised in the past, and that I told you still to send it to me. Whatever may be the future, I shall always love and treasure the casket for your sake, and in memory of what has been, and all your kindness. I should like a little crucifix if there is room besides the other things, and you will not forget the plans for the little white house, because I love it.

As for the inscription I do not know. I read these lines yesterday in a poem of my father's 'Man cannot make, but may ennoble fate By nobly bearing it.' Would they do, do you think? If not you must think of something better.

I dare not speak of the future, I can only trust. But if you will take comfort in the present, I shall feel that all has been right, and that I was not wrong to write this letter.

I will not say goodbye. Have hope and courage for my sake.

Yours
Emily Lytton

Ned received this letter that evening at Onslow Square and wrote back the same night:

My darling – your letter brings me hope and great joy. I fear no vow – I love you so – but you must not bind yourself. I will work and come to you without doubt. Should you ever be in trouble you must turn to me – without fear or doubt.

God bless you – I feel so unworthy: there is much before me – pray for me. I cannot – dare not write all that I would say to you. I must honour your own mother for your sweet sake and God forbid that I should ever ask of you anything but what is right.

Only I want so, to be near you. God bless my darling and keep all harm from her. I have prayed so hard for your love and now I pray for more with courage – will you join me? My prayer would not have been answered if there was wrong in what you did.

I have seen the *Holiest* grail and I can now go forth with great comfort. Pray that I may hold it.

The casket shall come and it shall be as you ask. Below the lowest tray there will yet be a space – look for it. I may not write again unless you can get permission from your own mother to allow me to see you. But 'tis wiser to wait.

I have four new 'jobs'. One for the Duke of Westminster [?] – one for Lady Stewart [alterations to Woodend, Witley, Surrey] – a good one – one for Lord Middleton [Viscount Middleton, work on the Peper Harrow estate, Godalming] and one for Mr Wickham [house at Mayfield, Sussex]. How I shall work for *you*.

How I look to the day when I may come forward – and in the space of silence – do not forget me. I trust you as

51

I trust God. Is this wicked, I don't mean it so. Do you remember that we thought the world a flat place? Now I find it round quite round and full of hope and blessings with more yet to come.

I must now go back to my shadow, but I know now what you have said and I am wondrous happy, knowing that light will come undimmed. I have hope. I have courage and God will yet bless us. I love to say 'us' and I may say

Yours
Ned

'Man cannot make but may ennoble Fate, by nobly bearing it.' [Underneath this he made a little drawing of the casket with a crucifix beside it.]

Emily was never one to obey her father's precept and nobly bear her fate. She was a fighter. Having confided all her feelings to old Mr Elwin and having been assured by him that 'The immense majority of weddings take place under circumstances less promising', she decided to appeal not only to her sister Betty but to her uncle Lord Loch, the husband of her mother's twin sister who had helped the family with his advice since Lord Lytton's death. Emily, unable to write to Ned herself, asked Barbara Webb to ask him to lay his financial position before Lord Loch. As a result of this Ned went to see Lord Loch early in December, taking with him his balance sheet from 1894 until November of the current year, '96. This showed that his office expenses had gone up in two years from £300 to £500 and that his fees had gone up from £826 to £1,803. Besides this he had £200 in the bank. Lord Loch was impressed with the steady increase in his income. If he took out a life insurance policy for £10,000, the premiums paid out of income, he would still have more than £1,000 a year to live on. Lord Loch's advice to Lady Lytton was to review the situation in a year's time during which the young couple should test their feelings for each other by not communicating at all.

Betty Balfour did not concur in the advice to forbid them to correspond, 'for this encourages the cherishing of an ideal and if you are to test the truth of their love they had better get to know each other better'. Thus Betty had written to her mother on 29 November from Dublin where Gerald was then Chief Secretary, pleading Emily's cause: '. . . he has made a remarkable start in a profession which calls forth some of the noblest faculties of a man's mind and which a gentleman of ability may be proud to follow. [Gerald Balfour's youngest brother was an architect.] That he has an exceptional gift is evidenced by the fact that at twenty-six [actually twenty-seven] with no social advantages at the outset he is already making £1,000 a year at his profession . . . So far I think his defect in my judgement has been a sort of frivolousness of talk which attractive as it is in its way seems to indicate a certain absence of seriousness.' Betty had now met Ned several times at London dances.

Emily, who went to stay with Betty in Dublin in December, pleaded her own cause with her mother: 'I do not think you will feel so unhappy about my poverty if I married. We should have about £1,000 a year to begin with, and that is nearly as much as Betty had, and you know I have not luxurious tastes. It would not be necessary for his profession that we should go into society, and a simple life is happiest when there is love to make it so. I know you have not been happiest in your great positions.'

Ned was not altogether lacking in social advantages. His first cousin, Nellie, daughter of Sir Thomas Gallwey, had married in 1886 Frank Stuart-Wortley who was to become Earl of Wharncliffe in 1899. The Lyttons, however, were proud of their ancestry which could be traced back to far beyond the first knight, Gilbert de Lytton, who went with Richard Coeur de Lion to the Holy Land, and Lady Lytton's father had been Edward Villiers, brother of the Earl of Clarendon, Foreign Secretary, and her mother, Elizabeth, one of sixteen children of Lord Ravensworth. Lady Lytton claimed to have over a hundred first cousins.

It may have been a letter from Barbara Webb that had most influence on Lady Lytton. Lord Lytton had loved Barbara, and anyone her husband had loved was loved by her. Barbara had written to her in an undated letter that although Ned was a great flirt this was the first time he had been 'seriously hit'. He was the only one of the Lutyens family she knew well; she had seen him constantly for the past year. The family was poor and his father would not be able to do anything for him, but she had the highest opinion of Ned's 'moral character' and he was 'extraordinarily clever and ingenious with a merry sweet temper – very engaging'.

Whatever the reason, or combination of reasons, Lady Lytton gave in at the end of January 1897. Emily wrote to Ned on 28 January saying that he might come to The Danes on the 30th as her accepted lover. He received her letter that same day at midnight and wrote an eight-page reply to catch the 3 a.m. post which was delivered at The Danes three hours later. He begged Emily to meet him at the station because he would be so nervous. Her mother, though, would not allow this on the grounds of propriety. Instead, she walked herself through the snow to meet him at Cole Green station. He captivated her at once; she was greatly concerned lest the patent leather boots he was wearing should suffer in the snow; by the time they reached The Danes she had consulted him about a house she wanted to build. He for his part loved her immediately. 'Your dear, sweet, pretty mother,' he wrote to Emily after the visit. 'I used so to dread her and feel such fear of her. Now it has all vanished, and I see her face only as one I have always loved. I hope your mother may always love me and that I may bring warmth to her heart these coming years . . . Will she be kind and trust me? I think so, her nature is so

54

generous and noble altogether.' His wish was granted: they remained devoted friends for the rest of her long life. Indeed, he understood and sympathised with her more than did any of her children.

The change in Lady Lytton's attitude to the marriage caused Barbara Webb to write to Betty Balfour: 'Your mother wrote a sweet letter *warmly thanking me* for having brought about the match!!! my brain whirls.'

CHAPTER THREE

Engagement
1897

Ned brought with him the casket to The Danes. I have known
and loved the casket all my life. It stands about nine inches
high, the upper part of green leather with brass handles and
a beautiful little brass lock with their entwined EL's chased
on it. The leather is tooled in gold in a diaper pattern, an
alternate E and L in each diamond. In gold letters round
the top is tooled the inscription MAN CANNOT MAKE BUT
CAN ENNOBLE FATE BY NOBLY BEARING IT, to which Ned
had added a line of his own BUT AS FAITH WILLS SO
FATE FULFILS. The bottom part of the casket is of wood,
painted with delicate flowered scrolls and an angel in the
act of blessing. It stands on ball feet lacquered red. Inside,
it is lined with flowered paper and contains lift-up trays for
its small treasures. As a treat we were sometimes allowed as
children to open it and take out its contents. These consisted
of a silver and ebony crucifix, most originally and delicately
designed by Ned, a brass pipe stopper (symbol of fireside
pipes) with a bird's head and EL engraved on the bottom
so that it could be used as a seal; a heart; an anchor (symbol
of hope); a little gold ring coated in white enamel with the
casket inscription engraved on it; a tiny blue leather-covered
bible with a magnifying glass lodged in an inner pocket, and

a white vellum book containing a poem in Ned's writing so small that it could hardly be read even with a magnifying glass. At the bottom was the roll of plans for the little white house embodying in its design their linked initials.

The engagement was announced on 3 February 1897, a day on which Ned was writing to Emily, 'I seem to have developed a wonderful capacity for loving and this must develop my capacity for work'. And two days later, 'I wish all the women in the world might be brought before me so that I might "choose" you before all.' Every letter of congratulation made him 'realise and wonder at the great fortune you bring me darling! and the responsibility of the great weight of love . . . Oh my darling I love you and the joy of being able to write instead of the dull ache of waiting and wondering'. And in the next letter: 'I feel I am so much a part of you, our lives so woven like threads in our linen, together and inseparable, making one great sheet of glory, made in heaven (not Belfast), so that it shall last till heaven ends, far beyond the end of this tired world.' He wanted to wrap her round 'as an apple wraps its core'. He loved 'that thing in the prayer book,' he told her, 'which says "whose service is perfect freedom"'. He wrote that E in Ned stood for Emy – 'the centre of all that is me NED', to which she replied, 'All that is ME loves all that is YOU and there is no room in my heart for anything but Ned.'

Emily told Elwin, 'I have found a companion more perfectly suited to me than I ever thought possible. Everything I have ever dreamt of or imagined, I find in him.' She described him as 'just my height or a little bit taller, has very dark hair which begins the day all smooth and sleek, towards evening gets beautifully rough and curly, very blue eyes, a pointed nose, a little curly fair moustache, and next to no chin'. She told Ned himself that many people had told her how good-looking he was but that she had never noticed his looks 'until at Milford I suddenly realised what a beautiful face you had. You have a beautiful brow and eyes and a very nice nose – the only falling away is the chin.'

They could not get married until Ned had saved enough to buy and furnish a house. Their engagement was to last six months. In March Ned paid the first premium on a life insurance for £11,000 and £100 lawyer's fees. Although he had been the first to suggest insuring his life he was in after life to tell me how much he had resented being made to do so by Lord Loch and what a difference the extra £200 a year would have made to him in the first years of his marriage. He and Emily often met during their engagement because she would come to London to stay either with the Balfours in Addison Road or with the Lutyenses in Onslow Square. She liked her 'large new family', especially Molly and Aileen whom she loved. She wrote to Elwin of her future father-in-law:

He has discovered what he calls the Venetian Secret – and is a little cracked on the subject. The effects of Nature, he declares, can be measured as accurately as the effects of sound – and he has invented an instrument for measuring tone and colour. But he can get no one to listen to him – and he is cut by his fellow painters. The sad thing is that his pictures, painted by the aid of this secret, are not very good, though he thinks them masterpieces. He is a splendid looking old man [then sixty-eight], very tall with white hair and beard. He has no regard for conventions but acts in the way that seems best to him. He has the nature of a child, perfectly pure and simple. He thinks all his children paragons. The mother is Irish and was a great beauty – she is beautiful still, with a soft, gentle face and voice. She is very religious of an Evangelical turn – but though she talks religion quite freely, not a word jars upon one, and she has not one touch of cant or hypocrisy, and her creed seems to be an unbounded love for all human beings. They do not go at all into society. The mother thinks it wrong, and the father is never happy away from his wife and his home.

Even when they were both in London and meeting every day, Ned and Emily still wrote to each other at least once a day, and when they were parted they wrote two or three times a day. There was nothing to choose between them in the loving warmth of their letters except that he, having read so little, expressed himself with far more originality. Her education had come entirely through reading and writing letters, and, of course, she spoke French very well from having lived in Paris. She hardly used her eyes at all for observation, had no interest in pictures any more than in music, nor in architecture apart from its being Ned's profession. It was probably Ned who told her that his father's pictures were 'not very good'. She fell in with all Ned's ideas for furnishing and decorating their house. This was just as well, for although he made some show of consulting her, he had very strong views and tastes on the matter. He owned that he did not care for comfort, one of the accusations often brought against him by his clients. He made many sketches in his letters of the furniture he was going to design for their house when they found one.

Shall I design a Dining Table? [he wrote in February] No, not green, do you think? It would be too ARTY. And then plain woodwork would look so nice peeping up through the blue table cloth. For I vote if E approves to have one little blue cloth for each person and not a great sheet of superfine damask! We shall have say two dozen of them kept in a press in the dining room . . . [drawing of dining table with comments] . . . Blue cloths – oak table, white china

59

and brass candles – coloured delft ware and green handled knives would make a most pretty and dear effect . . . The drawing Room which we should call

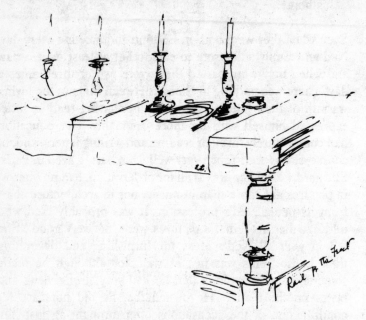

Parlour, will be just a simple room with what you want in it for use and no more – and everything to be as pretty as possible and so in some small way be worthy of my own darling darling E. . . . A good fireplace is essential in all rooms. Arm chairs and sofas etc covered with jolly stuffs . . . and a long range of low book cases.

And in a subsequent letter:

I see a white bed room with gay flowery curtains to window and bed – the bed of wood but of old gold and rather Italian in feeling – a high head and no foot – a cassone to stand at the foot. Look ye here [drawing] There are all sorts of impossible points about the above bed which must be worked out.

Red gold posts, blue curtains, red ceiling [to the bed] shelf for candles and the casket! wish I had paints here and a decent pen!! [drawing of washstand with comments] It would be jolly to keep all washing apparatus in a separate room – and make the Bed Room itself jolly – without cluttering it up with paraphernalia! [drawing of dressing table with comments] You *shall* have the dearest little glass in the world – and a three sided one too.

He 'shrank in terror' lest anyone should give them pictures. 'The pictures we shall have, if any, will be small, Italian in feeling, gorgeous in colour and in exquisite frames. Madonnas and St Georges to inspire our respective selves . . . But one really wants a house first.'

Ned even went so far in planning their home as to ask about 'conveniences' (night-tables). Must they have them? Must they have two? It was more furniture to fill up the room, and it was healthier to have them under the bed where there were draughts than close to one's head shut up in a cupboard.

61

They did not have night-tables, but the other furniture materialised almost exactly as he had first sketched it – a huge four-poster bed, but of light oak, not old gold, with posts of polished steel, a dressing table with a three-leaf mirror attached, a refectory table and linen press for the dining-room – all in light oak – and then the pale blue linen table-mats, old Delft salt-cellars, brass candlesticks, a white Wedgwood dinner service and green-dyed ivory handled knives.

They planned to have only the smallest, simplest house in London, or even a flat, close to Ned's office, until they could afford to build 'the little white house' in the country. They would need only two servants. They envisaged a perfect French couple who would do everything for them. 'I think we shall have an amusing establishment,' Emily told Elwin. 'Our house is to be all white and everything in it of the simplest kind and yet beautiful. Ned likes nothing that is not simple. He says the most beautiful things are always the simplest.'

Emily must have been particularly pleased when Ned wrote to her, 'Food matters not! Except how it is served, with quiet grace with all hospitable intent', for she had no conception of housekeeping. The most she had ever done at home was occasionally to pour out the tea and then she often broke a cup. She wrote that she did not care how poor they were; she would be the richest woman in the world because he loved her, yet she had no idea what it was like to be poor; the greatest hardship she could imagine was having to do her own hair. She told Elwin confidently that they would not have to entertain for Ned's work and need see no one but each other. They would always be two simple people in a little white house and would never let the world into their lives to spoil it.

Emily did make out lists of the linen they would need. Declaring that she loved sewing she offered to make the sheets and blue linen table mats herself, an offer Ned wisely declined. She estimated their probable immediate and annual expenses: plate would cost £63, linen under £50, servants about £50; £4 a week would cover food and washing, so they could easily live on £500 a year.

They were like children playing at house. She often wrote to him as to a child: 'My sweetest little boy-man', 'My own little boy husband to be', 'My own beloved little darling Ned'; and he called himself 'your little boy mate', 'your little husband to be'. In his sketches he always portrayed himself as small. Emily had told Elwin that he was hardly taller than she was, yet he was a tall man when I knew him, over six foot. Can it possibly be that he was not full grown at twenty-seven? The chin must have developed, for he did not have a weak chin. He went bald on top early in life and I do not remember him except with almost white hair.

When Emily wrote to Ned soon after they became engaged, 'How absurdly funny it is – that you are quite a stranger to me, and I really don't know anything about you – and yet I have given myself to you for ever', he protested that there was nothing about him she did not know. But it was true; she did not know him any more than he knew her; they did not know themselves. They had nothing in common except an intense romanticism. They both believed passionately in the happy ever after, that love would never fade, that they would never grow apart. They had no forewarning of the frictions engendered by two strong personalities rubbing together. He did not realise how much the sharing of books meant to her, how deeply religious she was, that running a home could never satisfy her ardent nature; nor did he know what a quick temper she had and how often she was prostrated by migraines. And she did not realise that his work consumed not only his time but his soul.

In spite of her belief that she would not have to entertain for him, she wanted to understand and help him with his work. She bought the *Architectural Review* to read in the train but owned that she could not make much of it. She feared that he lost commissions by his frivolousness; he did not assert himself enough, she told him.

> I have so much ambition for you [she wrote in one letter]. In that miserable time when I told you there was no hope I was wretched at losing you because I loved you so – and I wanted your love more than anything in the world. But my pride suffered too – because I knew that some day you would be a great and wonderful man, whom everyone would kneel to, and admire and praise. And then I thought you would have found someone else to love and would have forgotten me, and another woman would have the right I longed for to be proud of your greatness and success . . . And now the tragedy is swept away and turned into a beautiful and glorious poem. And some day *I* shall share your success and no other woman. You see I am very worldly after all, and I *do* want to be the wife of a great man, only I want my husband to be great through his own work and efforts – and not through money and titles which came to him without any trouble or effort on his part. My darling must become great, as great as he already is in my eyes.

Later in their engagement she was to tell him that she felt his work was separate from her. 'My work separate!!!!!!', he replied. 'It is that you don't come here and work with me and be there to decide and influence with her darling eyes all the beautiful work that shall come to my hand and head and Emy's heart.' How irritated he would have been if she had ever sat beside him while he was working and tried to influence him.

In a series of sketches he showed their daily life together as he imagined it would be: called in the big double bed at 7 a.m. by the maid with tea; breakfast; then Ned at his drawing-board while Emy talked to the fat cook; running into each other's arms at six in the evening; sitting close on the sofa together; then dinner with one guest, and from eight till twelve Ned back at his drawing-board. It is significant that he drew no pictures of what Emy would be doing between interviewing the cook and six p.m., nor between eight and midnight. Only once in his letters did he hint at children. He wrote that they would need six beds – and perhaps? – and there followed a sketch of a cradle. In another letter he wrote, 'The morning sun shall break upon your face and I shall watch my darling close beside me wake to life, and we shall steal into each other's arms and bid each other joy for another happy day now come.'

At least once a week Ned sent Emily a revised budget, including wedding-present cheques which had come in. Bumps had sent £25, the Webbs £25, his father £25, Lady Anne Blunt (Wilfrid's wife) £25, the Balfours £20, Elwin £20 (extraordinarily generous, for he was a poor man). Then there were smaller cheques and a few really good presents including old candlesticks from the Blumenthals at whose house they had first met and a moonstone and gold necklace from Wilfrid Blunt himself, and a pair of small early Delft horses from an unnamed friend. Ned was ecstatically in love, yet it was an anxious time for him – he was very concerned about money and always in a rush, working very late at his office, dashing all over the country on jobs (so many of his long letters to Emily were written in trains), going several times to Roseneath near Glasgow for Princess Louise's commissions for the Ferry Inn and Roseneath Castle, looking for a house in London, welcoming every new scrap of work, worrying that he might not get any work next year. The individual fees were so small – the highest during the first four months of 1897 being £75 – most of them £30 or £25, a few only £10 or £7. His estimate of what they would spend after they were married was £120 rent, £200 insurance, £500 office expenses; this represented

£16,400's worth of work, and £10,000's more work to earn the £500 a year they would need to live on. No wonder he declared in one letter, 'How I hate money.' I think he always hated it but was obsessed with the need to make it. If so much had not been expected of him from Emily's relations he would probably have worried much less about it.

Then more jobs suddenly came in in June. He hoped to earn £245 that month. They might have £350 in the bank by the time they married. Several of the best known of his early country houses were commissioned, built or a-building during 1897 – Binfield Lodge, Newbury, for Captain Ernest Rhodes; Sullingstead, Hascombe, Surrey, for Mr A. C. Cook; Fulbrook near Farnham for Gerald Streatfield; Orchards, near Godalming, for Sir William Chance, and Berry Down, Overton, Hampshire, for the Archibald Groves – as well as those mentioned in his letter of the previous October. Another commission was for alterations to the Bishop's Palace at Peterborough. This seems to have come through Princess Louise, for he wrote indignantly to Emily, 'The Princess warned me to be very careful – they say I can only build cottagey things and I am not to make Peterborough look cottagey – how can I make a few servants rooms and a coal hole look like a palace.'

By the end of June they had been able to fix the wedding day for 4 August and Ned had designed a wedding ring in 22 carat gold, very wide, with a division in the middle which made it look like two rings joined together. As each of his five children was born a heart was engraved inside. He afterwards said that he had always intended to have five children – five being a quiver-full.

*　　*　　*

Ned suggested going to Holland for their honeymoon because it was cheap; he reckoned it would not cost more than £20 or £30. 'Holland will be delicious,' Emily replied, 'but the time I long for most is when we begin to live and work together in our little white house. And then you must show me every stroke of work you do and make me understand it all.' But they were no nearer to finding a house although Ned had looked at several sent to him by Trollope's – in Amen Court, near St Paul's (he loved the idea of living in the shadow of St Paul's), Tower Square, Bankside, Chelsea, Cowley Street, Finsbury Square and Bedford Square. Lady Lytton was very much opposed to Bloomsbury: when people asked her where they lived how could she say in WC? Ned's father offered them a share of Onslow Square. When they told him they wanted to start life in a home of their own he was not offended. After seeing one particularly unsuitable house, Ned sent Emily a *cri de coeur*, 'O don't let's overhouse ourselves', in which she thoroughly concurred.

At the beginning of July their love was ennobled by the great sadness they shared in the death of Barbara Webb and their compassion for the heartbroken Bob Webb. Barbara died after great suffering on 8 July while Emily was staying at Milford. After her death Ned told Emily that he used to draw pictures for 'the blessed Barbara' while she was ill and write to her in fairy tale fantasies. It was much easier to write as a child, he said, and added, 'To write as a man requires more words than English gives . . . I often think that if I had but words at my command to speak my thoughts I should never be thought to be flippant and quite shallow. When the time comes for us to part – silence – just silence – will be my medium of expression.' There was something horribly prophetic in this.

*   *   *

Just three weeks before the marriage, Ned fell in love with a house which was unlike anything they had been looking for. 'Now darling,' he wrote on 14 July, 'if I were a Duke I should love to take my Emy to live at 29 Bloomsbury Square. The house is beautiful – large airy rooms, beautiful mantelpieces and staircase. You enter a square hall and a beautiful staircase is beyond. Three rooms which the great Norman Shaw used as his offices!! during his busiest period!! Such lovely doorways and cornices everywhere. Kitchen [in the basement] splendid, all in good working order and so good and simple.'

If they lived there, he said, he would move his office to the ground floor which had its own WC. The staircase rose from an inner hall to a skylight in the roof which made the house very light, and there was 'a delicious wooden gallery upstairs' from which one could look down into the hall. On the first floor were a drawing-room, a large back room and a large dining-room with a service lift coming up into a pantry beyond. On the second floor were three bedrooms and a bathroom, and on the top floor four bedrooms. Moreover, there was a garden at the back.

That evening he was writing again, 'The house is so delicious ... Although it looks grim and square outside [drawing], inside it is a paradise ... and there is hardly a dark corner anywhere, and all is fair and square, and spacious with any amount of cupboards and housewife's delights.' According to the sketch it had two windows on the ground floor with the porticoed front door on the left, and three windows on the three upper floors.

The house was on the east side of the square. All the houses on that side were to be pulled down in sixteen years' time. No 29 belonged to an old man, Mr Aldham Heaton, a decorator who had made a fortune working for Norman Shaw. He had recently spent some £2,000 on the house so it would need no repairs, and Mrs Heaton assured Ned that it could be run on three servants. The ground rent was £60 a year; Mr Heaton was asking £250 a year, including the rent, for the sixteen-year lease, but agreed to let Ned have it for £200. In that second letter Ned was already estimating the cost of living there: 'House, including ground rent, £200; taxes £60; Assurance [life insurance premiums] £190; Living £500; Clerks £400; odds and ends £100; Total £1,450. This means £29,000 of work in a year which I ought to get.'

Emily responded excitedly, so the deal was clinched, with vacant possession in November. At the same time Mr Heaton's son-in-law agreed to take over the Gray's Inn Square office. Neither Ned nor Emily seem to have realised how far away they had moved from the little white house: they had done the very thing Ned had prayed not to do – overhoused themselves.

CHAPTER FOUR

The Family and the Office
1889–1905

The marriage took place at mid-day on 4 August in the little
old church of St Mary's in the Park at Knebworth. Most
of Ned's large family attended; Frank was his best man and
Bill, assisting the local Rector, performed the actual marriage.
Emily, given away by her brother Victor, wore the traditional
white satin with an old Brussels lace veil and orange-blossom
wreath. Knebworth House was still let so a large tent had been
set up in the Park for a family lunch after the ceremony and, a
few days later, for Victor's coming of age celebrations. Emily
went away in a 'a pale grey travelling dress of moiré velours'
with 'black plumes in her small red straw hat'.

After four days at Warren Lodge, the house at Thursley
they had broken into in the moonlight, lent to them by
Bob Webb complete with excellent servants, and a return
to Knebworth for the day for Victor's celebrations, the
young couple continued their honeymoon in Holland for
another fortnight. By a miscalculation on Emily's part their
real wedding night had to be postponed until they got there. It
was a failure. They were both physically passionate, but Ned
had had no experience and Emily had received no guidance
from her mother beyond instructions not to refuse her husband anything and always to keep a pot of cold cream by the
bed. Like so many Victorian and Edwardian women whose

70

husbands regarded it as a supreme virtue to come to them 'pure', Emily was at first to suffer acute physical frustration and then disgust during the eighteen years they shared a bed. Moreover, they discovered in Holland one of their greatest incompatibilities: she adored the seaside whereas he detested it, comparing it to half an apple; she loved bathing, he hated it. For the first week they sat back to back on the beach at Scheveningen in two of those old-fashioned, high backed basket chairs, she facing towards the sea and he towards the land, reaching back uncomfortably to hold hands. For the second week he took her sight-seeing when she was so sore from his lovemaking that she could hardly walk and felt that she ought to have been resting.

On their return to London the Balfours lent them 24 Addison Road until they could get into their own house in the third week of December. Ned was fretting to open his new office so they moved in before the decorators were out. Ned went straight to his drawing-board while Emily went upstairs to find there was hardly any furniture and no carpets or curtains. Mr Heaton, when appealed to, immediately sent round some necessary pieces of furniture and matting for the floor of the only habitable bedroom, which was to become the night-nursery at the top of the house. The smell of the matting and the new paint and of Ned's pipe in the evenings in his office where she was obliged to sit for want of anywhere else, nauseated Emily who was already suffering from pregnancy sickness.

Soon the wedding presents and the furniture Ned had designed began to arrive, but for months they had nothing in the drawing-room except a huge Chinese screen (a wedding present), the red lacquer cabinet and the small pair of Delft horses. They had no electricity in the drawing-room or dining-room even though the wires were laid. The dining-room remained without electricity until the office was moved to separate premises in 1910.

Far from the whole house being white throughout, the walls of the nursery were painted a mixture of Antwerp blue and chrome yellow; those of the dining-room rose-madder mixed with black, and of the drawing-room black in semi-gloss with white ceiling and woodwork. Ned was to remain faithful to black walls for a large room for the rest of his life: the front drawing-rooms of all three houses we lived in as a family had their walls thus painted. There was nothing dead about this; indeed, the glossy black background reflected all the colours in the room. In an address to the Architectural Association in 1923 Lutyens was to say, 'Black is an important factor in all decoration . . . I often wonder why black is not more frequently used. If you want great dignity in decoration use black. It is conducive to magnificence.'

The great oak bed with the polished steel posts in which we were all born was soon in place in the main bedroom. On the mantelpiece stood the casket. A large Italian painted antique clock was on a bracket on the wall with a gilt angel-head on either side of it which we came to know as Tick and Tock. The bedroom had now acquired a light oak washstand to match the dressing-table with the three-leaf mirror, and a very small oak chest of drawers, also designed by Ned.

At first they did not have any pictures so as not to offend Ned's father. The old man was anyway hurt because they had not bought a picture from him; to have hung one by someone else would have been an added insult. 'We can't have a father picture,' Ned wrote to Emily soon after their marriage, 'they are so funny.' He was later to describe one of the 'funniest' – 'a black Venus to elevate the blacks in the eyes of the whites!! Venus is Aileen black all over laying up against a Surrey bank with a parrot in a nutbush and some geraniums under the hedgerow to give colour!!' Unfortunately I can find no trace of this delightful-sounding picture.

*　　*　　*

72

For several months after the move to Bloomsbury Square the house was in no condition to receive guests, but as soon as everything was straight they gave their first dinner party. It was all very well for Ned to have written, 'Food matters not! Except how it is served . . .': the thin gravy soup of that first dinner party, followed by 'salmi of duck', a few bones floating in the same soup, may have been graciously served but Emily burnt with shame and felt she could never entertain again. Oh, how different this was from the dear little white rooms of her dreams with the perfect French couple to look after them. In Bloomsbury Square they remained for years overhoused, understaffed and underfurnished.

At first they went out together. They stayed several times at Munstead House. Emily and Aggie Jekyll never really hit it off. During one visit Emily offended Aggie deeply by remarking on the delicious noise she made while eating toast; Emily had genuinely meant it as a compliment. Ned always held Aggie up to Emily as a model hostess, but even if Emily had had Aggie's gift in that direction she would never have been able to afford the Jekyll standard of living. She could not afford a well-trained cook and had no idea how to turn a bad cook into a good one or even into a better one. She had even less interest in housekeeping than talent for it.

In the early stages of her pregnancies she was to suffer acutely from sickness and never could make Ned understand how much she minded his pipe at such times. There is a pathetic letter from her written in 1900 when her second child was on the way, in which she tried to explain her feelings:

This is only a little line to ask you to be patient with your Emy. You are so endlessly good to me always – but just at present try Love and remember I am not feeling well – and it is a peculiar kind of illness which effects nerves and temper and everything. Try and be a little tender and thoughtful for me – especially if you would think and remember that smoke makes me feel so awfully sick. I don't mean I don't want you to smoke in the room – only try not to smoke in my face – or in cabs and small places. I know you would never do it if you knew how I hated it. You see you have a share in my sufferings – so you must help me to bear them too. Remember too that I have naturally a cross nature – I cannot help it – I try very very hard – but you must help me too. It is not easy for me to be cheerful and amiable as it is for you – so you must just remember you have taken me for better and for worse – and be patient darling. I do love you so but sometimes I feel too tired to be demonstrative and your smoke makes me feel oh! so ill.

Ned was deeply penitent. That his thoughtlessness was only a temporary shadow on their relationship is shown by a letter Emily wrote to him the following August for their fourth wedding anniversary, two months after the baby had been born: 'You are far, far dearer and more precious to me now than ever before and oh darling I love you so so so much that sometimes I wonder if it is too much. You are just the whole meaning and centre of my life – its aim and object – its beginning, middle and end – and every year my horizon widens and my world grows brighter and more lovely – as I love you more, and life binds us closer together.'

After she started a nursery Emily went out less and less until it became the accepted thing for Ned to be asked without her. And very few people ever came to the house apart from members of the family. When Ned had to be away on jobs, as he so often was, she would go and stay at The Danes or at Thursley. Although they never ceased to bewail in their letters the misery of being parted, she sometimes went to The Danes when they could have been together in London, for no other reason it seems than that she preferred being in the country; and every summer she would take the children away for two months to the seaside, either to lodgings or to some ugly rented house, while Ned remained alone in London. She had been brought up in the country, never liked London and never ceased to long for a country house of their own. Ned on the other hand did not much care for the country unless he had work to do there. He liked no sports except fishing and never wanted to go anywhere unless it led to a job. All the same, he frequently expressed his wish for 'the little white house' in the country as soon as they could afford it. That time might not be long delayed. By August 1902 he was writing, 'I have £860 in the bank and £180 accounts sent out – £1,040 – but then I have to pay out £60 or £70 this month, which spoils my £1,000 balance. But we are getting on aren't we? And I am I think working keenly and with some confidence and definiteness.'

*   *   *

The first Lutyens child, a girl, had been born on 8 August 1898. She was called Barbara (soon shortened to Barbie) after Barbara Webb. With her came our beloved nannie, Alice Louise Sleath, who was to remain with us until her death in 1937. We used to celebrate the day she came to us, 25 August; Father called it her nannieversary. Ned was thrilled with this first baby and was always drawing pictures of her in his letters. In spite of his thoughtlessness over smoking, everything to do with motherhood was sacred to him and beautiful. He even thought a pregnant woman beautiful, and he loved Emily to nurse her babies, which she continued to do on each occasion for a year or more. Robert, the only boy came next, born on 13 June 1901. He seems to have been named after Robert Webb rather than after Emily's father. Then on 31 October 1904 came Ursula. She was called after St Ursula in the

Carpaccio paintings of the saint in the Accademia in Venice. We had many mementoes of Venice, including two Fortuny tea-gowns which my mother often wore, yet I cannot find any evidence that my father ever went to Venice, and my mother did not go there until 1924. They must have fallen in love with the Carpaccio series from reproductions. Father had a pair of beds made for Barbie and Ursula, inspired by St Ursula's bed in the Carpaccio picture. We always called them the St Ursula beds although they were of mahogany with wicker-work head and foot.

Agnes Elisabeth was born on 9 July 1906. (She was always called Betty, a name she so intensely dislikes that she has asked me to call her Elisabeth in this memoir.) She derived the name Agnes from Arthur Chapman's wife who died in May 1906. Arthur Chapman was her godfather. Edith Mary was to be the last child; she was born on 31 July 1908. I was called after my two grandmothers. Elisabeth and I managed to shed our first names. I suppose we were lucky in that none of us was called Gertrude.

True, the Bloomsbury Square house was too large in that the rooms were very big and there were too many floors, yet there were very few bedrooms to accommodate us all. There was only one bathroom in the house, on the main bedroom floor. The service lift, worked by ropes, came up most inconveniently into this bathroom. On the top floor the two front rooms were our day and night nurseries. Nannie slept in the night nursery with Ursula, Elisabeth and me. There were three maids in one small room on that floor, including our darling nursery-maid – Annie McKerrow – who came to us when I was three (there had been other nursery-maids before her). The cook slept in the basement. A sewing woman came three days a week. She was called Miss Ada Drake and was by far the most saintly person I have ever known. She made all the children's clothes and most of Mother's. Father always called her Miss Sew-and-Sew.

76

After the first two children were born there grew up a division between the office and the rest of the house. The children were not allowed to go into the offices, and Ned's assistants were not allowed upstairs unless they were invited, which they often were for birthday parties or other celebrations.

By 1904 Ned had several assistants and some paying pupils. His net income by then had risen to £2,884. His genius was to find perfect expression in this opulent Edwardian age. It was the age of the great country house, with entertaining from Saturday to Monday. With bathrooms coming into fashion the rich, who did not want to build new houses, at least wanted to alter or enlarge their existing ones (Crooksbury was enlarged twice). In the middle of the decade Lutyens's style began to change from cottage-picturesque to the symmetry of the classical. He was probably influenced by living in a Georgian house with the classical features he had fallen in love with. In 1906, with the building of Heathcote at Ilkley, Yorkshire, for Mr Ernest Hemingway for £17,500, he reached what he called his 'Wrenaissance'; Wren thereafter became his lodestar; he had entered on 'the Great Game', another name he gave to classical architecture. He wrote to Herbert Baker about the classical Orders: 'When they are right they are curiously lovely and unalterable like a plant form ... the perfection of the Order is far nearer nature than anything produced on impulse and accident-wise.'

Not unnaturally some fellow architects, jealous of Lutyens's extraordinary success, attributed it to the advantages of his marriage. Only quite recently some critic in an article referred sneeringly to his 'clever marriage'. In truth he met nearly all his clients directly or indirectly through the Jekylls. Apart from the house he built for his mother-in-law and St Martin's Church, both at Knebworth, the commissions he did get through his wife might equally well have come if he had never met her. The Gerald Balfours, for instance, for whom he built a house near Woking, Fishers Hill, in 1900, he could have met through the Horners at Mells. Betty Balfour was a great friend of Frances Horner and often stayed with her. In the same way a commission, also in 1900, to build a house for a relation by marriage of Gerald Balfour, Alfred Lyttleton – Grey Walls, near North Berwick – could have come through the Horners whose close friend he was. When Ned was asked to design the British Pavilion for the 1901 Paris Exhibition it was probably because Colonel Jekyll was on the Committee.

What helped Lutyens as much as anything in his career were the illustrated articles on his work in *Country Life* whose proprietor and editor, Edward Hudson, he had met through Miss Jekyll, as I have already said; Hudson and Emily never got on well together.

Quite apart from not bringing Ned commissions, Emily was not able to help him overcome his deep sense of social insecurity resulting from his father's poverty and artistic failure and his own lack of a public school education. *Au fond* Emily was confident of her place in the social world derived from her father's eminence and her own 'handle', as she derisively referred to her courtesy title, but she was too shy to support Ned in society. Indeed, he fared better without her. The greatest help she gave him was in allowing him, or, rather, pressing him, to go out on his own, even to stay away for week-ends on his own. She always declared that in consequence she was the most popular wife in England. A lively, entertaining, attractive single man, who can be relied on to pull his weight, will always be an invaluable asset to any hostess, and he managed to hide his vulnerability and sense of social inadequacy behind a clown's mask. Ned might have lost many a job if Emily, never a social success, had had to be invited too. As it was, he was able to establish the perfect relationship with his clients; he flirted with his hostesses just enough to flatter them without irritating their husbands, and impressed his hosts with his profound knowledge of building techniques. He never underrated what he owed to his clients. In the first article of his ever to appear in print he wrote, 'There will never be great architects or great architecture without great patrons.'[1]

One relation of Emily's whom Ned occasionally met staying at Munstead House was her mother's eldest sister, Theresa, Mrs Charles Earle, who became well known in 1897 with the publication of *Pot-Pourri from a Surrey Garden* which went into at least twenty editions.[2] Without any of the beauty of her twin sisters or their grace (she was short and stout), she had far more intelligence, humour and liveliness. She combined many of the qualities of Gertrude and Aggie Jekyll, having a diversity of hobbies, including gardening, and being a great reader and a great home-maker. Although much poorer than the Jekylls she yet provided open hospitality and delicious food at her house at Cobham, Woodlands. Seven years older than Gertrude she was far more up to date, while sharing Gertrude's freshness of mind and complete honesty of opinions. She was the Aunt T often mentioned with affection in Ned's letters. We all loved her, for she had a special understanding of the young. I remember her quite well since she did not die until 1925 in her eighty-ninth year. Her son, Lionel Earle, one of my godfathers, was helpful to Ned in many ways after he became Permanent Secretary to the Office of Works in 1912.

Ned was probably aware of the rumours that he had made a 'clever marriage' when he wrote to Emily in 1906, 'I know my first love for you was awakened by your darling steadfast face – and my love for you was in no way influenced by my life chase after my work pursuits – I daren't say Art – it is either too common – or too big a word to use.'

[1] *The Work of the Late Philip Webb (Country Life*, Vol. 37, 1915, p. 619).
[2] This was followed in 1899 by *More Pot-Pourri from a Surrey Garden*, *A Third Pot-Pourri* in 1903 and *Memoirs and Memories* in 1911.

Ned made friends with many of his clients – with Herbert Johnson, for instance, for whom he built Marsh Court at Stockbridge, Hants, in 1901; with Ivor Guest (afterwards Lord Wimborne) for whom he carried out the first of many alterations to Ashby St Ledgers, near Rugby, in 1904; with the Mark Fenwicks for whom he built Abbotswood, Stow-on-the-Wold, Gloucestershire, in 1906, and Gaspard and Henry Farrer for whom he designed The Salutation at Sandwich in 1911. Edward Hudson himself was to become a life-long friend and admirer as well as patron. Ned had already in 1901 built Deanery Garden at Sonning, Berkshire, for him when the following year Hudson bought Lindisfarne Castle on Holy Island, off the coast of Northumberland, a part ruin with thirty bedrooms, and asked Ned to restore it. It is a fantastically beautiful place, three miles out to sea but attached at low tide to the mainland by a causeway. Now belonging to the National Trust it can be seen much as it was when Hudson lived there. Then in 1904 Lutyens built the new *Country Life* offices in Tavistock Street off the Strand, his first London building.

Hudson was a tall man, very kind, but unattractively plain. He was Ursula's godfather and often came to our nursery. He was devoted to Ursula who unfortunately disliked him and would never allow him to kiss her. He must have known this, for she would always turn her head away, yet he would persist in the attempt. He was very good-natured. We had a fire-screen in the nursery, the bottom part of which could be moved up leaving a gap at the bottom. It was perfect for playing French Revolutions, and Hudson was most obliging in kneeling on the floor and putting his head through the gap so that we could guillotine him. At Christmas time, when Father was in India, it would embarrass Mother dreadfully when he took her with all of us to Liberty's toy department, then the most expensive in London, to choose presents without giving her any idea of how much he wanted to spend.

But the client of Father's we saw most of was Arthur Chapman. We always called him Chippy. After his wife's death in 1906 he fell in love with Mother who was never in the slightest bit in love with him. For several years he came to stay at the seaside houses Mother took for the summer holidays, sharing the expenses. He seemed perfectly happy playing golf, amusing us children and reading aloud to Mother in the evenings. It was an odd arrangement which Father did not really seem to mind. When he once expressed some jealousy that Chippy did not have to earn his living and had nothing to do so that he could spend his time with Emily and the children, Mother reminded him sharply that Chippy was entirely self-made and that for years he had had to slave away in India without wife or home. 'And nothing bores you more,' she added, 'than to come away with me and the children. You have no occupation, no interest, outside your work' – which was true.

Another friend of Father's was James Barrie whom he had met through the Archie Groves of Berry Down. Ned designed the scenery for *Quality Street* in 1902 and was later to design the sets for the first production of *Peter Pan*; and he invented Nana. It was through our night-nursery window at Bloomsbury Square that the Darling children flew to the Never Land. William Nicholson, whom Father first met in 1902, became another life-long friend, as did also the Jekylls' younger daughter Pamela whom he had known since she was a small child and who married Reginald McKenna. McKenna, after he became Chairman of the Midland Bank, was to give Lutyens a great deal of work.

The family we knew best, however, apart from our Lytton cousins, were the Cecil Barings. Cecil Baring was a director of Barings Bank and afterwards became Lord Revelstoke. In 1905 Father began to restore for him a derelict castle off the coast of Dublin, Lambay. The work took several years to complete and involved many happy visits to Lambay where the Barings lived in a cottage while the work was going on. They also had a house in Bryanston Square and one at Chigwell in Essex. In 1902 Uncle Cecil, as we called him, had made a most romantic marriage with an enchanting American woman. The story, as told to me by Nannie, was that they had eloped after locking her husband in the refrigerator (I do not vouch for the truth of this). As a divorced woman she was not at that time accepted in English society, hence the retreat of Lambay. They had three children – Daphne, the same age as Ursula, Calypso, the same age as Elisabeth, and a boy, Rupert (the present Lord Revelstoke), three years younger than me. Cecil Baring was extremely good looking. I seem to remember that he had lost all his hair in an earthquake; if so it only enhanced his appearance. He looked like the marble bust of a Roman senator tinted pink. He also had the most beautiful singing voice, and whenever we were all together he would sing 'Green Grow the Rushes O' for which we provided the chorus. Mrs Baring, with broad features, had a most attractively alluring face. Father and Uncle Cecil planned that Robert should marry Calypso and that Father should design a house for them on Chelsea Embankment. Calypso was a tumultuously alive, wiry, wild, very naughty girl whom I found devastatingly attractive. I was jealous of her simply because I wanted to marry Robert myself. Father always seemed at his happiest with the Barings.

*   *   *

The Lutyens office remained at Bloomsbury Square until it was moved to 17 Queen Anne's Gate in August 1910. A. J. Thomas, a dumpy little man who smoked as many pipes as Father and who had joined him as an assistant in 1902 and was to remain with him for thirty-three years, was put in charge of Queen Anne's Gate. Thomas was allowed to do work on his own account, using Lutyens designs, in lieu of part of his salary, an arrangement that was to lead to trouble.

He did not get on well with the rest of the office and he and Emily never liked each other.

Fifteen years after Lutyens's death, some of his early assistants and pupils met at the Architectural Association to pay tribute to 'Lut' as he was generally called in the office. One of them, John Brandon Jones, told a story about the building of Heathcote in 1906, his first completely classical country house as I have already mentioned. Lutyens, showing his client, Ernest Hemingway, a rich Yorkshireman, the unfinished building, pointed out to him where the black marble staircase was to go. 'I don't want a black marble staircase,' his client said, 'I want an oak staircase.' 'What a pity,' Lutyens replied. Later, when they visited the house again, the black marble staircase was installed. The client protested, 'I told you I didn't want a black marble staircase.' 'I know,' Lutyens answered, 'and I said "What a pity", didn't I?'

Another assistant, Horace Farquarson, recalled that 'Lutyens was extraordinarily shy with his draughtsmen and they found it difficult to get him to criticise anything or answer questions; but darkly at dead of night he went round the boards, and in the morning we found them covered with little notes that he had made'. Oswald Milne, who worked with him on Marsh Court and many other early houses, said that he was 'a great worker. If not visiting a job, he stood working at his drawing-board in the front office – I do not remember him ever sitting down – legs apart and usually smoking a pipe. He spoke somewhat incoherently; he never explained himself; his wonderful fund of ideas and invention were expressed not in speech but at the end of his pencil. If we were in difficulties we would invite him to come and help us out. He would put a piece of tracing-paper over the drawing, and in a minute or two he had sketched half a dozen solutions to the problem'. Oswald Milne also recalled that 'Lutyens swept all before him when he arrived at the site . . . He had a wonderful way with his clients. He was marvellous, not only in dealing with materials but in

83

dealing with human beings. He always got them to spend what he wanted them to spend'. This is the reason why some people hesitated to employ him. He gained the reputation for being the most expensive architect in England, although, of course, he charged no more commission than any other. It is also the reason why some of his clients, such as Princess Louise, turned to Thomas: from Thomas they could get Lutyens designs without being wheedled into spending more than they wanted to spend. Lutyens's own lawyer, Francis Smith, who had married a first cousin of Emily's, employed Thomas to build their house in the New Forest.

Another early assistant, Nicholas (Beau) Hannen, who became the actor, declared that the three years he spent serving his apprenticeship with Lutyens at Bloomsbury Square were among the happiest of his life. It *was* a happy office in spite of the assistants being expected to work almost as hard as their master for only £2 a week, and often being asked to come back after dinner. Ned wrote to Emily in 1906, 'Two new pupils this morning. They *terrify* me.'

* * *

I saw very little of my father in my early years. In 1912, when I was only four, he started to go to India every winter for the building of New Delhi. He never came with us for our long summer holidays by the sea, and even when we were all in London he was frequently away on jobs. Between my parents' bedroom and the dressing-room there was a long walk-in hanging cupboard with brown holland curtains to cover the clothes. Father would play terrifying games of bears with us in that cupboard while he was dressing in the morning.

I never remember his being cross with us. The only punishment we ever received from Mother or Nannie was to be sent to bed. They would reason, 'If you are naughty you must be ill, and when you are ill bed is the best place for you.'

But there was one occasion when Robert was so naughty that Mother insisted that Father should punish him. Ordered to do something drastic, Father, the gentlest man in the world who could not bear any sort of violence, boxed Robert's ears so hard that it was feared he had broken an ear-drum. It was Father who cried far more than Robert.

Father left our education entirely to Mother. She had advanced views on everything; she did not believe in boarding schools so she sent Robert as well as Barbie to a co-educational day-school in Hampstead, King Alfred's, which had a remarkable headmaster in Mr Russell. I believe it was the first co-educational school in England. Elisabeth was the only one of us to go to a boarding school; she was 'difficult' and always wanted to be different. Mother often begged Father to help the children – to teach them to draw, for instance, but he maintained that one could not *learn* to draw; it was better to learn languages which could be taught, and, anyway, he felt incapable of teaching anything.

Father was a Fellow of the Zoo and would sometimes take us there on Sunday mornings to go behind the cages to see the animals being fed. It was not his fault that I hated these expeditions; I have always detested the Zoo with its abominable smell. And on Sundays we would go down to the dining-room after lunch to be given our weekly chocolate (no other sweets were allowed for the sake of our teeth, a deprivation for which I have every reason to be thankful), and Father would draw pictures for us. Many of these drawings were on paper with a fold in it so that when the fold was pulled open they revealed a surprise, such as a chicken having laid an egg or a woman having produced a baby. One drawing I remember showed a seated man with bare legs bathing his feet in a foot-bath. The 'legs' were two of Father's fingers stuck through holes in the man's torso and disappearing into the foot-bath. Some of his sketches were transparencies; – when held up to the light another figure was revealed. One of these showed Crippen lying in bed; there was a chest of drawers in the room and when the picture was held up to the light his dead wife appeared lying in one of the drawers. But I think his most successful pictures had horses in them. There was a lightness and gaiety about his drawings which I have never seen in anybody else's. He could make even an elephant look like a ballet dancer (he came to love elephants after he went to India).

After lunch on Sundays Father was supposed to amuse us in the drawing-room for half an hour. He had an unfair way of doing this. He would promise a shilling to the one who went to sleep first. Of course he always went to sleep first himself. The only indoor game he ever played with us was dominoes. Unfortunately he never taught us chess, a game he was very fond of. Later on he played chess with a man in India. They would send a move to each other by alternate mails so that a single game might last for months.

Father would give us £1 each for our birthdays. I have a letter from him written on my fifth birthday: 'My darlingest Mary, tell Nannie to put £1 away for you. This morning I woke at 5 – and I wanted my little daughters very badly. Don't forget darling I have given you £1 as I am dreadful at forgetting that sort of thing now. I love you darling and just put your arms right round yourself – and lift yourself high up and then kiss the tip of your nose. Your ever loving father, Father.' He always signed himself like that.

But Nannie would never have let him forget. I remember her waylaying him on the stairs more than once, 'Come on now, Sir, I want a pound from you for Mary's birthday.'

'Not now, Nannie – later – I'm in a hurry, and it's not her birthday yet.'

'No, *now*, Sir – you know what you are – and we shall be away on her birthday,' and the £1 would be extracted from him. I never saw any of this money. Nannie put it straight into the Post Office and my Post Office book disappeared.

Nannie had no awe of Father and oddly enough, considering how we all adored her, I do not think he really liked her. He was perhaps a little jealous of her. He preferred the elderly dragon of a parlour-maid called Walters, who was with us for years and who looked after his clothes as well as doing all the parlour work single-handed.

As far as I remember Father always wore a brown suit and brown shoes, a duck-egg green shirt and high starched butterfly collar with a narrow black tie. If he ever had a new suit it never looked new because of the ever-bulging pockets in which he kept note-pad, pencils, a knife for sharpening pencils, an india rubber, several little pipes, several boxes of matches (he smoked many more matches than pipes, for he was always allowing his pipe to go out) and his tobacco pouch. His note-pads, which he called 'virgins', were specially made for him. Measuring about eight inches by five they had to stand upright in his pocket with the top protruding. The pages were fastened by a string through a hole in the top left-hand corner which made them easy to tear off and give away. He must have given away thousands of these pages with what he called 'sketchicatures' on them.

Father used also to tell us nonsensical little stories which I, at any rate, was never tired of hearing. There was the story about a bishop who went away for the week-end. He was asked by his hostess on Saturday evening what he would like for breakfast next morning – and she gave him a choice. Here followed a long list of traditional English breakfast dishes. Having heard her to the end the bishop replied, 'Thank you, but all I want is owls' bowels on toast.' My own favourite among his stories was of the old lady who bicycled to church; the wind was against her all the way, so she prayed in church that the wind might change. It did, and was against her all the way going home.

Father never laughed aloud; he chuckled. I never heard Mother laugh aloud either except on one occasion. Then we were all so terrified that we ran out of the room thinking she had gone mad.

* * *

One of Father's houses that we knew as well as we knew our own was Homewood, at Knebworth, a couple of miles from the big house, which he had built in 1901 for our Lytton grandmother. (It was on the Knebworth estate and her son, Victor, had paid for it.) We always spent our Easter holidays there. It reminded Elisabeth of the old lady who once asked Father to build her a cottage full of very large rooms. Homewood was certainly not a cottage (I believe the definition of a cottage is a house in which the staircase appears as soon as you open the front door). It was a small house by the standards of the day and quite a large one by modern standards. It was on two floors only. It had three sitting-rooms and six bedrooms, two of them very small, and one bathroom, apart from the servants' quarters. What gave the house a sense of spaciousness was the very wide main staircase with shallow treads leading up from the inner hall and lit by the glass roof of the first floor landing. The stairs were carpeted in apple green with wide verges of glossy white paint. It was like 'the little white house' of the casket, although of quite a different design, and we loved it. There was no electricity and I associate it with the cosy smell of oil lamps which left black smudges on the ceilings. Our grandmother never used the bathroom. Throughout her long life – she died in 1936 at the age of ninety-five – she preferred a tin tub in front of her bedroom fire.

We often saw our Lytton cousins at Knebworth House when we stayed at Homewood. In 1902 Victor had married the exquisitely beautiful Pamela Plowden. They had four children – Antony, who was killed in a flying accident in 1933, Hermione, a year younger than Ursula who was her great friend, Davina, a year younger than me who was my great friend, and John, who was killed in the last war. Father, who did several small alterations for Victor at Knebworth House, admired Pamela immensely, not only for her beauty but for her impeccable taste and gift for home-making.

We were much closer, of course, to our mother than to our father. After tea every day Mother used to come up to the nursery for an hour and read aloud to Ursula and me. She read beautifully. Before I was nine and a half (I can date this accurately because at that age we went to live in the country) she had read to us all her favourite authors – Jane Austen, Dickens, Thackeray, the Brontës, Stevenson, Anstey, W. W. Jacobs, George Birmingham, Saki, and a great deal of Bulwer-Lytton (her grandfather) – books she had earlier read to Barbie and Robert. She would always knit while she was reading to us and was apt to drop a stitch at the most exciting moments. She knitted all our jerseys.

Elisabeth hated being read to, just as Father did, which made her feel neglected as a child because it was our chief contact with Mother. After reading, Mother would go and change for dinner and then come up and say goodnight to us in bed. She usually wore one of her two Fortuny tea-gowns – one in black, the other in sea-green – in which she looked very beautiful. These marvellous garments of very soft satin, accordion-pleated, could be tied in a knot for packing (another Venetian secret?). They lasted for years.

Periodically Mother would go to bed with a bad sick headache which was always preceded by dazzles in front of one eye which we called 'twinkles'. She had inherited these migraines from her mother and passed them on to Barbie and, to a much lesser degree, to me. She was always, unsuccessfully, seeking cures for them which led her to some very strange quacks and naturopathic establishments. Although capable of tremendous exertion when really interested in some activity, she had little natural vitality. As well as migraines she often suffered from back-ache, the result of a slight curvature of the spine, neglected in childhood. Father, on the other hand, in spite of his poor health as a child, or perhaps because of it, had splendid health and exuberant vitality. Apart from an occasional cold or bout of 'flu I do not remember him being ill until the severe attack of pneumonia he had in 1938 which nearly killed him.

CHAPTER FIVE

Emily's Discontent
1905–1910

After eight years of marriage Emily was lonely and dissatisfied. Ned gave her no companionship. Even when he was at home he persisted in the habit of returning to his drawing-board after dinner and working till past midnight. With a nannie and nursery-maid to look after the children she had little to occupy her. One might have expected her to do something about the quite large garden at the back of the house, but it was entirely neglected. Nor were there ever any flowers in the house; Ned, in spite of his love of gardens, disliked cut flowers or even pot-plants, indoors. Housekeeping irked Emily and the servants were a continual worry. Before her marriage she had played the guitar and sung to it; now she played it only to the children, and by the time I came along she had ceased to play it altogether, though she still sang, unaccompanied and in perfect tune, such songs as 'Polly Wolly Doodle', 'O dem Golden Slippers', 'Randall my Son', 'A Wearin' o' the Green' and dozens more. Ned never made any reference to this accomplishment of hers in any of his hundreds of letters to her. They never danced together after they were married although they both loved dancing, and only very occasionally did they go to a theatre.

Unfortunately for her married life her intellectual aspirations and emotional and spiritual yearnings could not be fulfilled by her love for her husband or her children. Moreover, sexual intercourse had become increasingly disagreeable to her so that she made every excuse to avoid it. So much is forgiven genius; genius will out, they say, but so will any overwhelmingly strong urge to self-fulfilment. The compulsion of a dandelion seed to become a dandelion is as great as for an acorn to become an oak. A letter she wrote to Ned in July 1905 gives prophetic warning of what was to happen to their relationship:

I have been *very* worried over household matters lately and let myself go – and then when my mind is in an irritable nervous state, and you seem indifferent and unsympathetic and far away from me, then black thoughts creep in, and I get so angry over any little trifle that makes an excuse. I think we might both try more and make more sacrifices for each other. I know your work must come first, rightly so, but you do owe me some little duty also. You always manage to make time for what you *really* want to do – fishing, patience – a book if you are interested in it – but you have *never* time for me – and you want to keep me don't you? I think I am worth some effort – and I get so afraid lest we drift further apart instead of growing closer. I don't think you feel it quite as I do for your work is so much to you – and you see so many people, and I don't think you have a complicated nature striving after many things, which I have. I just ache and crave for sympathy and understanding, and have it I must – and I want so that you should give it to me – and not let me find it outside my home. The deep things of life – God – religion in any form – mean so much to me – and you only scoff – till I have shut all those thoughts away from you [Ned believed that Christ's teaching was 'only possible at a mother's knee']. Then the children [there were only three of them at that time], their life

92

and their future, character, intellect – you don't seem to care – though perhaps you do. We never read a book together, you never tell me of your thoughts on any book you read. All I know of your work is its worries. I see so little of you – and when we do meet you are absorbed in your paper or a book – and often you never look up or listen when I speak. It is not that I don't love you – I love you so much I want more of you – not your body but your soul, your intellect, something big to take hold of and share, and when I am in a mood of longing for sympathy all you give me is criticism or jokes. Then I feel as if I bled inwardly, and I harden my heart like Pharoah, and go far away from you. Do try and bring me near while there is still time – be patient and gentle – and give me a little bit of your life. I am not exacting – if you would but make me equal to your pipe!

I must stop. Goodbye – I do love you and want a husband for my soul and intellect as well as for my body.

Ned responded by return from Marsh Court where he was staying:

My own darling love

Your sweet letter has burnt into me – and I feel so wretched as I greatly fear and know it to be just and true. I did not mean to be so wrong and thoughtless and I do love you very dearly in the best way and the way you most appreciate. I know this is so by the pain I feel at the knowledge that you have really suffered. Your dear sad letter makes me miserable now but I shall, we shall both be so glad that it has been written and you must help me and be patient with me and take me by the hand as though I was a little child.

Your happiness is of far greater count than all or any

work – and all the work in the world would count as nothing whilst you are unhappy and lost to me. My own darling forgive me – I long to get back to night but have to meet people here tomorrow.

I pray you may be kept patient with me for a little while. O Emmie my love I am unhappy for I love you so much and if you are unhappy so am I so with you. You have been worried and so brave and your bravery perhaps keeps me from realising all you have to go through. I have been very silly cruel and heartless though I never meant to hurt you and you do know how big things are and the all being of God. My heart is low and I am miserable and penitent and I can only come to you on my knees and beg you to make me better kinder and more worthy of you. You are, love, the light of my life you know.

Fishing, patience, Les Miserables are as nothing, and I count them nothing. Books – patience do help when I can't work and can't think so I have nothing to say. Fishing I do like but it is useful in other ways [as a social asset when staying away]. My work is first but before that you hold my whole heart and if you suffer by me one pang of pain or disappointment I feel lost. O Emmie love forgive your Nedi and help him – and I will try too.

Your own very loving Ned

He spoke the truth when he said she was the light of his life, and she continued to be so until his death, but, alas, he could not change. He tried to read more books because she wanted him to but he never really enjoyed reading. Meredith seems to have been the novelist he liked best and he quite enjoyed Hardy. He read Gibbon and struggled with Motley's *Dutch Republic*, skipping until he came to the part about the Armada which he found thrilling. As for religion, he was *au fond* a deeply religious man; it was the narrowness of all creeds that he disliked and scoffed at. He believed passionately in the God of beauty, whereas Emily was not yet emancipated from orthodox Christianity. What she feared might happen did happen: she found the understanding and sympathy she craved for outside her home.

But this was still six years away, years in which she still hoped to find companionship in him. At the beginning of May 1906, when she was staying with her mother for the Easter holidays, she wrote to tell him of one of her difficulties:

> I am terribly conscious of having no artistic perception what ever. I also am very shy at pretending to any knowledge and then being shown up to your artistic friends, and so feel it is better rather brutally perhaps to disclaim all knowledge about your work. All the same deep down in my heart I am tremendously – *desperately* proud of you and am dreadfully jealous of people whom I think can help you when I can't – Pamela [Lytton] and Mrs Horner.

This letter crossed one from him written in the train on 4 May on his way to Hestercombe, near Taunton, Somerset, where he was laying out the garden he and Miss Jekyll had designed for Mr Portman. He told her that Mr Hemingway had accepted and signed a contract for £17,500 for Heathcote. Other contracts recently 'signed and sealed' amounted to £34,000 'which means £1,730 for us. We shall be able to save this year'. He continued:

> Your mother said [in a letter] it was a pity that we had not our work in common; she and your father had and did everything together . . . Political life is so different and regards what I design and how I do it – I don't know. It just comes because I want it to – and if it don't I have to

grip inside and make or force it, and there is no speech that can ever describe it. My only words are foolish – quips and jibes – but you are all there in all my works and whether you will or not are a part of it and in it. And then it is so technical. The political life and those other professions are all based on literature which, at the best, produces a Pater or a Ruskin – in the arts. I don't want you to be either of these.

Two days later, again in the train on his way back to London, he took up the same theme once more:

I think I do wrong not to make the attempt and force myself to find a language to describe building and my aspirations in my work to you my own best and very true love and let the technicality go hang – and gradually we might get a language that we can understand in, and as my language improves your understanding of building will improve too and then it will be a joy indeed and we can sleep in each others sleeves in happiness, surely an Eastern simile. I shall try and write you now something – and you must tell me what you think – but dont be too critical – and if I write you on building darling I would like you to keep it absolutely private and to ourselves – burn them after reading – for one is bound to write what one may not mean, what one has to correct or to abandon with greater light – or differing feeling.

This shows not only the difficulty he had in expressing his feelings about building but the deep distrust he had of words. If he actually wrote something for her she must have burnt it. They never did find a common language for their very different aspirations.

*   *   *

In the autumn of this year, 1906, Ned agreed very reluctantly to go on a cruise in the Baltic. He had made a rule never to go anywhere unless it led to work. Nevertheless, he knew he had been overworking – his nerves were on edge, he was irritable in the office and his sleep did not rest him. His hostess on the *Miranda* was Miss Mary Dodge, a very rich American whom Emily was later to convert to Theosophy, but the invitation had come through the Jekylls. Herbert and Aggie Jekyll and their two young daughters were of the party; also Gerald Wellesley and Ozzie Dickinson, who became a life-long friend of Ned's and, incidentally, one of my godfathers. While Ned was away Emily and the children (Elisabeth had been born in July) stayed at Lindisfarne Castle, lent to them by Edward Hudson. The cruise was a huge success. Ned seems to have loved every moment of it. Apart from his honeymoon and a week's fishing with Victor Lytton in Norway in 1904, he had never had a complete holiday before. With a calm sea and plentiful meals, and nothing to do between meals but 'frivol' and make jokes to a highly appreciative audience, he described it as 'fairyland'.

He returned home on 24 September to be greeted by the news in a letter from Emily, who was still at Lindisfarne, that his mother had just died at Thursley. She had been ill on and off since January. On account of her health, as well as from lack of money, the Onslow Square house had been given up the previous year. Ned went first to Lindisfarne and then to Thursley.

Thursley is very very sad [he wrote to Emily] and very empty. The dear quiet presence is still there – but oh so quiet . . . all that country is so wrapt up with Mother and my first work: my rheumatic fever and all Mother was to me those days – came back . . . Molly told me that Father had said that he was glad to think he had never said an unkind word to her and that no word of his could ever have troubled her. It seems very merciful – o that I may think that too – should I have the grief of being the one of us that is left. Darling darling never listen to the unkind things I say.

The old man, then seventy-seven, was to live another nine years, looked after by Aileen in his blindness and by Priscilla Lacy, the nannie, who did not die until 1912 aged eighty-two. He shares the grave-stone in the churchyard at Thursley which Ned designed for his mother – a simple stone cross with a more complicated base.

Two days later Ned was writing again in the train on the way to a job near Manchester:

Angel Mother's death must bring us closer – nearer and dearer to each other. Without *you* I could not have borne it. With you and holding your love – no sorrow – though there and very real – can hold me very tight . . . O Ems, it was very, very heart rending. And through it all – greater than any promise of any life to come – came the knowledge of your great love for me – my whole love for you – our angel children. Wife. I cannot call you by a clearer or more perfect name. You have taught me the loveliness, the holiness of that darling word.

He inherited from his mother a gold ring she had always worn – the marriage ring of the Claddah tribe which had been given to her by Tom Moore. Thereafter he always wore it on the little finger of his left hand.

Emily responded to his grief with all her heart. For a time his mother's death did bring them closer. He wished he could get one or two really big jobs instead of 'a mass of little stuff' so that he would not have to travel so much and could spend more time with her.

Early in 1907 the chance of a really big job came along. He was one of eight leading architects asked to go in for a competition for the new London County Council Headquarters on the south side of Westminster Bridge. He worked on his plans most of the year. On 16 April 1907 he was writing, 'Very busy over L.C.C. I have got the plan to fit all right but the inards are yet many, many hours away from even approximate possibilities. The only news is that I have been elected to the Athenium [sic] Club. It makes my status good but is a horrid expense just at present . . . I *must* win this L.C.C. building – then we could have a country house of our own and you would be more quiet and happy.'

Emily went with the children to Rustington in Sussex that summer where Chippy was with her as usual. Ned sent her a brief character sketch of Miss Jekyll whom he was constantly in touch with over garden designs: 'Bumps is to have the lump in her nose cut out. She writes excitedly and full of arrangements for her operating table: very Bumpsaical. I believe if her head was cut off – she would love to arrange the guillotine and the basket to catch her head.'

Ned paid the family a short visit at Rustington in September and wrote on his return to London:

Glad to get back to my L.C.C. – what shall I do without it? Oh Ems love I do hate you being depressed about yourself and things. You have no cause to be and I do so want to make things easy and happy for you. In house matters you have never had a chance. In summer other peoples squalors and here the office complications fearful but darling the time will come and then we shall fit together into a dear little house of our own. It will be joy.

Emily replied to this:

99

I am so happy when your L.C.C. is making you happy. She is a mistress of as many moods as your wife! I wish I could follow you into it. You seem far away where I cannot come. Darling you can and do help me whenever we can talk openly, even if I am a little depressed. Only do realise it is not money or anything that money brings which will ever make my happiness. If I had a housekeeper she would worry me just as much as a cook. It is calm and inward serenity that I need and that does not depend on any outward thing.

In January 1908 Ned heard that an architect called Ralph Knott had won the competition. 'All my nine months work is lost,' he told Emily. 'You will be kind and not ask too much this year. Our dear little country house must wait a bit. All my little bits and pieces of work seem dull – But I shall soon pick up and be happy again.' The wasted work had cost him £1,000. He was writing a month later to Herbert Baker, who, though still a friend, was living and working in South Africa: 'The L.C.C. I feel sick of – bruised with. One was so in the dark as to what was wanted. The site so lovely, the conditions so difficult.' It was the loveliness of the site that had appealed to him more than anything; nor did he feel that Ralph Knott had adhered to all the difficult conditions.

In the winter of 1908–09 he was appointed consultant architect for Hampstead Garden Suburb and given the centre, including the Church of St Jude, to design. He also designed the Free Church. It was fortunate that he had this work, for Lloyd George's 1909 Budget in April – called the People's Budget – which increased Income Tax and Death Duties and introduced Super-Tax for the first time, fell heavily on the rich Edwardians who had been his best clients. With the death of King Edward in 1910 the great era of country house building came virtually to an end. Lutyens was never happy building for Governments or Councils whom he was unable to charm and coax and persuade not to spoil the ship for a ha'porth of tar as he did his private clients. Committees of grave officials were not always able to discern his intense seriousness under his flippant manner. The more uncomfortable he felt the more facetious he became. As he wrote to Emily in February 1909, 'A meeting of this sort always makes me uncomfortable. I imagine all sorts of horrible ignorant men, though they seldom are – yet I don't have the confidence they will agree with my rights and wrongs.'

He was to have more to do with committees when in October 1909 he was asked to go to Rome as consultant architect to the Royal Commission set up to represent Britain in the International Exhibition to take place in Turin and Rome in 1911. Victor Lytton was the Chairman of this Committee. Ned went first to Rome but could not resist stopping a night in Genoa on the way. It was his first visit to Italy and everything he saw thrilled him. In the train between Genoa and Rome he wrote a long letter to Emily:

The architecture – very little I have seen – cries aloud for sculpture and good housemaids . . . the lavish use of marble as stone; the splendid waste of space in the buildings and the economy of it in road ways marks the place. The very reverse of what we lay down as right in England. The lavish space given away in staircases makes me sick with envy . . . Another thing that astonishes me is *the fact* of the small amount of window area required to light a *room* – brilliantly well. The architecture – a good deal of it – is very badly finished off. Thoughtless, which would make me wild if it was mine. The great buildings on the hill tops excite me *fearfully* . . . I do wish I could have come here with Wren . . . Just past the Carrara mountains where the white marble of that name comes from. There is lots! left for me!! . . . Pisa. Just got an oh so short a glimpse of white

101

marble buildings with *lovely* red roofs against great blue hills lit by a setting sun – *lovely*, just what the world ought to be.

He ended this letter, 'Genoa thrilling . . . but nothing – nor anything can come up to my own darling Emy in London alone.'

After a very short stay in Rome he went north again to Turin where he met Victor and Pamela Lytton. He was very bored by the Committee meetings in Turin. 'During the long stupid arguments in a language I don't understand I sustained the courage of my friends by portraits of the Italians with and without their clothes etc. If there had not been some mild form of relaxation the while – I am sure there would have been high words and irremediable disasters in the tempers.'

He returned with the Lyttons to Rome where the weather was glorious. He wrote from there on 21 October, 'It is all very wonderful and to see the things one knows from illustrations – down a little street and then a corner and lo and behold stands some old loved friend in the form of a doorway, staircase or palace. I recognise some of them by their backs – backs which I had never seen . . . There is so much here of little ways of things I thought I had invented! no wonder people think I must have been in Italy.'

As he had hoped, he was asked to design the British Pavilion for the Exhibition. It was to be so much admired that it was afterwards built as a permanent home for the British School in Rome. This necessitated his going several times to Rome.

*   *   *

One of the last big private houses Lutyens was asked to build was in 1910 – Castle Drogo for Julius Drew, founder of the Home and Colonial Stores, for £50,000, and £10,000 for the garden. It was on the top of a hill above Drewsteignton in Devonshire. (Now the property of the National Trust, it took twenty years to complete. It was not until 1915 that Lutyens asked Mr Drew if Miss Jekyll might be called in to help with the garden. Up to this day it is the last castle built in England.) Ned was excited by the commission, though he wished that Drew 'didn't want a castle, but just a delicious lovable house with plenty of good large rooms in it'. Even though it was against his own interests he would often advocate living in an old house rather than a new one: 'an old house has a creative heart – a mother to a mistress'. Emily was all against large houses; she wanted a cottage with the smallest possible number of servants. Ned sympathised with her up to a point: 'I do wish we could live small and be quite independent – but I hate squalid houses and mean gardens. I want loveliness and cleanliness without conscious effort. And that means help and help means money.' And again, in August 1910 he was writing, 'I look at the big house from the other and best point of view. A centre for all that charity that should begin at home and cover henwise with wings of love those all near about her that are dependent, weaker and smaller.' He was essentially a feudalist, deploring democracy and railing against Asquith and, even more so, Lloyd George, whereas Emily was a socialist. It was another great incompatibility between them and their efforts to convert each other in their letters were, of course, hopeless.

*　　*　　*

Ironically, it was through Ned that Emily found the fulfilment she had been longing for and which was to take her away from him in spirit. She had tried to fill her emptiness with social work, becoming a visitor to the Lock Hospital for venereal diseases and, in 1907, joining an organisation called The Moral Education League of which she attended conferences in Manchester and Birmingham, but although she was happier with these occupations they did not absorb or satisfy her. Naturally she was drawn into the Women's Suffrage Movement. Unlike her unmarried sister Constance, however, who, in spite of a weak heart, went four times to prison for throwing stones, she never became a militant suffragette. The third time Constance went to prison, in January 1910, it was in disguise since she believed that on the two previous occasions she had received preferential treatment because of her title. This time she was forcibly fed without having her heart tested. When her true identity was suspected she was released. Emily went to fetch her from Walton Gaol, Liverpool, and brought her back to Bloomsbury Square where she remained very ill in bed for six weeks. Constance's brothers and sisters were extremely proud of her courage. Ned, alone of the family, sympathised with his mother-in-law who felt that the family had been disgraced.

My darling Mother [Ned wrote to her on 1 February 1910, four days after Constance's release], I do hate writing letters as a rule as you know! but I must write and tell you how much I am thinking of you and feel all the sorrow and heartache this Con-escapading brings you. It seems all so mean and mad and such a waste of energy and real courage, but I do wish you weren't so far away and I do wish to stand by and help you somehow and I do so adore your sweet patience, love and wonderful fortitude.

Darling Granny of my children I do love you so much, Your very, very loving Ned

And later on he was writing to Emily about her mother, 'Poor darling she does hate Con's work and all that – it is a real sorrow and sick at heart feel to her . . . She doesn't think I love her but I can't pour out to her the blandishments I give people who build!!! I love her with different metal. It is like stroking a cat to make it purr – pleasantness with a client is stroking – helps them to purr at all the different corners I have got to pull them round. It is all very mixed and the mixture of it all is perhaps the best metaphor.' And shortly afterwards: 'Do comfort your darling and most beloved mother. I do wish for her sake that she had one child who was of and with her world but I suppose it is human nature and the world is ever changing and our turn will come – our own children will give us pain in a new way peculiar to their generation and our very love for them will make it harder to bear. It means that we must stick close to each other to help each other and bear a common burden and counterweight of love.' He was right; his children were to give him pain.

CHAPTER SIX

Varengeville and Johannesburg
1910–1912

And now we come to the great transformation in Emily's life. In the spring of 1910 she and Ned paid one of their rare visits together to Monsieur Guillaume Mallet, a rich Protestant banker for whom Ned had built a house in 1901, Le Bois des Moutiers, at Varengeville in Normandy. Now Ned was building another house for him at Varengeville, Les Communes. Monsieur Mallet and his wife were both Theosophists, and during the visit Madame Mallet gave Emily the 1907 London lectures of Mrs Annie Besant, President of the Theosophical Society, to read. Emily was particularly struck by two passages in them which would probably not have appealed to her if she had not been influenced already by Ned's broad outlook on religion: 'We do not shut out any man because he does not believe in Theosophical teachings. A man may deny every one of them except that of human brotherhood, and claim his right and place within our ranks'; and, 'To us truth is so supreme a thing that we do not desire to bind any man with conditions as to how, or where, or why, he shall seek it.'

As soon as she returned to England Emily joined the Society. Not content merely to read about it she formed a new Lodge (the Society was divided into Lodges) with Dr Haden Guest (afterwards Lord Guest), and took lessons in public speaking so that she could travel round the country lecturing on her new faith. In spite of her shyness she was to become an excellent public speaker. That summer she met Mrs Besant when she came to London from the International Theosophical Society Headquarters at Adyar, near Madras, where she lived. Emily also went to hear her speak at the Queen's Hall (she was a superb orator) on an 'Ideal Form of Government' (which was later to form the basis of her Commonwealth of India Bill) and on 'The Coming of the World Teacher'. From this last talk Emily discovered that most Theosophists believed that every two thousand years or so a superhuman being called the Lord Maitreya, the World Teacher, came to earth to occupy a human body and found a new religion to help humanity along the path of evolution. (One of the tenets of Theosophy was reincarnation.) The bodies of Sri Krishna and Jesus had both been used in this way. Now it was almost time for the Lord Maitreya to come again. Indeed, it was already known whose body he was to occupy – that of a fourteen-year-old Brahmin boy living at Adyar, just south of Madras, called Jiddu Krishnamurti.

Emily's very soul was drawn to the idea of the coming of the World Teacher. She plucked up courage to ask Mrs Besant to lunch. This sixty-three-year-old woman, hatless, wearing long white garments, with her white curly hair cut short and with a strong rather beautiful face, had an extra-ordinary personal magnetism. Very small in stature, she had immense presence. Ned, who was there for lunch, liked her very much and was impressed by her especially when she asked him to design the new English Theosophical Head-quarters in Tavistock Square. She took greatly to him too; she called him Vishvakarman, the architect of the gods in Hindu mythology.

For some years Emily had been a semi-vegetarian in the hope of curing her migraines; now she became a strict one in accordance with humanitarian Theosophical principles, though she still ate cheese and eggs, eggs being considered birth control not murder. This complicated her housekeeping, for she still had to provide meat for Ned and the occasional guest. She decided to bring up her children as strict vegetarians also; thus I became a vegetarian by the time I was two. Even Nannie became a vegetarian since she could not bear to refuse us the bits of her breakfast bacon we nagged her for. We subsisted largely on milk, cheese, pease pudding and nut cutlets from Shearn's in Tottenham Court Road, shaped to resemble real cutlets with a piece of uncooked macaroni in a frill sticking out at the narrow end like a bone.

* * *

The idea that truth is to be found equally in all religions appealed to Ned. Emily was staying that summer of 1910 with Chippy and the children at East Runton near Cromer in Norfolk. Ned wrote to her in August, 'Your new vision brings you so close to me and I feel to share it and your thoughts in a way I have never done before. It seems a new and wider lease of love.' She too felt at first that Theosophy had brought them mentally much closer. They had now been married thirteen years and both declared what happy years they had been and that the next thirteen would be even happier.

While Emily was at East Runton, Ned moved his office to 17 Queen Anne's Gate, next door to where Edward Hudson lived at No 15. He engaged a caretaker and his wife for 25/- a week – Mr and Mrs Tribe who were to stay with him for nearly forty years. It was to be one of Tribe's jobs to fill six pipes every morning and lay them on Ned's drawing-board with a big box of matches. On 20 August Ned went down to the new office for the first time 'and found things wonderfully tidy – considering – and some of them working in full swing. I gave an office lunch to inaugurate the new house . . . I have moments both of exhilaration and terror'. There would be more room now in Bloomsbury Square for the family, and Ned hoped that more pupils would pay the expenses of the separate office. By this time he was charging his pupils 200 guineas a year.

*　*　*

In the autumn of 1910 Lutyens was asked by the Municipality of Johannesburg to build an Art Gallery in that city, founded by the exuberant Florence Phillips, wife of Lionel Phillips who had made a fortune out of the Rand goldfields. Mrs Phillips asked Hugh Lane to choose the pictures for the Gallery. Although Lutyens had so much other work on hand, including Castle Drogo, he hesitated to accept only because South Africa was now the territory of his old friend Herbert Baker. After written consultation with Baker, however, who was prepared to welcome him, warning him at the same time that there would be strong local feeling against the employment of any British architect for any major work in Johannesburg, he sailed for the Cape on 19 November. (After his departure a letter arrived from Baker telling him not to come after all.) Lutyens left Thomas in charge of the office. He had a list of sixty jobs to go through with him before sailing.

This was the first time Ned was to be away for Christmas and he was dreadfully homesick. From the ship he wrote, 'O Emmie I am so happy with you and in your love and hate to be away from you. Darling, my own sweet treasure, your own absolutely your own Ned.'

On the train journey between the Cape and Johannes-burg Ned was fascinated by all he saw. He found the landscape wonderfully beautiful. In Johannesburg he stayed with the Phillipses at the Villa Arcadia, designed by Baker. He declined an invitation to go down a gold mine, writing to Emily, 'I don't like men digging for potatoes they may not eat and gold they may not spend.' As well as the Gallery, he was now asked by the Government to design the Rand Regiment's War Memorial and a church on which Baker would work with him, and to be a consultant for the Government buildings in Pretoria for which Baker was the architect. He enjoyed the deference with which he was treated, 'though never forgetting the funny side of it all'. A praising newspaper article headed 'A Great Architect' made him 'sweat'. He intensely disliked the meetings with the Town Councillors and other officials. 'My silly innocent little jokes have a great success,' he told Emily, 'yet I was warned by everyone never to make one, yet I haven't met anyone who don't giggle and seem *glad* to. The town council etc are dead against Baker [for the Johannesburg work] and want to rope me in without Baker. This makes my position difficult – Baker is as good and generous as gold and I must be careful not to hurt him however advantageous to myself.' Baker was to write in his memoirs that during this time in South Africa he learnt something of Lutyens's 'wilful masterfulness which early success had developed in him' having worked hitherto only for 'rich and indulgent private clients'. Although Ned's Collins to Baker was very warm they must already have discerned many incompatibilities in each other.

On 1 January 1911, while Ned was still in Johannesburg, Emily was writing to him a really happy letter for once – waking 'to a New Year of hope and work and preparation for the coming Christ . . . All my great good fortune has come through you. You have made it all possible for me.' It was not to be long before she met the vehicle for the Christ. In the spring of 1911 Mrs Besant brought Krishnamurti, now just sixteen, and his younger brother Nityananda, aged thirteen, to England for six months. Emily was among the crowd of Theosophists who went to meet them at Charing Cross Station on 5 May. 'I had eyes for none but Krishna,' she wrote in her autobiography, 'an odd figure with long black hair falling almost to his shoulders and enormous dark eyes with a strange, vacant look in them.' It was love at first sight.

A new organization had just been founded within the Theosophical Society called the Order of the Star in the East, with Krishnamurti as its Head, whose members pledged their lives to preparing the way for the coming of the World Teacher. Emily at once joined this new Order and soon afterwards was made National Representative for it in England.

For the summer holidays of 1911 Mother took us all to Varengeville where the Mallets had lent Les Communes to 'the boys', as we called Krishna and Nitya, and their two Theosophical tutors. Chippy was also of the party and lodged with us in a farmhouse. Father wanted to come over for three days in August, but when Mother told him that he would have to sleep at the Mallets because there was no room at the farm he wrote that he would rather not come if he had to stay with the Mallets – 'It is so uncomfy – and I want to be with you – the family'. He came all the same. It was a very unhappy visit. There was no chance for him to be alone with Emily except for one walk they took together.

I couldn't talk to you a bit [he wrote on 11 August in the train on the way back to England], so I got inside myself and smoked (a form of meditation!) to be scolded and then I said things sounding and affecting cold – longing, *aching*, all the time for a wild hoorah to say I loved you.

You talked of divorce and we both no doubt as little children do attended our own funerals. Then I went away and then you cried. Then I went all pink with compassion for the darling wife I love, have loved and always will love that I was so unkind and unhelpful to. I am so sorry for my bad temper for that is what it is – very very sorry sad and so ashamed and now I am away from you I feel wretched yet I don't want to be back to see you at odd abstracted moments – living away from you – and seeing you only amidst nursery broils. Even our delicious walk felt guilty and stolen. You were Nannie and I was Mallet conscious, and the today wouldn't forget the tomorrow and there was no real unselfconscious joi de l'âme in it. And another condition – our rare encounters find my body self rampant, aggressive, horrid, so there seems no time when the physical imprickles can be forgotten and laid aside to our common happiness. We have no common occupation. I cannot forgo my work with its everpressing claims and you your interests with their compelling claims. Your Theosophy has brought us closer perhaps than any other subject. Its breadth is great but I dread the definitions and their articles and the isolation from the world of man's affairs to which by necessity and will I must belong. Why need we suffer the tyranny of creeds and the narrowing beliefs of men in men. The fencing in of God with palings to his ways. Darling of course I love you. I love you dearly, very dearly, altogether whole heartedly but I do feel the time will come when you will pass me by, so kindly – but pass me by you will and I shall be so lonely and the empty house I go to is as a sign – a prophecy of what will come.

I have been so cross with everyone in my office lately and being cross with you frightens and depresses me. It must effect my work and its quality too.

There is much more of this long sad letter to which Emily replied by return:

Such a sweet darling beautiful letter and it touches me to the soul. You are quite wrong in thinking I am leaving you behind, I am only beginning very very slowly to grow up to you. You were *not* cross the other day – you never are. How

I wish I could make you understand how much I love you – only you will count my kisses, and lip kisses especially, and I can't pay in those coin. At the same time I am so happy just walking hand in hand with you and laying my head against your arm. I love to feel your physical presence and to be close to you but it is all spoilt to me when that sensual touch is dragged in. Coming to me I should like so much better if it was just natural and occasional as it should be at our age, and not the intruding presence every time I hug you.

Before receiving this reply he had written again from London: 'I only know I love you more than I can tell you and hate myself for all my failing to you. The knighthood that I promised you seems to be not mine to give. Deep down I have complete faith in your love for me and take hope in it that I may yet awake in you the wife I know you are and mean to be – my real helpmate and confidant . . . Don't take any personal heed of my letters – just understand I must cry out to you. I find no fault in you. It is just a mea culpa, mea culpa . . . Be just a little pink to me darling and read all this I dare not re-read as a blue wave from me around your feet.'

He poured out his relief when he received her answer to his first letter, having counted the days until he could expect it:

. . . such a darling letter. No, I couldn't sleep that Tuesday and lay awake for hours thinking of you and realizing that I must have lost your love through my own thoughtless ill doing. And I wrote to you in a spirit difficult for me to analyse – a spirit of childish wilfulness – almost resentfulness and hardly know what I said through my love and anguish of love for you and I thought, having posted it, that you would – must – resent it and had you answered hardly I should have felt I had lost you and had I lost you I should have had no salvation in it at all at all . . . Do trust me darling and put your arm round my neck and whisper in my ear things you cannot say aloud. I shall be content and happy – *oh so happy*. Of course I was cross – bitterly cross that other day and you were as I know you were and together we built a bonfire that flared and thank God has burnt itself out to leave the softest of white grey ashes. And these ashes I wear upon my head and shoulders and worshipped you the while. Now a darling God grant forever. I know you dread the body physical and with me it flares and burns and behind it all there is my steady white light that belongs to you . . . Your dear eyes burn steadfast through my soul and pin me yours for ever darling – God sent Emmie.

Emily's response to this was to tell him all she had suffered on their honeymoon. Perhaps his expressed hope that he might still awake in her the wife he wanted had frightened her, otherwise it seems an unnecessarily cruel reply to his loving letter:

Remember that I married you, loving you and wanting you physically as much as you wanted me. I don't reproach you one instant for what happened after because you were just selfish and did not think and I was silly too. At the same time you can't believe the nightmare the thought of my honeymoon is to me – a nightmare of physical pain and mental disappointment. I was in constant and unceasing pain and you never left me alone. If ever you doubt my love remember what I went through then, and then think, that in spite of that I love you a thousand times more now than then. I know and fully sympathise with the disappointment you feel but remember I have never refused you except when I was having babies. If I could not respond to your feelings at least I have

114

let you come to me as often as my husband has a right to ask.

It seems extraordinary that he could ever have wanted to make love to her again after this terrible confession, his reply to which, if there was one, has not survived. I think it should be remembered that he was living at a time when average Englishmen did not expect their womenfolk to enjoy sex, when compliance was enough to satisfy them, when they had no shame in bringing an action for the restitution of conjugal rights, and when they were conditioned to regarding the bodies of their wives as their personal property.

Emily did not tell him – perhaps she never told him – what she was afterwards to tell me, that there had been a long period of frustration before she became revolted by sex. She had been a very passionate girl and Ned's quickly-satisfied love-making had left her night after night unappeased and resentful. Millions of women married to inexperienced men must have found themselves in this same condition, too innocent to understand their own bodies and too ashamed to seek help. The sad thing is that Ned, adoring her as he did and loving the human body, would probably have made a wonderful lover if he had known how, or realised her need.

This whole upset must have drawn him towards his children, for on 21 August he was writing a long letter to Robert, then aged ten, illustrated with drawings of knights fighting dragons, and ending 'O Robert boy I love you and pray to glow with pride of you for your own dear sake and the beloved Mother's'.

*   *   *

Mrs Besant and the boys returned to India in November but were back again the following February, 1912. Mrs Besant soon went back to India leaving the boys in England until

115

1920. From 1912 onwards Krishna and Nitya came constantly to Bloomsbury Square; thus I cannot remember a time when they were not as familiar to me as my eldest siblings, or even more so because they were much more often in our nursery than Barbie and Robert who by this time were leading a schoolroom life. Mother felt that her role now in the Theosophical movement was to look after Krishna as her own son. She had found her Grail just as Father embarked on the most exciting adventure of his career – the Highest of the High Game.

CHAPTER SEVEN

Delhi

1912–1913

At the Coronation Durbar at Delhi in December 1911, which was attended by King George and Queen Mary, the King announced the creation of a new capital at Delhi. Up till then the Supreme Government of India under the Viceroy had been at Calcutta for the four winter months and at the hill station of Simla in the Punjab for the rest of the year. Delhi was chosen by the Government because it was said to be central, to have a healthy climate and ease of access. Lord Curzon, who, although he had no official position at that time, possessed great influence as an expert on Indian affairs, campaigned in England against the project on the grounds of expense; he estimated that it would cost the Indian tax-payer £12,000,000. The European as well as the Indian population of Calcutta were no less vociferous in protesting against their capital city being relegated to the status of a provincial one.

As for the Indians as a whole, they were very much against the choice of Delhi. They wanted an all-year-round capital to save the expense of moving the Government in summer. The climate of Delhi may have been healthy but it was so abominably hot in summer that the Government would still have to move up to Simla, and intensely cold indoors in winter. Moreover, it had been for generations the Mogul capital before the British came to power and this did not

117

please the Hindus. The only thing about the choice that satisfied all sections of Indian opinion was that, according to tradition, every new city built at Delhi presaged the collapse of a dynasty.

The ruins of six other cities lay scattered over the great plain west of the River Jumna. Old Delhi, as the seventh and existing city came to be called after the new one was built, was the creation of Shah Jehan, who also built the Taj Mahal at Agra, and dates from 1638 when he began to build the Red Fort on the banks of the Jumna.

At the beginning of 1912 Lord Crewe, Secretary of State for India, approached Reginald Blomfield, President of the Royal Institute of British Architects, to recommend an architect to serve on a commission of three experts to advise the Government of India on the siting and laying out of the new capital. Blomfield recommended Lutyens on the strength of his country houses, now well known from the *Country Life* articles, his work in Johannesburg and for the Paris and Rome Exhibitions and for Hampstead Garden Suburb. Sir Richmond Ritchie, Permanent Secretary for India, then sent for Lutyens and asked him if he would be willing to serve on the Commission. Lutyens agreed to be a member on the understanding that he would be allowed to design the central Government buildings. It was a brave try to secure for himself the position of chief architect, but he never lacked courage, and, besides, he had just heard that another architect, H.V. Lanchester, with a flourishing Eastern practice, was going to Delhi in the hope of landing the job. Ritchie told Lutyens that the decision as to who should design the buildings rested with the Government of India, particularly with the Viceroy, Lord Hardinge of Penshurst, who regarded the scheme very much as his own. Nevertheless, Lutyens felt sufficiently encouraged by Ritchie to agree to join the Commission.

The other members were John Brodie, City Engineer of Liverpool, and Captain George Swinton, who retired as

118

Chairman of the London County Council in order to go to India. They were to sail for Bombay from Marseilles on 1 April 1912. On 21 March Lutyens was received at Buckingham Palace by King George who had strong views of his own about the new city and who took it for granted that Lutyens was to design it.

Emily was not at home to help Ned pack for what he called his 'miraculous pilgrimage' (she was in Holland with Mrs Besant and the boys), but she returned in time to see him off at Victoria Station on 28 March, the day before his forty-third birthday. He left Thomas in charge of the office with his power of attorney and took with him only one assistant, E. E. Hall, who had been in the office since 1902 and who was to work with him on Delhi for all the years it took to build. In the train he wrote to Emily. 'This is just to put my arm about you and God bless you for your wonderful and patient love. It is all very wonderful and exciting . . . If we do a fine thing and get our chance it will be the most wonderful thing that ever happened.' For once he left a thoroughly contented wife behind him.

the tiger is an awful beast

Some of Father's most witty and enchanting drawings appear in his letters during his voyages to and from India, incorporating the letter-heading of the P & O writing paper

119

in an infinite variety of images. He sat at the Captain's table on all his voyages, was convivial, interested in his fellow passengers whom he described with wit and concern, and took part in the life of the ship as well as working hard in his cabin. (On his later voyages the Captain gave him an office on the bridge.) From India he wrote long diary letters to Mother by every mail and picture letters to his children in turn. One joint letter to his children was signed, 'Ever your five-hearted Father who loves his bairns to absolute distraction.' His letters from India give a detailed record of all he saw, did and felt. He also wrote by almost every mail a special little love letter to Mother for her eyes alone.

Dozens of native bearers were waiting to be engaged on the quay at Bombay, as they always were in those days when a ship came in. Father, slow off the mark, found that all the presentable looking ones had been snapped up by the other passengers; the only one left for him was 'an old scallywag dressed in an uncouth dhoti'. This was Pershotum who was to serve him with loyal devotion for eighteen years. I came to know Pershotum well when I went to Delhi in the Twenties.

Always smiling his toothless smile he was at the same time wonderfully efficient, managing the other servants, arranging dinner parties and protecting Father from all household anxieties. He hero-worshipped Father, loving his jokes even when he could not understand them.

The Commission stayed at the Maiden Hotel in Delhi on this first visit and were given a bungalow for an office. Lutyens had a Government architectural engineer and a draughtsman attached to him. It was the Commission's assignment to find twenty-five square miles of ground at not too high a cost, close to the existing city, with a good water supply, fertile soil and room for expansion while in no way interfering with the sacred ruins and tombs of the half buried former cities.

A ridge of hills, running north and south, lay to the north of Delhi. This ridge was as sacred to the British as any Mogul tomb to the Moslems, for it was from here that the British had beleaguered Delhi in the Mutiny in 1857. On a triangular plain east of this ridge, the 1911 Durbar had been held and, before that, the great Assemblage of 1877 at which Lord Lytton had proclaimed Queen Victoria Empress of India. King George had laid the foundation stone here for the new city, but it was symbolical only since there was no room for expansion. The ridge broadened and continued south-west of Delhi, and it was eventually a treeless plain to the east of this southern ridge, called Raisina, between Indrapat to the east and Malcha to the west that was recommended by the Commission. The site was rather dry, so one of the many problems was irrigation: trees would not grow without water, yet too much water would bring mosquitoes and malaria.

Before coming to this decision, the Commission had been over all the possible sites on elephant-back in temperatures of 104°. Father came to love what he called 'this fearful and beloved creature', though at first, 'oh the green fear of me when I saw this great beast shy at a train, and oh the feelings of mine going down steep ravines into mullahs and up again over stony places'. On one occasion he rode a female elephant who 'walked crabwise over rough ground changing the angle of her crab at every other step. I was made to straddle her too just behind the Mahout and nearly split myself up to the collar stud. I felt everything depended on this stud.'

He found India 'thrilling yet baffling' with 'an enormous amount to love and admire'. He loved the birds and 'the sacred Brahmin cream-coloured bulls' that wandered about the streets, and was terrified by 'the fearsome insects'. 'The housing of the people here seems extraordinarily unintelligent,' he wrote, '– both for the white and Indians and the sanitation is nil. The absence of drains is all right but the eventual disposal of things is awful. The milk, butter and supplies generally pass along the same road, the open carts carrying all horror and the baskets of filth on the heads of women so that flies move freely from one conveyance to another ad lib.' He always impressed on us that smelly drains were acceptable; it was drains that did not smell that might be dangerous.

It soon became apparent to Lutyens that he would have to contend with many more obstacles to the realisation of his hopes than he had bargained for. First of all, the Public Works Department were resentful that the new capital had not been left to them to build; then it became known that Lanchester had actually been invited to India by the Hardinges and had 'the ear of the Viceroy'; furthermore there was a prejudice against Lutyens in some quarters owing to his reputation for exceeding his estimates. (The tenders for the British School in Rome had been more than double the estimates.) Over and above all this, Indian opinion had to be placated as far as possible, and Malcolm Hailey, the Commissioner for Delhi, won round. After the Viceroy, Hailey had more power than any other man in Delhi to interfere with the Commission's recommendations and block Lutyens's appointment. All these difficulties were intensified by the frequent quarrels that developed between Swinton and Brodie. Swinton talked too much and too loosely about Delhi to reporters and mere acquaintances and 'jumped to conclusions before thinking'; this infuriated Brodie. Lutyens, finding himself between 'a map thumping illogical jumper [Swinton] and a brow-furrowed slow pacer' at first tried to reconcile them and then to keep clear of their disputes. While they argued he began to make preliminary sketches for the new Government House. What worried him more than anything was to hear that the Viceroy was strongly in favour of an Eastern style of architecture for the central buildings, including pointed arches for windows and doorways. Lutyens, who disliked the pointed arch, foresaw a fight over this.[1]

On 19 April at the Viceroy's written request (he had not yet come to Delhi), the Commission went to Jaipur and then on to Agra to study both Hindu and Mogul architecture. Lutyens was not impressed with the ruins of Amber, the old Hindu city of Jaipur, nor with the new pink city, only a hundred years old, laid out with wide avenues. At Agra he wrote of 'The Fort, the Taj and other wonderful mad beautiful things in spite of folly'. More than a month later he was writing:

> Veneered joinery in stone, concrete and marble on a gigantic scale there is lots of, but no real architecture and nothing is built to last not even the Taj. The Taj and some other of the tombs have charm. They are empty of people, quiet, square, simple and green and this is only when money is spent on repairs, upkeep etc. When in ruins the buildings, especially the Mogul, are bad and have none of the dignity a ruin can have that has been the work of any great period . . . Personally I do not believe there is *any* real Indian architecture or any great tradition. They are just spurts by various mushroom dynasties with as much intellect in them as

[1]In 1920, when speaking to the students of the Architectural Association, he was to state his objection to the pointed arch: 'I do not like the pointed arch. It is too easy to get out of one's difficulties with it. One cannot alter the round arch, but there is no difficulty with the pointed, therefore there is not the same discipline.'

any other art nouveau. When Italians came over they brought with them some loveliness but never anything more than two dimensional work and they imported no architects [only] craftsmen . . . Colour they have or God gave them when the earthquakes or convulsions made the stone. Marbles of a most lovely texture brought by bare feet and hands – a quality our butlers once had in the balls of their thumbs and expended on our spoons. 300 years ago and for a period of 150 years the Moguls produced their architecture. 150–200 is and must make an art nouveau and gives no space of time for any tradition.

He sent Baker two 'recipes' for Indian styles:

Hindu: Set square stones and build childwise, but, before you erect, carve every stone differently and independently, with lace patterns and terrifying shapes. On top, over trabeated pendentives, set – an onion.
Mogul: Build a vasty mass of rough concrete, elephantwise, on a very simple rectangular-cum-octagon plan, dome in anyhow, cutting off square. Overlay with a veneer of stone patterns, like laying a vertical tile floor, and get Italians to help you. Inlay jewels and cornelians if you can afford it and rob someone if you can't. Then on top of the mass put three turnips in concrete and overlay with stone or marble as before. Be very careful not to bond anything in, and don't care a damn if it does all come to pieces.

*   *   *

It was not until 28 April that the Commission met Lord Hardinge who had come to Delhi on his way up to Simla from Calcutta. They spent over two hours with him. Lutyens liked him and found him sympathetic. He was very anxious for them to settle quickly on a site because their choice affected the siting of the temporary 'tin Delhi' which was to be erected by the following year at a cost of £500,000 to house the Government until the new buildings were ready for occupation. Afterwards they saw Lady Hardinge who was 'very cordial and pleasant'.

By the time the Commission went up to Simla on 20 May they had decided to recommend the Raisina site. They stayed at the Grand Hotel at Simla. Ned wrote to Emily about this preposterous seat of Government on a narrow five-mile ridge nearly eight thousand feet above sea level: 'The hills and depths below are heroic. The building and conception of the place by the P.W.D. [Public Works Department] mind is beyond the beyond and if one was told the monkeys had built it all one would have said – what wonderful monkeys. They must be shot in case they do it again. It is inconceivable – and consequently very English! – to have a capital as Simla is entirely of tin roofs.' He preferred the heat of Delhi to the cold of Simla, and found the hills boring compared to the plains. He was praising, though, of the Civil Service: 'The whole country is run by pleasant-blooded Englishmen – all young in the modern sense, all with responsibilities beyond their years, but all waiting for the clock to strike and tell them to go home and enjoy their pensions. Nice men of nice feeling but absolutely art unconscious.' At a horse-show at Allandale, a valley 1,200 feet below Simla, he was greatly moved when in a jumping competition, 'the only man who went over clear and without a fault was an Indian on a really nice animal, riding beautifully. And the men and women and children, English and native, gave him an ovation. This gave me the choke and I had to hide a tear and pretend dust was in my eyes. I don't think you would find that spirit in Africa.'

The members of the Commission dined with the Hardinges

at Viceregal Lodge (an inoffensive pile put up by the Public Works Department in 1888 on a lofty site chosen by Lord Lytton). Ned also lunched twice with them on his own and found it 'fun to be received without the others'. One morning he was invited up to see Lady Hardinge:

> She was very kind and Lord H. came in and I had a good talk about Delhi and architecture and it was all quite satisfactory and I am to make sketches for Government House [which he had done already] and Lord H. is quite keen and agreed with my view as to the architecture of the country and how the problems should be met. He said that he wanted the two cities one and not two – the new and the old, so I scored all round and feel very happy. I asked Lady H. about Lanchester. She said he was only coming for a month and they had to be tactful to him. I asked her if there was any chance of my doing the buildings. She said Yes, of course, who else!! This doesn't commit the Viceroy but it does, I hope, point to the mind-wind . . . The amount of building required for Delhi is colossal!!! Great fun.

Ned established with Lady Hardinge, a daughter of Lord Alington, the old happy architect-client relationship. It was to her that after committing some minor offence he was to make that most irresistibly gracious of apologies: 'I will wash your feet with my tears and dry them with my hair. True, I have very little hair but then you have very little feet.'

The Viceroy had imagined that the new Government House would cost no more than £200,000; it came as a great shock to him therefore when Lutyens told him that it would cost a million. Nevertheless, Ned was able to report to Emily on 9 June that Lord Hardinge had agreed to spending that sum, that he would like Lutyens to design Government House and the great Court in front of it and possibly the Secretariat buildings as well, and that he, the Viceroy, had written to Lord Crewe to tell him as much. So now everything depended on Lord Crewe. 'Lord Hardinge is delightful to work with,' Ned added, 'wide-viewed – non fussy and autocratic!!'

It had been decided that there was to be a two-mile long processional avenue running west from Indrapat to Government House at the foot of the Raisina ridge. Outside Government House there would be a forecourt and then the Great Court flanked by the two Secretariat buildings. Thus, for the whole length of the wide, tree-lined avenue, to be called the King's Way, Government House would be visible between and beyond the Secretariat buildings. It is important to remember this layout for an understanding of future developments.

Having sent in a written report with their recommendations the Commission was allowed to leave India when the monsoon broke towards the end of June with the understanding that they were to return in December. In his last letter home Ned declared himself to be feeling very well, happy and content.

*   *   *

At the end of August when Lord Hardinge returned to Delhi and saw the site recommended by the Commission, which had been pegged out for his inspection, he declared it would not do; it was too hot, it had no views and no room for expansion. (This last criticism was inaccurate – the Commission had all along borne in mind the need for expansion.) Lord Hardinge then jumped on his horse and galloped off over the plain with Malcolm Hailey to a hill some distance away. From the top of this hill there was a magnificent view over the whole of Delhi and he decided at once that this must be the site for the new Government House which would be clearly visible from all parts of the old city. The top of the hill was not large enough

127

to accommodate Government House, but the engineers who were with the Viceroy assured him that the top of the hill could easily be blasted off to form a sufficiently large plateau.[1] This hill, Raisina Hill, slightly to the north-west of the site chosen by the Commission, was the place finally decided upon for Government House, and the land to the east of it became the new city. The Commission in London was duly informed of the Viceroy's decision.

Back in London in July Lutyens began working hard on his Delhi plans. Lord Hardinge was urging Lord Crewe to confirm his appointment as architect of Government House but Lord Crewe refused to do so until he had received and studied the Commission's full report. Lutyens was not particularly perturbed when he heard at the beginning of September that the site of Government House had been moved to the top of Raisina Hill. His building would still be on level ground so that it would not effect the design, and the King's Way would still run east to west, though now the ground would gradually rise so that Government House, on the brow of the hill, would appear at the end of the two-mile vista with the Secretariat buildings on the slope below it. What did worry him extremely, however, was to hear that Lanchester had just returned from India 'boasting that he had the Viceroy in his pocket' and that he had persuaded him to put the building of the Secretariats out to competition. Lanchester had also told Lord Hardinge that Lutyens's avenues were too wide. If the idea of the competition was adopted it would mean that he (Lutyens) might have to collaborate with some unknown architect – at any rate an architect not of his own choosing. If he had to have a collaborator he would prefer it to be Herbert Baker or Reginald Blomfield. For the moment he took no action, hoping that the competition idea would be dropped.

Lutyens was also worried when he heard that the King

[1]*My Indian Years* by Lord Hardinge of Penshurst, p. 72 (1948).

was now in favour of a Mogul style of architecture. 'Fancy Shakespeare being asked by Elizabeth to write an ode in Chaucerian metre,' he wrote indignantly to Emily.

*　　*　　*

Although Ned had not returned to England until 19 July, after a four months' absence, Emily went off to East Runton at the end of July for the summer holidays with Chippy and the children. It is apparent from Ned's love letters to Emily from India, especially the ones written towards the end of his long absence, that he hoped she was missing him as much as he was missing her and that their relationship would be closer on his return. But he did not visit her once at East Runton, probably because when he got home he found that her feelings about his love-making had not changed. Although from India he had been begging for more news of 'our beloved children', she was pressing him at the beginning of September to give 'a little more time and thought' to them:

> Robert is full of artistic leanings and you can help and guide him if you will. I can't help influencing the children according to my own ideas and if you never give five minutes to them you can't expect them to understand your ideas. You owe *some* responsibility to your family as well as to your work. You can give them such great things, but it means trouble and patience. They love you dearly as does your neglected wife but it is difficult to put you much into our lives when you are never there. Could Robert go to South Kensington for painting lessons?

Ned saw no good in this. He reiterated that one could not be taught to draw. What he wanted Robert to learn was geometry and 'sciography' – the science of drawing shadows. Anyway, he added, the only time he had tried to teach Robert anything Robert had lost his temper. Later on, when the family were in Cornwall, Ned advised Robert to draw the rigging of a boat: 'Every rope has its use and purpose, its size to meet the strain put on it – blocks and pulleys to give due leverage – see how its clipper shape is built up. A boat is a good thing to observe and learn from.'

But Emily, by complaining of Ned's neglect, had in some measure been paving the way to obtaining his consent to take Barbie and Robert to Genoa to stay with a Theosophical couple, Mr and Mrs Kirby, to meet Charles Webster Leadbeater, a controversial figure in the Theosophical movement. An ex-curate in the Church of England, Leadbeater had joined the Society in 1883, gone with Madame Blavatsky, its founder, to India, developed clairvoyant and other occult powers and, after her death, worked closely with Mrs Besant. On a tour of America in 1904, some adolescent boys were put in his charge by their parents for Theosophical teaching. Back in England two years later he became the centre of a scandal when two of the boys accused him of homosexual practices with them. An inquiry was instituted by the British Section of Theosophists in London at which Leadbeater's defence was that he had always recommended masturbation to his pupils as a prophylactic against impure thoughts. This explanation was not accepted; he was obliged to resign from the Society and was warned to leave England and never to return there. After Mrs Besant became President of the Society in 1907 he was reinstated. His home was now at Adyar but he had come to Europe that summer on one of his rare visits. It was he who had 'discovered' Krishnamurti at Adyar from the beauty of his aura.

Ned, who knew all about the Leadbeater scandal, very understandably objected to the Genoa plan when Emily put it to him:

I have absolute faith in your judgement and true seeing and sympathy with me [he wrote on 29 August] but I don't like Leadbeater on top of so much else. I get nervous darling when you are from me but he seems in many ways a foolish man, a dangerous man and one claiming powers that are not quite sober-minded . . . I do want you to go carefully and not be led into depths where none can swim. Don't tell the children darling or anyone of my feeling. I hold their affection by necessarily so slight a thread and a word from you might cut it!! You see darling how completely I am in your power.

He wrote this about the children because Emily had told him how very anxious Barbie and Robert were to go to Genoa. A week later he was writing again:

I do believe in a force – spooks – call it what you like, as a very real and material force and as dangerous as electricity and as little understood and which, unlike electricity, has not been harnessed. That it has more to do with the 'soul' than electricity or any other element has is not proved. I believe in this power and believing it hold it to be a very dangerous one, especially for young people and destructive where the person adopting it has family ties and mutual responsibilities. The subject is a thrilling one – as thrilling as almost any. But I should rather a child of mine went tiger shooting on foot than dabble with magic and brain magnetism as a child.

If a man without worldly or family ties can give his whole mind and life to it – as a German scientist would to a blue bug of Bombay! – all right, and he may die slowly of blue bug plague!! But it would be wrong of me with all my joyous responsibilities to embark on any blue bug crusade. So I feel that occultism is far wiser let alone until such time as it is recognised and converted into a harmless and no doubt most useful domestic animal. [Sketch of a fierce tiger and a smiling cat.]

Emily replied that after all she had heard for and against Leadbeater she wanted to have the opportunity of judging his character for herself – she thought it only fair and she might never have another opportunity of meeting him. Ned gave way: '. . . of course I say yes – *go* and enjoy yourself and be happy darling. Have no qualms or doubts. Be happy and healthy in body and your mind will be true – for such is the way of God.' Later on he was to own to her how miserable he had been over 'the Leadbeater influence'.

After an initial disappointment, Emily became very attracted to Leadbeater. He was 'perfect' with the children. She was struck by his 'wisdom and level-headedness and joie de vivre'. He was then a man of sixty-two. When I knew him, some twelve years later, with his long white beard and twinkling eyes, his resemblance to Bernard Shaw was remarkable.

Nothing could have been more diverse than Emily's and Ned's interests at this time. While she was in Genoa in September, he went to Balmoral to show his Delhi plans to the King and Queen. Of course the King had ideas of his own, made suggestions and wanted modifications, while at the same time saying that the design for Government House was 'beautiful'. Ned seems to have wooed him away from the Mogul style, for he was able to write to Emily, 'I think it is all satisfactory. I feel happy about style and those difficulties. Next week I must try and win Crewe and get it settled.' But Lord Crewe, when Ned did see him, although 'nice and gentlemanlike refused to say anything or commit himself as to my doing any, all or none of the Delhi work. But I hope it is all right. Lady Crewe said she was frightened of my coming as she didn't like geniuses. That, silly as it was, comforted me'. This was a time of great frustration and anxiety for Ned.

When towards the end of October he heard that the Viceroy was still in favour of a competition, he managed to persuade Sir Richmond Ritchie at the India Office that it would be a mistake and to obtain his consent to asking Baker to join him in Delhi in order to support him. He then cabled to Baker inviting him to come to Delhi as his collaborator if he did get the job. On 29 October he received a reply accepting the invitation. In many ways Ned would have preferred Reginald Blomfield to work with him, and, indeed, Blomfield had a strong claim since it was he, it may be remembered, who had recommended Lutyens to Lord Crewe to serve on the Commission, but Ned thought it only fair to choose Baker in return for Baker's co-operation in South Africa. Baker himself had great reservations about working with Lutyens – he foresaw that it would be difficult to collaborate with him and he consented to do so only on the understanding that they should work on equal terms in separate spheres. If they were appointed it was agreed that Baker should do the Secretariat buildings. Baker never accepted that he owed his appointment to Lutyens. In his memoirs he was to write:

> In the early autumn of 1912 . . . I had had hints that I might be asked to go to Delhi as joint architect with Edwin Lutyens for the new Capital. I knew that on the strength of my Pretoria buildings my appointment had been recommended by Lord Hardinge, but on great pressure from home, he, rightly, appointed Lutyens. When he was out there, however, the Viceroy decided that Lutyens must have a collaborator, and then I also was appointed.[1]

This does not tally with the facts since Lutyens had not been appointed by the time he cabled Baker, and if Lord

[1] *Architecture and Personalities*, p. 63.

Hardinge had had Baker in mind on Lutyens's previous visit, Lutyens was certainly not aware of it. He had to set out for India on his second visit in November without knowing whether his appointment was secure or whether there was to be a competition for the Secretariats. Swinton and Brodie travelled with him again; Baker was to join them later.

* * *

On his arrival in Bombay on 12 December Lutyens received a letter from Lady Hardinge welcoming him to India but saying that the Viceroy 'for high considerations of state felt bound to have an Indian styled city'. Lord Hardinge, having visited Kashmir and other places on an autumn tour, was now wholly in favour again of an Eastern style quite apart from considerations of state. Lutyens had worked for six months on his plans and knew that the Viceroy had it in his power to nullify all that effort.

Lord Hardinge telegraphed to the Commission in Bombay asking them to visit Dhar and the ruins of Mandu in Central India on their way up to Delhi. At Mandu Lutyens immediately divined the faulty skeleton below the picturesque ruins of the Durbar Hall which had so enchanted the Viceroy: '. . . a great stone building with sloping buttresses and a series of huge stone pointed arches which once carried a flat stone roof (now fell in!),' he told Emily. 'When you consider the roof 25 feet wide requires 36 to 40 foot wall thickness to support it it becomes ridiculous and an impossible type to adopt for any practical or secretarial purpose. And then when the roof was on would be as dark as dark could well be if you want the darkness visible.'

He came to the conclusion that what was needed was a synthesis of Eastern and Western styles which was something very different from grafting Eastern excrescences on to a Western building. He was to explain this in a letter to Sir

134

Valentine Chirol, a great lover of India, who was in Delhi as a member of a Royal Commission on Indian Public Services:

> I do not think Lord Hardinge yet realises what great architecture might be and should express.
>
> It must be constructive. Architecture will always find her noblest expression in stone. Every different material will influence that expression.
>
> Though Lord Hardinge has great taste and is certainly what one would call artistic, I do not think he realises the use of ornament in relation to construction, where it should begin and end, and what is integral and what applied. He begins with ornament instead of construction . . .
>
> To express modern India in stone, to represent her amazing sense of the supernatural, with its compliment of profound fatalism and enduring patience, is no easy task.
>
> This cannot be done by the almost sterile stability of the English classical style; nor can it be done by capturing Indian details and inserting their features, like hanging pictures on a wall!
>
> In giving India some new sense of architectural construction, adapted to her crafts, lies the great chance of creating what may become a new and inspiring period in the history of her art . . .
>
> By this you will see where I am fearful of a Viceroy's arbitrary insistence on features and insertions. He, as I can well understand, is fearful of my obstinacy. I have no wish to be obstinate, but only to serve the Viceroy, and so India, to the best of my ability.[1]

He may not have wanted to be obstinate but obstinate he

[1]Hussey, pp. 280-81.

135

was in his aesthetic integrity. What did delight him in Indian buildings was the Mogul gardens with their pools (called tanks), fountains and running water. I have seen some of these gardens myself in Kashmir. The water cascades over a long wide stone stairway, each step differently carved so that the water music is constantly changing its tune.

*   *   *

The Commission arrived in Delhi on 20 December. Three days later the Viceroy made a state entry into the new capital to take up residence in the temporary Viceregal Lodge in the 'tin Delhi' three miles north of the city. As his elephant procession from the station passed along the Chandni Chauk, the chief shopping street, a bomb was thrown from a window at the Viceroy's elephant. Lord Hardinge was badly injured, a mahout was killed and the elephant slightly wounded. Lady Hardinge, sitting beside the Viceroy, was miraculously unhurt.

On the 26th Lady Hardinge asked Lutyens to breakfast with her; she then told him her story of the bombing. Left alone on the elephant with one dead and, for all she knew, one dying man, she never lost her head or her nerve. 'I do think she is a wonder,' Ned wrote to Emily. 'The bomb will delay us. The Viceroy's fixed on an adaptation of the Indian style but I can't fight him yet. Talking with Lady H. it seems all right. The suggestion is that I, Baker, Swinton and Jacob [Sir Swinton Jacob], the latter a sort of walking dictionary on Indo-Saracenic art – should do the whole caboodle.' The idea of the competition had evidently been abandoned.

Lord Hardinge took a long time to recover from his very painful wounds. He needed several operations to remove particles of the home-made bomb which had contained screws, nails and gramophone needles. After ten weeks in bed he went to Dehra Dun to recuperate. It was not until the middle of February 1913, therefore, that Lutyens's appointment and that of the other architects was officially confirmed. (Sir Swinton Jacob resigned a few months later and Captain Swinton seems to have faded out of the picture. Lutyens and Baker were left as co-architects with equal status.) By the middle of February Lutyens had also heard that he had been elected an Associate Member of the Royal Academy. 'I do rather dread your pop journeys,' he wrote (Emily had been lecturing all over England on the coming of the World Teacher), 'and now I am an A.R.A. will you ever help *me*? Ever?? or not. How I don't know but just at these soirees etc. etc. – R.A. students and Lord! I have to make a speech now on my return to the assembled R.A.'s.'

Lutyens had been to Bombay to meet Baker when he arrived on 7 February. They had not met since Johannesburg, though frequent letters had kept them in touch. After telling Emily that it was such a strength and comfort to have Baker there Ned was writing by the next mail, 'I don't think he treats architecture as seriously as I do. He makes her the handmaiden of sentiment.'

Baker had come to India determined that the Secretariat buildings, if he was to design them, must share the same eminence as Government House – that the whole complex of Government buildings must stand on the plateau – what he called an acropolis. This would necessitate blasting a much larger area on the hill-top to level it, and pushing back Government House four hundred feet from the brow of the hill. Lutyens, not wanting to oppose Baker so soon after his arrival, reluctantly gave in to his insistence in spite of Brodie's pointing out that if Government House were to be set back, most of it would disappear from view at some point along the two-mile approach of the King's Way. Both architects assured him that this would not be allowed to happen, though how they intended to avoid it was not explained. It seems extraordinary that Lutyens, with all his experience,

137

should not have realised that this was bound to happen. Did he trust to Baker's assurance that it could be avoided, telling himself that Baker, with his knowledge of *kopjes* must know best? Or was he too occupied with his plans for Government House to give the matter his whole attention?

Before he went home at the end of March Ned hoped that he had persuaded the Viceroy to admit 'the influence of a Western style – i.e. logic, and not the mad riot of the tom-tom'. At the same time he was dismayed by Hardinge's short-term view of building: 'The Viceroy thinks only of what the place will look like in three years time,' he told Emily. '*300 is what I think of*. I mentioned ten years in regard to something, and he said it was so far ahead it was not worth considering. This is building an Imperial City!'

Lutyens's relations with Hardinge were never the same after the bomb outrage. Lutyens believed that he had 'lost all energy of mind' as a result of his wounds. But Lady Hardinge was as charming to him as ever. She cordially invited his wife to come out with him on his next visit. Ned, greatly pleased, passed this on to Emily. She replied:

Now remember when I go to India I go as a Theosophist and that means that I have brothers waiting for me in every town where there is a T.S. Lodge. When I arrive at Bombay I don't want to be met by the Governor's launch, but I *know* I shall be met by kindly brown faces – who will greet me as one of themselves. You go to India and mix only with the official class and look at Indians always from a long way off – you can never get to know them like that. I have a password to their hearts which I will show you when I come.

Ned was so terrified by this letter that it was years before he asked her again to go with him to India.

CHAPTER EIGHT

Frustrations and War
1913–1914

Lutyens received several new commissions as soon as he returned to London in the middle of April 1913 and he still had much work to do on old ones, especially Castle Drogo and the TS Headquarters in Tavistock Square. It had now become essential to have a separate office for his Indian work, so on 8 September he moved that part of his practice to 7 Apple Tree Yard, larger rooms than in Queen Anne's Gate and very well lighted. Apple Tree Yard is the mews behind St James's Square on the north side, and No 7 belonged to 7 St James's Square, a house which Lutyens had built for Gaspard and Henry Farrer. They had no use for the mews at present and let Lutyens have the upper part of it at a very low rent. E. E. Hall was put in charge of this Indian office.

Lord Hardinge had now gone back on his agreement that Government House should cost a million pounds and had publicly announced that the whole of the new city would cost only four million of which £500,000 was to be allotted to Government House. This meant that Lutyens had to cut down the scale of his plans; at the same time he was still not sure whether the Viceroy was going to insist on hanging Mogul excrescences on the façade and the use of the pointed arch. The round arch was an integral part of Lutyens's design.

Baker was prepared to compromise over the question of the arch. Lutyens, who cared passionately about it, wrote to Baker in August, 'I should like to ask him [Hardinge] to what country the Rainbow belongs! One cannot tinker with a round arch. God did not make the Eastern rainbow pointed to show His wide sympathies.'

Ned told Emily in August when they were parted as usual for the summer holidays:

I am finding it difficult to concentrate myself and I want your help. You have the power of concentration and I am beginning to realise I have wasted you in not training myself to concentrate in need. I think this is a loss from not having gone to a public school. I wish I had that power now I know I must do this thing [Delhi] and do it to the exclusion of all else without distraction. With my great amount of varied work I find it difficult to do one thing without thinking of 101 other things at the same time.

In another letter he begged Emily to be careful of money for a little longer until 'India is on the way and then I do want to save and to avoid money worries as it spoils work, temper and everything goes wrong.' And again: 'I hope in a year or two I shall be easier with money and not be so cribbed about it . . . Oh, I do want sometimes – just to get out of it – and be something other than an architect at the beck and call of everyone.' And a week later:

I am rather hipped being alone in London. There are many places I could go to – but dont want to, it seems waste of time – and unnatural being for ever en garçon in other people's houses. I want a home of my own of which I form a part.

I have rather let you slip from me – all your thoughts

140

are away from mine and mine from yours. As a professional man I must make my profession of first importance and then so much beyond hangs on it. Your comfort, happiness, the education of children and a roof above our heads. Except for the people I build for I have no friends and now if my work is to be for Government you cant make a friend of a Government.

While Ned was in London battling with his many problems Emily was having the happiest summer of her life. The Mallets had again lent Les Communes at Varengeville to Krishna and Nitya and their two tutors. Mother took us all there for the second time to be near them and we stayed in the same farmhouse as in 1911. This time I remember it quite well; I celebrated my fifth birthday there and Barbie her fifteenth. Mother, Barbie and Robert spent most of their time at Les Communes with 'the boys' but we all came together for picnics and games of rounders. For the first time since his wife's death Chippy was not with us, and he never joined us again for a summer holiday although he continued to dine regularly with Mother in London. He was extremely jealous of her new friends and interests.

There was an inner Society within the Theosophical Society called the Esoteric School (the ES). Members of the ES, to which Mother, Barbie and Robert now belonged, believed that there were some superhuman beings living in Tibet, called Arhats or Masters, who, having reached a stage of perfection in evolution after many hundreds of lives, and who might therefore have passed into Nirvana, had chosen to remain on earth in human bodies in order to help humanity along the path of evolution. Those members of the ES who aspired to enter the Path chose one or other of these Masters and endeavoured to become his pupil. The first step on the Path was when a Master agreed to take a pupil on probation;

the second step was when a Master accepted him (a bond which could never be broken); the third was Initiation when the pupil became a member of the Great White Brotherhood. There were five Initiations altogether, the final one being that of Adapthood which took innumerable lives to achieve. Krishna had taken his second Initiation; Nitya and the two tutors their first. Mrs Besant and C. W. Leadbeater were said to have taken their fourth already.

These occult steps were taken on the astral plane while asleep and it was only Leadbeater who was qualified to tell an aspirant when he had taken a step. Mrs Besant, who had been clairvoyant at the beginning of her life in Theosophy, had voluntarily relinquished her occult powers in order to take up work for Indian Home Rule which was considered of vital importance to the Masters, and she now relied entirely on Leadbeater in all occult matters.

On the night of 11 August while at Varengeville Emily was put on probation by her chosen Master, Kuthumi, and a week later Barbie and Robert also took this first step on the Path. The news reached them by cable from Leadbeater from Adyar. Emily, according to her diary, was so 'radiantly happy' that her 'cup was brimming over'. Pupils of the Master would be particularly valuable in preparing the way for the coming of the World Teacher. Emily realised that she and the children would never have taken this step if she had not gone to Genoa to meet Leadbeater the year before.

One of the requirements for discipleship was absolute physical as well as mental purity. According to the teaching of the E.S., even conjugal sex was taboo for pupils of the Master. Emily had discovered that the Mallets, who were both pupils, now had a *mariage blanc* after producing two children. This strengthened her in the resolve that she had already made to break off sexual relations with Ned, though it was to be another year before she found the courage to tell him so. She gave him a strong hint of it when she wrote in

August, 'I am afraid holidays make me rather selfish – I love the entire freedom – a room to myself being one! . . . I have never had such a happy holiday before and I hope to come home full of strength for all things except a baby!'

Ned did not come to Varengeville this year, and Emily did not tell him the details of these occult experiences which would have seemed to him, as to most people, quite crazy. When he asked her towards the end of August why she did not take him more into her confidence she replied, 'Your critical faculty is terribly over-developed, and I think this makes me more afraid of telling you things than I need be. I feel you will lay bare and ridicule my dearest beliefs.' This highly developed critical faculty, which we were all aware of, made him at times an intimidating parent, though in the case of the Masters and discipleship it would have been difficult for any man with his feet on the ground not to be critical. He doubted all creeds, let alone occult hypotheses. He had recently expressed again to Emily his distrust of words: 'I can think better of things when unsaid and unspoken than the drift wood of words that spoil reflections in the water – and blot out the skies therein. However, nothing matters as long as one's own pools are clear – and in mine I ever see my darling's face reflected.'

Towards the end of the holiday she must have told him enough to disturb him deeply, for on 18 September he was writing that although he loved her letters he did not like reading them twice: 'Darling they frighten me – the aloofness. Oh Emmie darling I do so rely on your moral courage – your truthfulness. When I see your darling face in my mind's eye I have no fears.'

To this Emily replied in her last letter before returning home:

Yes, my darling, in some ways it is true I am aloof in thought, but then so are you. You are just as far away

143

from my thought when you are absorbed in building as I am when absorbed in Theosophy . . . I want you to know, and to know it not as a joke, that the one all absorbing thought for me in this life is the coming of the Great Teacher. It is the great reality and everything else in life is subordinate to that idea . . . Now I know this will make you rather unhappy darling, but at least respect my confidence.

In her autobiography Mother afterwards expressed herself with the greater truth of hindsight:

From the time we left Varengeville at the end of September I was never really happy away from Krishna. My husband, my home, my children faded into the background; Krishna became my entire life, and for the next ten years I suffered all the difficulties of trying to sublimate a human love.

It is probable that she herself did not recognise her true feelings at the time. Krishna had a horror of sex which was one of the reasons why she fell in love with him. In those early years he returned her love with his whole heart, wanting to be with her as much as she wanted to be with him. This caused a great deal of jealousy among his other disciples who did their best to separate them, making out that his love for her was detrimental to his spiritual progress. One of these jealous people wrote and complained of her to Leadbeater who, in consequence, saw to it that she did not take any more steps on the Path until she became more detached. It was to be nine years before the Master Kuthumi accepted her – years in which she made pathetic entries in her diary such as 'Failed', 'Failed again' as the great occult festivals went by when advancements were expected. These were not miseries that she could have confided to Ned. For their very different reasons they were both almost equally unhappy in these years.

*　　*　　*

Before Lutyens set out for India for the third time in November 1913, financial arrangements had been made regarding Delhi. By the terms of the architects' agreement with the Government of India they were required to visit Delhi once a year for as many years as the Delhi Building Committee, which Lord Hardinge had now set up, thought necesssary. (It was then expected that the main buildings would be finished by 1918.) Lutyens and Baker were to receive 5% of the actual cost of the work, 1¼% of this to be given on completion of the plans. They were also to receive £1,000 a year each for acting as advisers to the Government on all architectural matters to do with the new city; first class return steamship fares, first class railway travel in India, a daily subsistence allowance of 30/- and a fee of £5 a day each while away from home. All office expenses were to be paid out of their own pockets. Lutyens was to be responsible for Government House, its gardens and staff quarters, and Baker for the two Secretariat buildings. They were to agree between themselves which other buildings they were to be responsible for.

Baker had suggested that all fees should go into a joint account called the Pool Account from which their office expenses and five guineas a day when either party was away from home should be paid. Lutyens had verbally agreed to this when he had last seen Baker; subsequently it had been pointed out to him by his lawyer, Francis Smith, that Baker would inevitably draw a far larger proportion from the Pool Account, not only because office expenses were higher in South Africa but because he would have the extra journey to and from the Cape and an annual holiday of three weeks in England en route for India. When Baker arrived in London in

November, Lutyens told him that he wanted a legal agreement drawn up laying down Baker's proportion of the Pool. Baker was bitterly hurt by this, feeling that it should be a matter for mutual trust. When they set off for Marseilles together from Victoria Station on 13 November the atmosphere between them was frosty. 'Baker is better,' Ned wrote next day from the train, ' – not that funny face. But he is awfully hurt and bruised. We have not mentioned the subject but he said something about happy days being over which is absurd as it is only a money question and a lawyer safeguard in the interests of my family. I hope he will come to see it. He is very rude and uncouth when cross – a pity and we have so much to do together.' By the time they reached Bombay Lutyens had made a proposal to which Baker agreed: half of their total commission should go into the Pool; of this half Baker should be entitled to draw 60% and Lutyens 40% for expenses. The other half of the joint commission should be divided equally.

This year in Delhi they had their own bungalow, the old Mill House – a large communal room for meals with a bedroom and bathroom leading off it at either end. They were also given an old motor car – a necessity since their bungalow was three miles south of Delhi whereas the temporary Viceregal Lodge was three miles north of it. The site for the new city had been cleared and the roads and avenues laid out but there were still several tombs in the way which were to prove a great nuisance. On the whole, this third visit to Delhi was a wretched time for Ned. In order to conform to Lord Hardinge's published estimate he had virtually to redraw his plans for Government House. Then the Viceroy, having the year before asked him to make his central dome higher, now wanted it lowered which would make it disproportionately low compared to the domes of Baker's Secretariats which were already ten feet higher. But at least Hardinge had come round to his ideas for a fusion of Eastern and Western

146

styles; there was no more talk of the pointed arch. Still, he felt so dispirited by the end of the year that he was writing, 'O Emmie is it worthwhile this awful long separation.'

On 14 January 1914 he was writing again, 'The Committee go to all lengths to make things fit Hardinge's preconceived ideas as to what costs should be. It is too silly and they all laugh at him and his methods. It is a great pity. However, I am cutting down vigorously but there is a point beyond which I cannot go.' And a week later: 'I cannot get Baker to alter his drawings to fit mine. He wants to get on and make a start but I shall not be party to a misfit and ugliness of that sort to save trouble. What good would it be in 20 years time to save a few weeks or months or days of labour now! It is absurd.' And by the next mail: 'Baker is so accustomed to cheap work and getting over difficulties in a slovenly way that he is no real help.' On 4 February he was writing again:

No one looks at plans or takes interest in them comprehensively. Only the cost is counted. So I wrote to Lady H. to tell her that the engineers thought they could be cut down if the dome was omitted and the upper part was built plastered and that although the new plan had advantages over the old one I gave 5 or 6 points as disadvantages. No one ever tells them the truth and as these were points they had been specially insistent on I thought I had better mention them. So Tuesday she came down post haste and she and H. E. had been miserable over my 'black letter'. Baker never helps. He won't face difficulties, just slurs them over and does something muddy which I can't bear doing without a fight.

He then heard that the Hardinges wanted the plans enlarged again although there was no more money available. No wonder he said that the new city should be called

Bedlampore. He had just received a copy of Lawrence Weaver's lavishly illustrated folio book on his early work which had recently been published by *Country Life*. 'It does make me hot,' was his comment. 'I do wish he had not mentioned Delhi so often and O dear it is just a catalogue of mistakes and failures. Clients who when I first started – I don't mean Chippy of course – did not know enough to direct and afterwards enough to lead.'

Emily had written to ask him what his feelings were for India now that he knew it better. 'I don't think I am in love with India,' he replied on 9 March. 'No one seems well here – no vigour . . . The squalor, unkempt ugliness, the dirt, the lassitude is depressing – and oh the flies wherever natives are left alone – horrible. I don't think I am only pro-government. My want of school training etc. puts me out of real sympathy with any form of bureaucracy – the ever going for the second best instead of the best – the spirit of compromise.'

Ned himself was one of those ailing at this time. He was passing blood, a worrying symptom caused, apparently, by dysentery. His longing to get home was overwhelming. In March, feeling very ill, and harassed by the Viceroy's chopping and changing, he signed a minute the significance of which he failed to realise. This was an agreement that a gradient of 22½ had been chosen for the slope of Raisina Hill up to the plateau on which the Government buildings were to stand. Since the exact levels of the Viceroy's Court and the Great Place in front of the Secretariats were not to be settled until the following year, Lutyens, as he afterwards told Baker, regarded this as a preliminary, not a final, decision. Baker on the other hand was to maintain that in signing the minute Lutyens had realised that at some point along the two-mile drive of the King's Way, Government House would almost disappear from view and that he had accepted the fact.

Perspective drawings for Government House, made by W. Walcot, were exhibited at the Academy in May this year 1914.

One of them was a view of the main vista along the King's Way showing the Secretariats on Raisina Hill with Government House behind them just as Lutyens imagined the scene would look. What he did not realise was that Walcot had drawn this from an imaginary point thirty feet above ground so that it was not a true representation. I believe this drawing was in large measure responsible for Lutyens's failure to grasp the truth.

* * *

While Ned was still in Delhi Emily had written to him trying to explain her feelings for Krishna and Nitya – how she had first been drawn to them because their mother had died when they were very young and she had felt they were homesick and lonely in a strange land with Mrs Besant far away, and how she and Krishna had gradually come to feel for each other as mother and son. 'I know your feelings for Indians makes this hard for you to understand,' she went on, 'but I have no such feelings, and they seem to me like my own boys.'

Ned replied to this:

I loved your dear letter and know how you feel and what you feel. And you must know too what I feel and I feel some things very strongly indeed. The colour question is one and there is no compromise. I want darling for you to know this and realise it. There is one limit beyond which I should prefer death. O darling love for the love I hold and you do love me darling? Don't darling go so far as to blast our happiness. I have tried to be kind, wise and patient and my love for you has been and is so true darling. It is impossible to use the word unselfish to you but darling just think and try and be selfish just a little for *me* who loves you so dearly.

He was frightened for Barbie. She and Nitya were of the same age and he probably knew that Nitya was very devoted to her. Emily evidently realised this for she hastened to assure him that Barbie was just as much against mixed marriages as he was. All the same, loving Krishna as she did, Emily must have found his letter very alienating. It was another great divide between them. Ned found it hard enough to accept the mother-son relationship, wincing to hear Krishna call her Mother or Mummy as he invariably did – but he was always charming to him. Krishna for his part was extremely fond of him, and admired and respected him greatly. I never heard Father utter a word against Krishna. Most unjustly it was Mrs Besant he blamed for Mother's absorption in the World Teacher; he was to become increasingly bitter against her.

At Bombay on his way home, on 28 March, the day before his forty-fifth birthday, he received a depressed letter from Emily which made him deeply regret the one he had written to her about the colour question. 'Oh, darling,' he replied, 'it [her letter] raises all that mothership love for my darling wife which you find so difficult to understand and which I don't attempt to. I accept it as a great God gift.'

He returned to England in the middle of April without having heard whether his revised plans had been accepted or not by the Delhi Committee. The lease of 29 Bloomsbury Square was up that summer; the house was to be pulled down. In his absence Emily had found a new house for us on the west side of Bedford Square, No 31, one of the houses Ned had turned down during their engagement.[1] At Aden he had received a letter from her informing him that the £350 premium she had been authorised to offer for the new house had been accepted, with vacant possession on 24 June. As well as the premium, he was 'under covenant' to spend £700 on the house in exchange

[1]Hussey states that the numbers of Bedford Square have been changed. This is not so. The house we lived in is still numbered 31.

150

for a long lease. The great advantage of having another house on the Bedford Estate was that he was given permission to transfer the Bloomsbury Square mantelpieces which he loved so much. Emily had wanted to save him trouble but it was foolish of her to have settled on a house in his absence. He never liked it.

*　　*　　*

The weather was perfect during that spring and summer of 1914 before the outbreak of the Great War. At the end of June Ned began decorating the Bedford Square house. He went out a great deal at this time. Cecil Baring, Edward Knoblock, William Nicholson, Edward Hudson and E. V. Lucas were his closest friends apart from the Jekylls and the Horners. He could no longer say with any truth that he had no friends apart from clients. As well as Mells, the Horners had a house in Lower Berkeley Street where he met most of the members of the Liberal Government. He also became friendly with Lady Cunard that summer and although disliking opera went occasionally to her box at Covent Garden, and met at her house in Cavendish Square George Moore and Sargent among others.

A great row was blowing up at this time over the building of the Theosophical Headquarters in Tavistock Square. The revised estimates had come out more than double the original ones. There was much excuse for this because Mrs Besant from India had asked for alterations and additions as well as flats at the top of the building. The Committee in London representing her, which included Emily's Theosophical colleague, Dr Haden Guest, had insisted on doing without a contractor and employing direct labour. Now the Committee had sacked the foreman Lutyens had appointed without consulting him and decided to employ only Trade Union labour. Ned wrote indignantly to Emily, 'I do not think it right to ask

151

a man his political tenets before giving him work,' to which Emily replied that he must reconcile himself to the fact that Trade Unions had come to stay. But far worse, Dr Guest was now making accusations of dishonesty against Lutyens's office, particularly against Thomas, which he would neither substantiate nor apologise for. Lutyens wrote a long letter to Mrs Besant relating all the circumstances of the trouble and saying that he had no option but to resign.[1] He was quite firm for once: he told Emily that he would never have Guest in the house again; she must choose between Guest and her husband. The war took Dr Guest away to France to run a hospital and I do not think he ever did come to the house again. But the whole episode left an aftermath of bitterness. Ned did not feel that Emily had wholly supported him; she had even reproved him for exceeding the estimates, knowing nothing of the circumstances.

This trouble was still going on when war broke out on 4 August, their seventeenth wedding anniversary. Emily was already in the country with the children for the summer holidays in a furnished house at Sulhampstead, Berkshire, close to Folly Farm. Folly Farm was a house Ned had first altered in 1901 and was now making extensive alterations and additions to for the new owners, Mr and Mrs Zachari Merton. Mrs Merton came over frequently to visit us. We were all very fond of her, calling her by the name Father had invented for her – Mère-toni – which suited her perfectly. Middle-aged, rich, fat, plain and with a strong German accent, she was wonderfully kind and possessed the attraction of good grooming from a French maid.

The war was brought home to me when the pony who drew the lawn mower was taken off to the Front, leaving his leather shoes behind him.

[1] The unfinished building was sold to the British Medical Association at the end of the war, and in 1924 Lutyens completed it for the BMA.

Ned's letters to Emily from London in August were concerned almost exclusively with the war. Money had been tight even before war broke out – Governments were slow to pay – but now he realised that all private practice would come to an end. It was a great relief to him to hear that Delhi was to go on. And yet he was busier than he had ever been because by 6 August nearly the whole of his office staff had volunteered. One gets a strong feeling that he wished he could have joined up himself. He lunched most days at the Athenaeum to hear the war gossip. At a dining club, called the Other Club, he met Winston Churchill, Lord Roberts, Kitchener and other war leaders. Emily had taken the Sulhampstead house so that he might frequently come and stay, but he preferred to spend the weekends at Mells or at Munstead. Pamela Jekyll's husband, Reginald McKenna, was now Home Secretary.

At the beginning of September Emily moved with the children to Bude in north Cornwall where Krishna and Nitya were now living. Ned had just written his letter of resignation to Mrs Besant and was very depressed and worried about money. He told Emily on 3 September that £2,500 a year for living was all he could afford. 'If you can't do this I had better sell Bedford Square as soon as I can and go somewhere smaller altogether. Of the 2,500 I could take 300 and go away. I could easily go to India earlier. I feel I am no help or use to you and can only hinder you. Your friends cannot be my friends and there it is.' Another cause of his depression was the breaking up of the house he had loved so much. He already hated the new house into which the furniture was to be moved on 26 September.

Emily replied that she did not know what to say or do to comfort him:

Would it help if I went away for a bit right out of your life [she wrote]. I could easily do it without any trouble. I can offer myself to the Front in some capacity and give you six months or a year in which to use all your influence with the children. I love you very much and can't bear you to be hurt and I will do anything I can to make you happy. But the fact remains, as you have put it, my friends can never be your friends – my beliefs only move you to contempt or fear. I *can* make your friends my friends – or some of them – and when I am at home I will try harder to encourage your friends and make a happier life for you. But I claim the right to my friends and my beliefs. I will never worry you with them. I will never even ask you to respect them. Use all your influence to give our children the friends you wish for them – the beliefs which are yours. I will stand aside loyally I promise you, *if* you will take over the responsibility . . . About money. You know darling I could be happy in a cottage with no servants, only I cannot do the impossible. I cannot run a big house like Bedford Square with less than seven servants and I cannot feed seven servants and five children and ourselves under £10 a week and that with great care. Do not think I am not doing my best to economise in every way. After this term stop all education if you wish, sell or let Bedford Square, make any arrangements you think wise, only don't ask me to live in a big house and pig it like Onslow Square. Let us face our difficulties together with tolerance for each other's point of view.

To give up all education seems a strange economy. Ned replied on the 7th to Emily's letter, 'Of course darling own Emmie our children cannot spare you and I can easily be spared – if not so I couldn't go to India and that would mean ruin – an impossible capitulation. I read your letter once and it crumpled me up . . . Darling, let me and I will stick by you and love you in every way to my full power to do all I can that you will love best of me.'

154

Emily chose this moment to shoot the bolt she had tried to prepare him for. She spelt it all out in a seven-page letter dated 11 September. The gist of it was that if their love was to continue it could only be, on her side, by a severance of their physical relationship. She felt that she had now done her duty to him and to her country with regard to children and could never face another. 'It has come to this – if I continue to bear what is becoming unbearable it must certainly kill the great love I have for you. On the other hand if the physical dread is removed – I will be more tender and loving to you than I have ever been – I fully and firmly believe we shall find unity and peace we have never known.' She had taken this step at this time, she said, because she knew that a double bed would, in the new conditions, be torment to him, and in getting into the new house it would be easy and natural to have single beds.

Ned's reply to this blow, anguished as it was, shows more than anything, I think, the gentleness of his nature:

14 September

My own darling—

I am so looking forward to your coming tomorrow [she was going to London for one night to see about the new house] I cannot write or do anything I feel ill and depressed.

You have indeed put a pistol at my head and although I accept and would do anything to retain your love yet the day may come when all I hold true may turn to dishonour and shame.

I cannot give up work. I should leave you and all dependent on me too badly off and yet all my confidence and hope seems gone to water. I am NOT asking your pity darling but just sympathy.

The thought of India so hopelessly far and alone for months without a friend, in a world of Bakers, makes me sick. Sick at heart am I. My failure belongs to me alone

155

and I must bear it. I almost wish I could just 'go out' and leave it all.

I feel further away from Theosophy than ever I have felt before. I think I know what you feel better than you know what I feel.

I write this now darling that I need not speak too much of myself tomorrow and try only to show that I love you truly

Your very very sad and loving Nedi

That same evening he was writing again: 'My own sweet darling, my own love, wife. I had expected this but it seems hard somehow. It would have been easier could I be faithless to you and before I knew you to the woman I prayed God to give me as my mate and wife. When I first saw you – 18, 19! years ago I knew you at once. You must try not to be frightened of me and God help me to be kind and chivalrous to you. I cannot do without your love and oh darling I want help and a lot of comfort. Where can I turn but to you?'

Would it have made it easier for him if she had gone off with another man? As it was he could at least keep his misery private. One can be sure that his friends and acquaintances at the Athenaeum and the Other Club had little idea of his desolation. He always had the gift of outward cheerfulness in society. I doubt whether even his best friends ever penetrated to the depths of his loneliness.

On 26 September he moved into Bedford Square and wrote next day from Temple Dinsley, the house he had built for H. G. Fenwick in 1908:

A perfect day and my heart just yearns and aches for you. Leaving Bloomsbury Square wring, wranged me. That is all past now – gone. You will say I should rejoice? The happiness of Bloomsbury Square reads as one long failure. I think, believe and hope I have achieved security for you but I seem to have lost more than it was worth. No matter what the future brings, I know I have loved you whatever has come about. I do love you what may come. I will love you darling wife. I just ask your patience, help and try to understandiness. I feel very lonely and lost and full of fears and anguish. I do hope I get a letter from you tomorrow and one that will help your ever very very loving Nedi.

Emily sent him infinitely loving, gentle letters every day, trying to make him feel how much happiness still lay before them. These letters soothed him even if they were of no real comfort. At forty-five he had the choice between celibacy with the effect it might have on his work and temper, or loveless sex from which he revolted with all his romantic soul. However, he did his best to be cheerful, writing to Emily on 1 October, the day before she joined him in Bedford Square, 'Away with all dull care in the thought of your coming back and this is just to welcome my own wife home to a new house and a new life wherein I shall strive to be more gentle, patient and loving in all these ways you would appreciate.'

CHAPTER NINE

India, Spain and Folly Farm

1914–1917

The move to Bedford Square did not make much difference to the lives of us children. We still had a square garden to play in where the wounded soldiers in their blue cotton uniforms with red ties came in increasing numbers to play bowls. On the south side of the square lived Raymond Asquith, who was married to the Horners' daughter, Katherine, and their three children. Raymond was killed in the war as was also the Horners' son, Edward. That extraordinary angular bird with the flamboyant plumage, Lady Ottoline Morrell, had her territory on the north side of the square. She looked gloriously eccentric even to me who was accustomed to seeing some very odd people in our own house. Barbie and Robert still went to King Alfred's School and Elisabeth to her boarding school, while Ursula and I had lessons in the morning in the dining-room from a hated (by me) PNEU[1] governess in which some neighbouring children joined. And an equally detested Mademoiselle came two afternoons a week to teach us French.

Father never became reconciled to the new house in spite

[1]Parents National Education Union, an organization started by a Miss Mason to train governesses to maintain a certain standard of education.

of doing a great deal to it. At the back he had built on two little rooms with glazed doors from two half landings, the lower one as a sitting-room for Barbie and the upper one as Mother's meditation room where she could burn incense and have her holy pictures round her. We used to go to her in this room every morning to recite a Theosophical prayer: 'I am a link in the golden chain of love that stretches round the world and I promise to keep my link bright and strong.' Mother had also instituted Christian prayers in the dining-room every morning after breakfast, something she had never done, oddly enough, before she became a Theosophist. All the household attended except Father. I remember the little kitchen-maid bursting into tears one morning while we were singing 'For those in peril on the sea': her brother was crossing to the Isle of Wight that day.

Father had covered the walls of the small outer hall with what he called silver paper but which looked like that lead-coloured lining to antique tea-caddies. The drawing-room, as at Bloomsbury Square, had black walls, white wood-work, yellow curtains and an emerald green painted floor, highly varnished and strewn with old Persian rugs. A passage on the ground floor led to two rooms at the back which were occupied all through the war by a family of Belgian refugees called Delville. Beyond those rooms were three small servants' rooms. We still had all the furniture Father had designed for Bloomsbury Square, as well as some good antique pieces. And we also had some pictures now, most of them given to Father by Sir Hugh Lane in payment for work done in connection with building a gallery in Dublin to house Lane's collection. In 1912 Father had designed a beautiful Palladian-style gallery in the form of a bridge to go across the Liffey, but the scheme had come to nothing. Lane's pictures in our house included two portraits of old ladies who Father claimed as his ancestors, and a huge painting of the Pannini school. After our grandfather's death in 1915, the portrait of General de Wagenheim always hung in our hall.

Mother still slept in the great oak bed, Father preferring to sleep in his dressing-room rather than have twin beds. Having endured this arrangement for nearly a year he asked to have a bedroom prepared for him on the drawing-room floor. He could no longer bear to go upstairs or see the casket, the symbol of his dream life with Emmie in the little white house that was never built.

I was not aware of any undercurrents of unhappiness during my childhood. I never heard my parents say a cross word to each other. My childhood was blissful and secure, but now I understand why it was that after we moved into Bedford Square, when I was six, Father never came up to the nursery. The nursery was part of 'upstairs' – the 'upstairs' that represented all he had lost. In cutting off physical relations with him, Mother had virtually cut him off from Elisabeth and me who rarely as yet went down to the drawing-room.

No one but I ever liked the Bedford Square house. I loved it. The main rooms faced east; it was cold and so damp that mushrooms grew even on the walls of Barbie's little sitting-room. The atmosphere of the house was said to be so bad that not long after we moved in Mother had it exorcised by a Roman Catholic priest.

There were only our night and day nurseries, a bathroom and two small rooms for Robert and Miss Drake (Miss Sew-and-Sew) above the main bedroom floor. Our day nursery was a lovely large room at the back of the house with a bow window looking on to the tower of the YMCA building in Tottenham Court Road (now demolished and replaced by the Y Hotel).

*　　*　　*

160

Father went off to India again for the fourth time on 4 December 1914 leaving Thomas in charge of the London office as usual. For this first wartime voyage he started from Tilbury instead of from Marseilles. Because of the fear of

submarines he was issued with an inflated waistcoat. According to Robert, instead of wearing it, he blew it up and sent it home from Tilbury with instructions that if he were torpedoed his wife and children should stand in reverence while it was deflated, listening to 'Father's last breath'. Mother cried when he left which touched him deeply. She wrote that she hoped it would comfort him to know how sad she had been to let him go whereas at other times his departure had been almost a relief because it removed what she dreaded.

In spite of all their talk of economy Father was writing to Mother from boardship to ask her to arrange astronomy lessons for the whole family that summer. 'Try and get a mathematician and not an astrologer – a Cambridge don! – One wants to understand the merry go round of the universe as though it was the palm of one's hand . . . I don't see why one should not teach a child and we are all children or should be (except naughty ones!) the meaning, view and intention of conic sections, the differential calculus, etc., etc. without the necessity of any sums or figures and without the puzzle world comprised within the numerals.' I am sorry that nothing came of this plan and that I am still completely ignorant of the differential calculus and conic sections. Nor do I altogether understand his letter. Did he wish to free us altogether from the boredom of arithmetic?

It made a great difference to Father to have William Nicholson with him on this voyage. Nicholson was feeling the war pinch and Father had arranged for him to go out to Delhi to paint the Viceroy. Poor Lord Hardinge was in a bad way. His wife had died in July and his elder son had been killed in France.

Nothing but the foundations of the central buildings for the new city could as yet be seen. In the middle of January 1915 Father told Mother that going up the river in a launch with Nicholson he had seen some lovely eagles: 'I am glad Government did not have the building of our birds!!! Mud beaks and corrugated iron feathers with a noisy machine that smelt of oil inside.' He continued:

I have a great deal of designing to do. Parks, roads, buildings etc. besides Government House and much work going on one must see to. It goes slow – the work. And they are not spending so much this year on account of the war. About £500,000 instead of £700,000. Baker has been very troublesome and serves ever Mammon rather than the righteousness of good and what I consider fine building. He is very selfish too. It is a bore. He has great, good qualities and can be very charming and is to those in his own interests . . . I do wish sometimes I had been to a proper school. I should have got on better with most people and knowing them and understanding them got my way with greater surety. Especially in this country and I would not have hurt and offended you so awfully. Robert [he would be fourteen in June] is going just the same way only more so. He is more indulged and has less discipline than ever I with my 7 brothers got. And he has not felt the awful pinch of real poverty I knew. I wonder if he will ever become an architect – it is the way where I could help him most. I should like him to become a decorative painter in the grand manner but what does matter is that he is keen on what he does and takes it up from love of it . . . The danger with Robert will be the danger of dilettantism. An office and drill of it might be good for him – the necessity of application and accuracy in drawing.

Father was still desperately unhappy about his relationship with Mother. They were both offering by almost every mail to go away if it would make the other happier. 'I hope to God I shall not stray and go wrong,' he was writing in February. 'I don't think I shall. The misery after! would be too horrible to bear. I want no other wife. But if I did I should tell you for I hate secrets.'

By the middle of February he was able to report that he had sent home money for Francis Smith to invest. That would make their total savings £10,000. With his £11,000 life insurance and the £5,000 coming to Mother on her mother's death, she would have a total of £26,000 if he died tomorrow. He wondered whether they could possibly afford to build a country house yet.

P & O. S. N. Co.
S.S.

when my father goes to sea
He takes my mother away from me

when my father comes home from sea
He brings my mother back to me

Father returned home in April. On 19 May this year, 1915, Charles Lutyens died. Since Father and Mother were together, there is no record of Father's feelings. He now had an exciting new commission. The Duke of Peñaranda, younger brother of the Duke of Alba, whom he had met with Lord Wimborne at Ashby St Ledgers, asked him to build a palace for him on one of his estates, El Guadelperal, near Toledo. At the end of June Father went to the Liria Palace in Madrid, belonging to the Duke of Alba, to discuss the project. Peñaranda was everything Father most liked – 'a charming person, 33, young, simple in a nice way, full of fun and life'. Father made a second journey to Spain in October when it was arranged for him by the the India Office to catch a P & O liner from Gibraltar to Malta and Cairo, and thence to Bombay. On this second visit to Spain he went to Toledo and inspected the site for the new palace. His detailed descriptive letters from Spain during this second visit run to over twenty pages. He was enthralled by all he saw and the people he met.

On 16 November he was in Cairo having joined Baker at Gibraltar and encountered five submarines in the Mediterranean. 'The Cairo mosques are much better built than anything I have seen in India,' he wrote from Cairo. 'They are remarkable – with qualities of real building and not that love of Dicky (shirt) front order so loved by the Indians (Moguls).' The Pyramids by moonlight looked 'monstrous large and made one wonder if the very hills were built by men of a race of giants to the Egyptians as they are giants to our times – and yet with their material magnitude there seems to be some spiritual motive as great and as impressive and marvellously mysterious'. Part of the Sphinx was hidden behind scaffolding.

Before embarking on another ship to Bombay he had been to Thebes and Luxor. The ship ran aground in thick fog in the Suez Canal. Father sympathised with the Captain who then asked him to come to his cabin on the bridge. He showed Father his chart and his report, calmly taking it for granted that his career was ruined. 'I wonder why it is,' Father wrote to Mother after this incident, 'that I get the confidence of working men, who cannot write or write well – seldom of men who write and base their lives on other peoples words.' He never based his own life on the words of others.

He arrived in Delhi on 4 December to find, to his joy, four letters from Mother. This winter of 1915–16 was to be Lord Hardinge's last as Viceroy. His health was beginning to deteriorate. Work already begun on the new city was going ahead but no new work was to be sanctioned unless it in some way helped the war effort. Lutyens was working on the details of a column to stand in the Viceroy's Court, to be called the Jaipur column in honour of the Maharaja of Jaipur who was giving the money for it. The decoration on the main buildings had now come under discussion and the need for stonemasons. Lutyens had found that Indian masons worked very well under English foremen. He longed to start a Delhi Centre for the training of Indian craftsmen for whom he had a great respect but he could get no Government cooperation for such a scheme.

Work on the King's Way, begun in 1912, was now so far advanced that Lutyens became fully aware for the first time that because of the angle of the slope of Raisina Hill, Government House would disappear from view, except for the top of the dome, for about a quarter of a mile along the two-mile processional way. When tackled, Baker reminded him of the minute he had signed two years before agreeing to a 22½ gradient. Lutyens replied that he had only signed it on an understanding that a model for it was to be made. Baker maintained that 'the pitch of the road' was 'inherent in the nature of the raised platform which was agreed to as a basis for the plan for the central buildings in 1913'. It was Baker's opinion that 'in a two-mile vista a prospect which for part of the distance hides and then reveals itself again is rather an attraction than otherwise'. There is some truth in this; the approach to the palace has a pleasing mystery. Rising up to its full splendour as one gets close, it gives one a shock of delighted surprise which would be missing it if were fully revealed along the whole length of the avenue. But to Father it was a disaster. As he pointed out to us, it was as if the Arc de Triomphe were suddenly to disappear half way up the Champs Élysées. He felt that Baker had betrayed him, deliberately allowing him to fall into a trap.

Since there was still time to rectify the mistake Lutyens appealed to the Delhi Committee. A cutting could be made in the slope between the Secretariat buildings; this, it was estimated, would cost only £2,000. Baker made a strong protest against the cutting on the grounds that his Secretariats would then be on either side of a sunken road so that little would be seen of them by processions passing along the avenue to the palace. The Committee anyway refused to recommend this extra expenditure in wartime, nor would Lord Hardinge, on whom the final decision rested, have sanctioned it. Lutyens could only hope that the new Viceroy, Lord Chelmsford, would be more sympathetic. The cutting could still be made next year, though the longer it was left the more it would cost.

Father felt intensely lonely at Delhi this year with everyone against him. 'O Emmie have you no heart left,' he cried out. 'You will perhaps some day remember my aching heart and desolate home when you so gladly make your great renunciation of us all.' He was able to send home another £1,000 that year for investment, bringing their savings up to £11,000.

He and Baker had to travel back to England together at the end of March, arguing all the way. When Father told Baker that he was going to bring the whole matter before the King, Baker merely laughed. Later that summer Queen Mary visited the Apple Tree Yard office to look at the altered plans for Government House. 'I made no jokes and now feel a loser!!', Father told Mother. 'She was rather prim and sticky and horribly shocked to find Government House had been cut down.'

Hardinge's own superficial and dismissive account of his dealings with Lutyens shows clearly the kind of man Father had to stand up to: 'I had no trouble with Baker, whose plans were admirable, and within the figure prescribed for the estimate, but Lutyens' plans, though beautiful, were made absolutely regardless of cost and had to be reduced in every way, which created some unpleasantness. He told people, the Queen amongst them, that I had quite spoilt his plans, but I think I was generous in allotting to him more than half a million sterling to build Government House.'[1] It may be noted here that the London County Council building, the competition for which Lutyens had lost, cost seven million pounds. Had he won this competition he would probably never have got Delhi, but financially he would have gained immeasurably. He earned hardly anything from Delhi; building costs, on which his commission was based, were low in India whereas his office expenses in London for the Delhi work were as high as for any English commission.

*　　*　　*

In June of that year 1916 a fresh cause of disruption arose between Father and Mother. Mother had inaugurated what she called the English Home Rule League in support of Mrs Besant's All India Home Rule League. On 18 June she held the first meeting of her new league at Bedford Square. Next day a leading article appeared in *The Times* headed 'A Mischievous Movement', not mentioning her name but saying, Cranky people in this country do many mad things, but surely

[1] *My Indian Years*, p. 96.

the maddest is to encourage a "Home Rule" agitation in India at a moment when we are just entering upon the greatest crisis of the war'. Mother made quite sure that it should be publicly known that she was the originator of the League by publishing a letter in *The Times* next day defending it.

In her autobiography Mother was to write that she believed her husband minded her meddling in Indian politics more than any of her other activities. Knowing that she was about to form this League he had written from Delhi:

If you come to India on a *political* mission I suppose I shall have to chuck Delhi and leave it to Baker which will spell ruin for us . . . Your politics religious and educational have beaten me . . . if my wishes and principles as regards our children are ignored – then I must make some arrangement towards finality but o! darling – do think it over so that we can make some modus vivendi. I can see no way out but with your help . . . It is no good both being unhappy and I would rather it is me than you.

Mother received what she called 'a very impertinent letter' from Edward Hudson after *The Times* article appeared, accusing her of harming her husband: she had a genius in her care and ought to make looking after him her sole object in life. No doubt many of Father's friends felt the same but did not have Hudson's courage to tell her so. It was Mrs Besant who put a stop to these political activities, and no one but Mrs Besant or Krishna could have done so. 'I think you should keep out of this,' Mrs Besant wrote to her from India, 'as it would irritate my dear Vishvakarman, and this would be wrong.' It was generous of Mrs Besant thus to refer to Father after the row over the TS building and his resignation.

In the same month, June 1916, a far-reaching event took place for Father: in Lady Cunard's box at Covent Garden he met Lady Sackville who was to play such a major role in his future and bring him a great measure of joy. He was also elected to the Garrick Club that summer where he was to spend some of his most convivial hours. Moreover, it was to be the happiest summer of our family life. Kind Mrs Merton lent us Folly Farm for the holidays, complete with her excellent servants. After all the misery of the past few years it is particularly pleasant to dwell on this holiday at Folly Farm. It was the first time the whole family had lived together in a house of Father's designing. I remember it so well. It was a delicious house to live in with a great sense of space and luxury. William Nicholson was staying there painting murals for the dining-room so that the house was pervaded with my favourite smell of artist's studio. There was an enormous jigsaw puzzle laid out in the dining-room on which we all worked from time to time, keeping Nicholson company. In the high hall was a wooden balcony painted red, behind which was a window giving on to the long first floor gallery where Prydie, Nicholson's first wife (a sister of James Pryde), would sit for hours on end playing the pianola. In other parts of the house I remember yellow glossy paint. I believe there was a bedroom in which all the furniture, designed by Father, was painted primrose yellow.

When, many years later, I lived at Munstead Wood for three months, the atmosphere there took me back to Folly Farm even though the houses were so different. Father gave all his houses a special feeling of his own. There was never anything in them to jar – rather, there was a sense of order, of harmony, that was both inspiring and restful. Outside one wing of Folly Farm was a cloister surrounding a pool or tank. It must have been a fine summer because we spent so much time sitting out there catching the goldfish with bread pellets attached to string, and putting them back again. There was another long stretch of water in the garden, herring-bone brick paths, and a sunk Dutch rose garden.

Eddie Knoblock was staying as well as the Nicholsons, and some of Barbie's friends. Miss Jekyll, who had laid out the garden for the Mertons, was persuaded to come for a short and rare holiday at the beginning of September and enjoyed playing the pianola as much as Mrs Nicholson did. After her departure Father wrote to her on 9 September hoping that she had got home all right and was not too tired.[1] He addressed her in his letters in a deliciously affectionate way – simply 'Toute Suite', and signed himself Nedi.

We played tremendous games of Crazy Croquet at Folly Farm on a very large, smooth lawn – the perfect game for all ages and any number of players, for there were several sets of balls and mallets. Fishing and croquet were the only outdoor activities Father enjoyed. He could not play tennis and he hated swimming. In his gentleness he could not bear to kill anything, not even the 'fearsome insects' in India. The exception was fish, but here he could tell himself that fish had no feelings; like so many other people he had more than once caught a fish baited with its own eye.

Father was not there all the time – he had to carry on his work in London – but he stayed for long week-ends. It was the nearest he ever came to having a country house of his own. But in some ways it was better than his own; Mrs Merton had a superlative cook and supplied every luxury (I can still remember the rich feeling of my fat satin eiderdown), and he had no worries about the expense of the holiday.

I had my eighth birthday there on the last day of July, and Barbie her eighteenth eight days later. Barbie had been working as a VAD at Waverley Abbey, a hospital near Aldershot, and at the end of the summer was to go and work at Dartmouth House in Charles Street (now the English Speaking Union) in a hospital run by Pamela Lytton. Barbie

[1]This and other letters to her from Father are in the University of California, Berkeley.

was tall and beautiful with Father's colouring, very blue eyes and dark hair, and with his long legs. Father was extremely proud of her. She had reacted strongly against Theosophy, was now ashamed of Mother's friends and as determined to get out of her milieu as Father had been to get out of his. She had great social gifts as well as intelligence and wit, and soon achieved her ambition of being accepted in smart society. I was in great awe of her. She and Robert had ceased to be vegetarians. Robert had also reacted against Theosophy but was still friendly with Krishna and Nitya. At fifteen he was very good-looking with abounding charm. He was also wonderfully talented in several directions; he could draw, paint, write, play anything on the piano by ear and had a beautiful singing voice with perfect pitch. But he had had no discipline either at home or at King Alfred's. He often played truant from school, forging Mother's signature on a note excusing him, and spending the afternoon in our local flea-pit in Tottenham Court Road – or so he told me. In consequence of this he had very little power of application. If he had had money he would, as Father had said, have become the perfect dilettante, for he had superb taste. Mother once told me that Father had been jealous of Robert as a boy. I can find no trace of this in Father's letters.

Ursula would be twelve in October. She was not pretty but she had a face of great charm with a slightly tip-tilted nose; she was the only one of us with curly hair, and the only one who never at any time came under the influence of Mother's ideas. She was Father's favourite – he never made the slightest attempt to hide it. She had been so delicate as a baby that it was feared she would not live and this had drawn out all his protective instinct. Because he showed that he loved her best she adored him. She was always a favourite with all grown-ups, including our terrible governesses. She was very clever and advanced for her age. She could paint well too, dance beautifully, write wonderful letters and, later on, do exquisite needlework. Her bad fairy had put two curses on her: she was easily discouraged and easily bored. She wanted to go to art school or into Father's office as an apprentice but gave up the ideas without any protest when Father disapproved of them; then she wanted to study ballet but this again was frowned on by Father. None of the rest of us would have been put off doing what we wanted to do because of parental authority.

Elisabeth, just ten, the 'difficult' one of us, was as alive as quicksilver, generous, lithe, impulsive, like a fish in water. She had wanted to be a boy; she always wanted to be different. It was for this reason that she was the only one of us to go to a boarding school, and later she took up composition because no one else in the family knew anything about it. Not only did she have great musical talent but a great power of perseverance. As for me I was fat and phlegmatic, living almost entirely in my own world of imagination, never bored so long as I was left to my own devices and completely self-sufficient except for my creature comforts. Looked after by Nannie and Annie, seldom required to do anything I did not like, I lived in a state of conscious bliss. Adults impinged hardly at all on me except when I was in love, but then I nearly always was in love. Nitya was the object of my most constant in-loveness, but at Folly Farm I fell in love with Prydie Nicholson and with one of Barbie's girl friends. The cause of in-loveness is a mystery. As a child I did not want any communication with my loved ones; to be in their presence was enough, though when they left the room I experienced a sensation of the sun going in.

In some ways I had an intuitive understanding of Father. I understood, for instance, that behind the endless games of patience he played, which so irritated Mother and were later to irritate Lady Sackville, his imagination was working hard. Then I knew that his facetiousness hid a sense of inadequacy in uncongenial society. I played the fool and won popularity in just the same way when I went to a day school in London.

When Father was with his true friends he still loved fun and jokes – what he called 'vivreations' – but his fun was far more spontaneous. His happiness that summer was like a blessing on the house. I have a very clear picture of him in my mind, facing me on the croquet lawn at Folly Farm, wearing his usual London clothes, his pipe in his mouth, his mallet poised between his long legs for a shot. I can see him in a dinner jacket, in tails and in a morning coat – in a top hat, a solar topee and a black trilby, but I cannot see him in country clothes and doubt whether he ever wore them.

*　　*　　*

Queen Mary's visit to Apple Tree Yard led to an invitation to Buckingham Palace in the autumn where Lutyens was able to lay all his grievances over Delhi before the King. The King deplored the change in the plans due to economy. Lutyens wrote to Lord Chelmsford, the new Viceroy, that the King had said:

> . . . it did not matter how long the Palace took to build, so long as it was, when built, worthy of India and its purpose, and that if money was not forthcoming now, parts might for the time be omitted and façades left unfinished as is usual in Italy, until such time as money was available to complete them . . . His Majesty objected to the rise in the level from the Great Place masking and impairing the dignity and approach of the Palace.[1]

It rather sounds from this as if the King had been subjected to the suggestive treatment familiar to so many of Ned's clients – but Ned evidently left Buckingham Palace convinced that not only had he received commands which happened to

[1]Hussey, p. 364.

coincide with his own views but that the King's wishes were enough to convince Authority.

He set out for India from Southampton on 10 November that year 1916 greatly encouraged by the King's support, and on leaving London wrote far more cheerfully to Emily, 'Always remember my love and when I am older I shall be able to hold you without fear and we shall be a very happy and contented Darby and Joan with lots of grandchildren and lots of leisure to enjoy being together.' He went again via Spain in connection with his work for the Duke of Peñaranda. This time he met King Alphonso with whom he made a hit. 'My visit has been a great success,' he wrote on 17 November, 'I know a King and like the feeling of it. So very different from ours! . . . I wish I could describe King Alphonso to you. His change from good fellow to King – as when he is recognised and the guard turns out – is direct yet imperceptible and absolutely unconscious. Chameleon like in his attitude with men and situations – yet always Alphonso.'

In the Mediterranean the P & O liner which Father had joined at Gibraltar was attacked by two submarines – 'little black devils'. It was a two-hour running battle, the submarines' shells falling short of the ship and the ship's shells falling short of the submarines. Eventually the ship got away but 'it was very nerve destroying and left no comfort for the rest of the voyage and the peace of Port Said is bliss'. He arrived in Delhi on the day before Christmas when everyone was away so it was not until the middle of January 1917 that he met the Chelmsfords. Lady Chelmsford was a sister of Lord Wimborne. Father found her 'quite intelligent about plans'. At least she really looked at them, and Lord Chelmsford was more sympathetic than Lord Hardinge had been.

Father was getting on no better with Baker: 'His goody goody talk about "right" things drives me wild as he never practises what he preaches and buckles up at the first difficulty and lets his work go hang! and folks here don't know

175

and don't care for the difference. He lives in the furrowed clay of his own despondency ... They are getting rather tired of Baker here and are turning to me. Baker never does any work without "instructions". As I am paid £5.5.0 a day for advice alone I fill every spare moment designing something that may or may not be used.'

Lutyens's plans for the staff bungalows were considered too expensive by the Delhi Committee whereas Baker's 'bungle ohs' were approved. Lutyens asked to be relieved from 'the anguish of designing jerry-villas' in exchange for building all the bungalows along the King's Way. This request was granted, and he was also given the job of designing the All India War Memorial at the eastern end of the King's Way. This delighted him, and he was further elated by the news that another £130,000 was to be allocated for Government House, though with the proviso that it was not to be used to alter the levels of approach. But his chief work that winter was in designing the garden for the palace. The Government of India had 'commanded a Mogul garden which means terraces, water ways and sunk courts' he wrote.

Before he left Delhi in April 1917 it had been decided that no fresh building was to be put in hand until the end of the war and that therefore the presence of the architects would not be required in Delhi until that time came. It meant a great financial loss to Father. He must have looked forward to his home-coming with a certain amount of dread. It had been a bitterly cold winter in England and Mother had practised rigorous economies, much to Barbie's indignation. Although Father had been urging Mother to economise he could hardly have appreciated her means of doing so. All bedroom fires had been stopped; there were two meatless meals a week for the whole household, and he had received an ominous announcement that 'Mrs Andrews was cheap and quite a good enough cook in wartime'.

CHAPTER TEN

Sackvilles and Cenotaph
1917–1920

In June 1917 General Fabian Ware, Director of the newly constituted War Graves Commission, asked Lutyens, Baker and Charles Aitken, Director of the Tate Gallery, to go to France to report on the military cemeteries and the monuments that should be erected in them. They went on 9 July and were billeted in a château close to the military Headquarters near Boulogne. Every day they were taken on a long motor drive to inspect the temporary graves. Father, who was deeply moved, wrote to Mother from France on 12 July:

The battlefields – the obliteration of all human endeavour and achievement of destruction is bettered by the poppies and the wild flowers that are as friendly to an unexploded shell as they are to the leg of a garden seat in Surrey . . . The grave yards, haphazard from the needs of much to do and little time for thought. And then a ribbon of isolated graves like a milky way across miles of country where men were tucked in where they fell. Ribbons of little crosses each touching each across a cemetery, set in a wilderness of annuals and where one sort of flower has grown the effect is charming, easy and oh so pathetic. One thinks for the moment no other monument is needed. Evanescent but for the moment is almost perfect but how misleading I surmise is this emotion and how some love to sermonise, but the only monument can be one where the endeavour is sincere to make such monuments permanent – a solid ball of bronze!! . . . *Very private.* Just had a pleasant talk with Gen Ware. His idea is that I am made top dog to carry it all out!! Employing Baker etc!

After his return from France Lutyens advocated 'One great fair stone of fine proportions' as a monument in every cemetery. He also pressed that there should be uniformity for every grave, with headstones of an unvarying pattern. For once Mother was entirely with him over his Great Stone: '. . . it appeals to *my* side of life as houses don't. I see so much true symbolism in it. I hope you get it through. Baker must be dotty! A five pointed cross for each of the colonies. Too silly. And India left out which will cause bitter hurt and what about the Jews and agnostics who hate crosses.'

There now followed between Lutyens and Baker a controversy over the Stone versus the Cross almost as bitter as that waged over the gradient at Delhi. Lutyens wanted his stone to be entirely non-denominational; Baker insisted on the symbolism of the Cross. Lutyens wished he had someone to fight his battles for him and leave him happy with his work which in itself was 'sufficiently full of anxieties'. In the end the Commission compromised. They decided that while all the cemeteries should incorporate Lutyens's Stone of Remembrance, Christian cemeteries should include the Cross of Sacrifice, designed by Reginald Blomfield, and cemeteries of other faiths their own religious symbols. But the arrangement was evidently not adhered to, for in August 1919 Father was

178

to write, '300 stones to 1000 crosses – not fair'. And in September 1919 he was writing, 'I made a "mot" to day in company at the club talking of monuments and crosses. I said that every cross the Church put up to commemorate the war was a faggot to her pyre.'

That winter of 1917 was a particularly bad one for Father financially. No new work was coming in, he would not get his £1,000 from Delhi nor his five guineas a day and he had to give his time free to the war graves.[1] 'Oh, Emmie, money is difficult,' he wrote despairingly. 'I don't know what I shall do. Only I can make it and war stops everything. I don't think I *could* last two more years: it would take *all* my savings. I don't see how closing down Bedford Square would help. I still owe money for getting into the place. I wish it was a better house.'

*　　*　　*

Ever since their first meeting at the opera on 24 June 1916, Father and Victoria, Lady Sackville had been seeing a great deal of each other. She had found him 'charming' on that first evening and their friendship had ripened rapidly. He had been forty-seven when they met and she fifty-four. The illegitimate daughter of Lord Sackville by Pepita, a Spanish dancer, Victoria Sackville (she took her father's name) had married in 1890 her first cousin, Lionel, who became the third Lord Sackville in 1910 and inherited the great Elizabethan house, Knole, in Kent where Victoria had lived with her father. Before Ned Lutyens got to know her, Sir John Murray Scott, a very rich bachelor, had been her adorer for more than ten years. On his death in 1912 he had

[1] That is, in his advisory capacity. The principal architects for the war memorials received a salary of £400 a year in 1918 which was raised to £600 in 1919.

left her £150,000 as well as the contents of a house in the rue Lafitte in Paris, then valued at £350,000, inherited from the widow of Sir Richard Wallace whose secretary he had been. Murray Scott had also given her a house in London, 34 Hill Street.

Victoria's friends called her B.M. (*bonne maman*). To Father she became MacSack and to her he was McNed, and her daughter, Vita Nicolson, became MacVita. (The origin of the Mac was the marriage of the Jekylls' elder daughter Barbara to Francis McClaren. Pamela Jekyll was already married to Reginald McKenna, so on Barbara's engagement Father had written to her that it was obvious one had to be called MacSomething to be loved by a Jekyll.) Lady Sackville's nature was one of extravagant generosity veined with incredible meannesses. Her passions in life were giving small perfect luncheon parties, decorating houses and acquiring furniture and *objets d'art*. When I knew her in the Twenties she had grown too fat but she was still beautiful with a perfect complexion. She never used make-up. Her slight foreign accent and her general ambience of deliciously scented opulence were a great attraction to me. She always seemed to wear a hat with a veil, even indoors, and to be dressed in sables, the softness of the fur emphasising the softness of everything else about her (except her will). She was lavishly cushioned in warm security.

She was very unhappy at the time she met McNed because her husband Lionel had a mistress and was treating her, his wife, with great coldness. She did not know how long she would be able to bear to remain at Knole in these conditions, much as she adored the place, and was therefore thinking of building a house at Hove as a bolt-hole. She and McNed had not known each other a month before he was begging her, according to her diary, to let him build the Hove house, saying that he would charge her only 5% on any work he did for her. 'His ideas agree with mine thoroughly,' she noted in her diary on 27 July 1916, 'and I am tempted because it would add great value to the house later on.' She wanted him to build for her because she believed he was 'a great genius', while he for his part felt that at last he had found the ideal client – kind, generous, rich in her own right, who had faith in him and was prepared to cosset him. Her style of living in contrast to our own would have put Mother at an impossible disadvantage had she looked on Lady MacSack, as we called her, as a rival. Even Aggie Jekyll's housekeeping was put in the shade. MacSack gave McNed all the delicacies he would never have dreamt of having at home – foie gras, lobsters stuffed with caviar, soufflées, perfect sauces and the best wines.

By the time McNed returned from India in May 1917 the Hove plan had fallen through and they began looking together for a house for her at Brighton. She had also decided to buy a smaller house in Mayfair to replace Hill Street and allow him to do it up for her. He had already made some alterations to Hill Street and done some minor work at Knole. They had now become sufficiently intimate for her to record in her diary on 25 June after a day in Brighton, 'He told me in the car that he had never, never loved another woman or touched anybody but his wife, who refuses him now. I believe him, and his men-friends say the same.' She was struck by the purity of his nature: when he lunched in a party with Augustus John at the Eiffel Tower he had been disgusted by the sex talk.

But soon they began to quarrel over what he wanted to rebuild for her. No sooner was a plan decided on for the new London house in Brook Street than she changed her mind. The house had not yet been bought but he had made innumerable drawings for it. She would love his ideas and then find some fault with them, usually on the grounds of expense: it would be all right if she had £20,000 a year, she said. As it was her capital had dwindled considerably owing to her extravagance and her net income was now only £4,000 a

181

year. Besides, she believed that her taste in interior decoration was much better than his; he was not bold enough and cared too much about 'the grammar' of architecture. For him, her taste was too flamboyant, verging on the vulgar. He wanted a free hand to build her something really perfect. Successful collaboration between them was almost impossible. 'I must get my friends moulded in my way or else I can't work with them,' she wrote characteristically on 9 September; and later she was to note, '. . . even if I had to work with Michelangelo, I would prefer to do my own jobs, according to my own inspiration.' What she wanted was a tame genius. They were alternately fire and water to each other.

She was either praising his genius and the sweetness of his nature and finding him 'brilliantly amusing' or else trying to cure him of making jokes and warning him not to be so outspoken, especially when meeting people for the first time. She recorded that she had written him a letter 'begging him to get some new clothes and not to go making puns all the time. I do it for his good, as people mind it so much, and he will get unpopular, and may lose some work through boring people, such as Sybil Rocksavage [later Lady Cholmondeley].' And another diary entry reads, 'The poor man has got no one to look after his things; no collars, no handkerchiefs, no ties, everything wants mending. Emmie, instead of attending to him, goes and saves souls.' Walters, the parlour-maid who had looked after him, had now left, but no doubt MacSack was exaggerating his neglected condition. Lavish in everything, she would have expected a man to have many more clothes than he needed. It was natural for her to blame Emily who had been with McNed to Knole for the day on 22 September: '. . . she is so grey, so joyless and such a contrast to McNed who tries to be so nice to her.'

But in spite of constant friction over building, MacSack and McNed had some very happy times together and became more and more emotionally dependent on each other as becomes apparent. One happy occasion was when McNed took her and Vita on 25 August to see Gertrude Jekyll at Munstead Wood. 'She is 74,' MacSack wrote, 'very ugly in her features, but has a very fresh and clean skin, and charming voice and timbre de voix, and a very kind smile. She was charming to V. and me . . . we had a charming talk in French. She admires Vita and so does McNed. I like her immensely. She is such a Grande Dame.' On a subsequent visit she wrote of how overjoyed Miss Jekyll was to see McNed. 'She loves him, and follows him about with such loving eyes and treats him like a child.' Miss Jekyll was aware that she was a *grande dame*. She had told Logan Pearsall Smith that she belonged to the 'armigerous' class, meaning entitled to bear arms. '. . . armigerous people have certain expressions of their own,' Pearsall Smith reported her as saying. 'They don't for instance, say *overcoat*, but *great-coat*; they *have* tea or coffee or sugar, they never *take* them; they never take anything into their bodies but pills and medicines, and these they don't talk about; armigerous men never say *vest*, they say *waistcoat*, but expect their tailors to use *vest* in speaking to them or in sending in their bills. It would be an impertinence for a tailor to use the word *waistcoat* to an armigerous person.'[1]

In the autumn of 1917 Augustus John painted a portrait of Father which Lady MacSack went to John's studio to see. She found it 'horrible', saying that it made McNed look like 'a sickly Japanese instead of his pink and jolly face.' However, she liked a first unfinished oil sketch and bought it for £100.[2]

The Christmas of 1917 was the first Father had spent at home since 1911. He made what I now realise must have been a great sacrifice for our sakes – he went 'upstairs' and

---

[1]*Gertrude Jekyll, A Memoir* by Francis Jekyll, p. 197 (Cape 1934).
[2]The finished portrait now belongs to Lord Ridley and the unfinished one to Nicholas Ridley, MP.

got into bed with Mother so that we could find them there together when we went in early in the morning, as was our Christmas custom, to open our presents all together in, or on, the big bed after singing carols outside the door.

On Boxing Day, Mother's forty-third birthday, he took us to lunch at the Berkeley Grill, an unprecedented and unforgettable treat. He had done some work for the Berkeley Hotel, including redecorating the Grill Room, and was allowed to take his family there free on festive occasions. (A little sitting-room he designed, panelled in silvery wood, has been transferred intact to the new Berkeley in Knightsbridge.)

On 29 December Father went to Spain again so that he was away when his name appeared in the New Year's Honours List of 1918 as a Knight of the Order of the Indian Empire. It was announced at the same time that he had been made chief architect for the War Graves Commission. 'Yesterday I found the hall table stacked with telegrams and letters to Sir Edwin,' Mother wrote to him, 'so I brought them down to Knebworth [Homewood] that we might all enjoy them. A very amusing wire from Diana Manners [whom Father had met at Knole]: "The King and I are agreed – well done." A very nice letter from Baker to me.' (Baker was knighted in 1926.) There would no longer be any need for Father to hang his red braces round his neck as he had once done when attending a dinner where orders were to be worn and he had none to wear. When he went to the palace to be knighted a very nervous man next to him asked what the procedure was. 'Quite simple,' Father told him. 'The Lord Chamberlain will call out your name and lead you up to the throne; then all you have to do is go down on one knee on a cushion and sing God Save the King.' 'But I don't even know the words!' 'Don't worry, the King will help you out with them.'

*　　*　　*

The zeppelin raids on London had now become so bad that in February 1918 Ursula and I with Nannie, Annie and a cook for our vegetarian food were evacuated to Church Stretton in Shropshire. We remained there until July 1919 in a series of furnished lodgings in the Carding Mill Valley. (I see in a letter of Mother's that our first lodgings cost £3.15.0 a week.) Elisabeth joined us for holidays and Mother paid us occasional visits. Ursula went daily to a boys' tutor and I to a governess in the town. Barbie was still working in Pamela Lytton's hospital, while Robert, having given a false age (he was not yet eighteen) had joined the army as a cook. In April 1918 the lease of Bedford Square was sold, presumably at a loss, and Father and Barbie, and Mother too when she was not with us or travelling around lecturing, moved into furnished houses, first No 9 Montagu Street and then 15 Queen Anne Street. Father and Barbie were closer at this period than they had ever been before or were ever to be again.

At this time, while Father was so much alone in London, he was seeing Lady Sackville continually and spending almost every weekend at Knole. The idea of a new London house had been given up, but in May 1918 she bought three houses in Brighton, Nos 39 40 and 40a Sussex Square with a large garden reached by a tunnel under the roadway. McNed immediately started making plans for knocking the three houses into one and redesigning the garden. MacSack complained that he crabbed everything about the houses and made 'stupid remarks about their grammar', said that they were not 'grand seigneur enough' for her and wanted to alter everything in them. 'He never remembers how little money I have got now, and is too ambitious for me.' She was having to sell capital and some of her jewels. She noted that many people would not employ 'the great Lutyens' because he had a reputation for being extravagant and not allowing them to have what they wanted. She conceded, however, that 'McNed remodelled 40, 40a and 39 in half-an-hour in the most wonderful manner. I must admit his genius: it never struck me more forcibly than today, which was fairy-like as if he had touched the houses with a wand.'

She bought a great deal of new furniture for the Brighton houses and in August removed van-loads of her own possessions from Knole. On 5 September she moved into No 40 Sussex Square while building was going on around her and while she continued to go to Knole for the weekends. On her birthday, 23 September, she wrote that she was fifty-six 'and I am still malade, which pleases me rather, as I am cracking the record, I think.' Evidently all passion was not spent. She had been used to male adoration all her life and was still a physically very attractive woman.

*   *   *

Father and Mother celebrated the Armistice alone together in London on 11 November 1918. Father was now on the lookout for another house where the family could be reunited, something much smaller and easier to run than Bedford Square. In spite of the war being over, building was not to start again in Delhi that winter so Father did not have to go to India. In the New Year of 1919 he went to Spain again and then on 27 February to South Africa to report on designs for the new University of Cape Town, a commission he had hoped to get himself but which had been given to J. M. Solomon, a disciple of Baker's. He was allowed to take a secretary with him and chose a young man interested in architecture, Herbert Ward, the son of a sculptor of that name who was a friend of William Nicholson's. Herbie Ward, an old Etonian, had joined the Royal Flying Corps at the age of seventeen, had been shot down over Germany, taken prisoner and been the first war prisoner to escape. Father was glad of the company of this vital, talented young man, who was still only twenty-one, with whom he shared a cabin on the

Balmoral Castle. 'Wardie', as Father called him, has many recollections of that time. At first he was disconcerted when Father told the other passengers that he, Wardie, 'went to bed with two little animals – two little calves'. The soup at dinner prompted Father to tell a story of an elderly American lady who ate so many clams that her stomach rose and fell with the tide. He also told a story of a woman who was petitioning for divorce on the grounds that her chain-smoking husband used her open mouth in the early morning as an ash-tray. When the cheese was brought round he would murmur, 'How sweet the name of cheeses sounds in vegetarians' ears'.

When they sighted Madeira Father held out his arms and cried, 'Madeira, my God, to thee.' He confessed to Wardie how desperately shy he had been as a young man; he had overcome this, he said, by deciding to behave like a puppy which rolls on its back and relies on helplessness to provide immunity. 'I now say whatever comes into my head and hope that no one will kick my round, soft tummy.' What really impressed Wardie were the delicious pictures Father drew of an appropriate house for the Captain of the *Balmoral Castle* who was to retire to Gravesend after the return voyage.[1]

In Cape Town they stayed with Solomon in a house called The Woolsack designed by Baker. 'A nice little house,' Father described it as, 'but full of schoolboy errors, a sort of early me.' When Father was asked to be the guest of honour at a dinner given by Cape Town's exclusive Owl Club he was, according to Wardie, in such a state of nervous anxiety over his speech that for two days beforehand he lost his appetite. When the moment came for him to stand up he began, 'Gentlemen, I cannot claim to have t'wit t'woo you with high flown words . . .' but he was so inaudible that his audience did not immediately catch the wit of this opening.

[1]These drawings, edited by Margaret Richardson, have been published in facsimile by the Scolar Press.

Father returned from South Africa on 25 April. Not long afterwards Lady Sackville left Knole for good. She had discovered Lionel kissing his mistress under the tulip tree in the garden – out of doors in broad daylight where the servants might have seen him; it was too vulgar; she could stand it no longer. McNed happened to be staying at Knole for the week-end when she left. She motored him back to London on Sunday afternoon, 19 May. 'I did not tell him everything during our drive to London,' she wrote in her diary, 'so as not to distress him. But he sees that I cannot stay at Knole any longer. He was so nice and friendly about it all. He suggested all sorts of charming plans to distract my attention.' One of his plans was for a little guest-house in the garden, but four days later she lost her temper with McNed when he told her it would cost £10,000. 'I must really suppress McNed finally. I can't allow him to spend my money like water.' This quarrel was soon made up like so many others.

Early in June Father was dining one evening with William Bridgeman (afterwards Lord Bridgeman) at his Adam house, 13 Mansfield Street near Cavendish Square, when he heard that the house was for sale. After dinner he went all over it, fell in love with it and decided then and there to buy it. It was Bloomsbury Square all over again. Far from being a small house, easy to run, Mansfield Street was huge and with what Mother called 'a wicked basement'. And all this time he and Thomas were complaining to Lady Sackville of Mother's terrible extravagance. The price was £10,000 for a 999-year lease with a very small ground rent. I always understood that Lady Sackville most generously gave Father most of the money for the premium but this is not so, for there is an entry in her diary for 26 June 1919, saying that she had seen Thomas about 'the Mansfield mortgage and given him £7,800 security' in case she died. It seems from this that she had taken out a mortgage on the house, and she charged him interest on the loan. By September 1923 he had paid back

£7,500, and the following year he gave her another £500. We were not to move in to Mansfield Street until the autumn.

* * *

Father must have been aware since the Armistice that a war memorial would be needed for London and had no doubt made sketches for it in the hope that he would be asked to design it, but it was probably not until the end of June or the beginning of July 1919 that Lloyd George, the Prime Minister, sent for him and told him that the Government wanted a 'catafalque' erected in Whitehall as a saluting point for the march past of allied troops on Saturday, 19 July, during the peace celebrations at which Marshal Foch and General Pershing were to be present. Father said that it should not be a catafalque, which bears a coffin, but a cenotaph, which is an empty tomb. He remembered a massive stone seat he had designed for Miss Jekyll being once compared to some celebrated cenotaph. Thus this hitherto obscure word became associated with the best known of all modern funerary monuments. Since it had to be ready in ten days' time it could only be a temporary structure of wood and plaster.

Father evidently sent in his design very quickly for there is a letter from him to Mother dated 7 July 1919, telling her that Lord Curzon, the Foreign Secretary, 'has approved my structure in Whitehall – but wanted it if possible less catafalqué so I am putting a great vase or basin on it – to spout a pillar of flame at night and I hope smoke by day.' At the end of this letter he drew a small rough sketch of the monument as it was finally built.

Among Lady Sackville's papers are two sketches of the Cenotaph as well as two drawings of it in pencil and coloured chalks. One of the sketches is dated July in her writing but no day is given. What is interesting is that she owned a third sketch of a completely different design, showing a recumbent

189

soldier on the top of a much squatter monument. She claimed in her diary at a later date that McNed had first designed his memorial while dining alone with her at Hill Street, so this third sketch may possibly be his very first design for the Cenotaph.

Father also made a drawing of the Cenotaph for Vita Nicolson in pencil and coloured chalks, inscribed in his own hand 19 July 1919, the day of the march past. Lady Sackville was away at Bradford-on-Avon on this day and he had dined with the Nicolsons in Ebury Street. He also made a drawing of the Cenotaph for Sir Frank Baines, Head of the Ministry of Works, showing it at a slightly different angle from Vita's and Lady Sackville's, and he sent two drawings of its other side to Miss Jekyll. As well as these there are five sketches of it and one worked up drawing from the office, not in Lutyens's hand, dated July 1919, in the RIBA Drawings Collection.

Father was hurt not to receive an official invitation to attend the march past but the Cenotaph was greeted with such enthusiasm in the press for days afterwards and received so much praise all round that Mother, away as usual for the summer holidays, warned him not to get a swollen head! He was naturally thrilled by his success (as Mother was also) and inspired by it. It was the first time his name became known to the general public.

The simplicity of the Cenotaph, its non-denominational character, its universality and timelessness, caught the imagination of the hundreds of thousands of people who passed it during the peace celebrations. It was so perfectly right for its setting and for the mood of the time that within a week it had become a national monument. The only inscription on it – To the Glorious Dead – was suggested by Lloyd George. It is the best known and best loved of all Lutyens's work. In his own words 'the plain fact emerged and grew stronger every hour that the Cenotaph was what the people wanted, and they wanted to have the wood and plaster original replaced by an identical memorial in lasting stone'. Doubts were raised by some about the site and the effect of the structure on the flow of traffic in Whitehall – it would be better in the Mall. Others, including the Archbishop of Canterbury and Lord Wolmer, a friend of Baker's, asked why there was no cross on it. 'Lord Wolmer refers to my cenotaph as an "article",' Father told Mother on 30 July. 'I have asked the P.M. to answer that Indian troops have to salute the cenotaph, now that it is one article we want not 39 but he wont.'

Among Father's letters is an incomplete draft of a letter from him to Sir Alfred Mond, First Commissioner of Works, dated 29 July, which reads: 'I should like the permanent monument to be where it now stands, of Portland stone with all the refinement digestion can invent to perfect it. The site has been officially qualified [dignified crossed out] by the salutes of Foch and the allied armies and by our men and their great leaders. No other site could give this pertinence.'

On 31 July it was reported in *The Times* that the Cabinet had decided at a meeting the day before that 'the cenotaph to "The Glorious Dead" should be re-erected as a permanent memorial on its present site in Whitehall . . . It is understood that the Cabinet was largely influenced in their decision to retain the Whitehall site by a moving letter from Sir Edwin Lutyens which Sir Alfred Mond read to the assembled ministers.'

Father also wanted coloured marble flags for the permanent structure instead of silk ones. Silk flags, he maintained, would get bedraggled and would need to be frequently renewed. But in this matter, to his intense disappointment, he was overruled by the Cabinet. He was to have stone flags, though not in colour, on his great war memorial at Étaples, and beautifully dignified they look.

What it is that gives the Cenotaph its magical quality I cannot say. The experts point out that the horizontal lines are not horizontal at all, but curves on a circle with its centre 900 feet below the ground. What is apparent to everyone is that there are no perpendicular lines: the four corners would, they say, meet at a point 1,000 feet high if they were continued upwards. No wonder, as Father told Vita Nicolson, that the calculations filled a manuscript book of thirty-three pages. I never saw the temporary monument which was pulled down the following January, but I became gradually conscious of the mystery and majesty of the permanent structure which was built in time for the Armistice Day unveiling ceremony of 1920. For years afterwards men instinctively raised their hats when they passed the Cenotaph, even when they were on the tops of buses.

* * *

We were spending the summer holidays of 1919 in a furnished house at Thorpeness in Suffolk. Barbie and her great friend of the moment, Cynthia Curzon (who was to become Oswald Mosley's first wife), celebrated their twenty-first birthdays while we were there. Several of Barbie's other friends had taken houses close by and there were plenty of young men to dance with to the gramophone. (The tunes I remember best from that summer are 'On the Level You're a Little Devil' and 'I Found a Rose in the Devil's Garden'.) Barbie received several proposals, I believe. Robert spent some time with us there. He had been demobilised in January and gone to Trinity College, Cambridge, to read history. It was possible to go to a university just after the war without passing an examination. He does not seem to have learnt anything at Cambridge except how to make *crème brûlée*. Father, who was shocked by the amount he was smoking and the bills he was running up, had written to Mother in May about one dinner bill, 'There is a liberality about it that belongs more to the actor than the gentleman.' Yet he did

The casket with some of its contents, 1896

Emily Lutyens soon after marriage, 1897: ink drawing by an unknown artist

Emily Lutyens in 1915

E.L. asleep, drawn by the same artist at the same time

Drawing of E.L. by Edmund Dulac, signed and inscribed 'between Dover & London Sept 1st 1922': brown and blue chalk

Krishnamurti at
Castle Eerde,
Holland, in 1926

Lady Sackville eating out in the loggia at White Lodge. (*Reproduced by courtesy of Nigel Nicolson*)

E.L. at Mansfield Street in the 1920s in his favourite seat, known as the Napoleon chair. It was a copy of a chair in a contemporary drawing of Napoleon's study

Top: Queen Mary's Dolls' House, with drawer extended to show
the garden designed by Gertrude Jekyll. (*Reproduced by gracious
permission of Her Majesty The Queen*)

The Dolls' House Library. The bound volumes contain original
MSS by the best-known authors of the day. (*Reproduced by gracious
permission of Her Majesty The Queen*)

From left to right: Captain Swinton, Edwin Lutyens, Herbert Baker

Viceroy's House, New Delhi, looking west, showing the Viceroy's Court and the Jaipur column, 1931

.L. with his grandson, Matthew Ridley, after receiving the KCIE in 1930

E.L. in the Racquet Court at Mansfield Street with plans for the Liverpool
Cathedral, 1930

Liverpool Cathedral, 1929. This model was exhibited at the Royal Academy in
1934. © Country Life

not want Mother to be cross with Robert, for he was writing soon afterwards, 'Scolding leads to excess and he is such a baby boy still.'

When Mother returned with us to London at the end of September we went straight to 13 Mansfield Street which Father had been busy preparing for us. It had an apple-green front door (later painted black) as in Bedford Square and the same brass knocker in the shape of a double dolphin, so that from the outside it appeared familiar, but inside it seemed a palace with a huge hall paved in black and white marble squares from which rose an imposing staircase with marble pillars at its foot. (I did not know then that they were scagliola.) The staircase wall went all the way up to a pretty glass roof which made the house very light and spacious. It had the same aspect as Bedford Square; the main rooms faced east and were very cold.

The house was not only wider than Bedford Square but went back much further to incorporate what had been the stables and coachman's quarters in Mansfield Mews. The stables and coach-house had been turned by the Bridgemans into a great billiard-room with a parquet floor which became our day-nursery, and immediately above it was a racquet court reached by a separate staircase. At that time there was no entrance into the mews. Also on the ground floor were the morning-room in front, with a red-painted floor, a large dining-room and a serving-room. The grand staircase was something of a sham for it went up only as far as the drawing-room floor. After that there was nothing but a narrow stone staircase leading from the basement to the top of the house, with a service lift, pulled by ropes, in the well. On the first floor were a large front drawing-room, a back drawing-room, and then Father's bedroom and bathroom which led to the racquet court. On the main bedroom floor there were only four bedrooms – a smallish one for Barbie in front, our large night-nursery also in front, Mother's bedroom above the back drawing-room and beyond that Ursula's room, over Father's bedroom. This room had been partitioned to form a passage leading to the only bathroom and lavatory on that floor. We had no spare room and when Robert was at home he had a bed in Father's room. On the top floor were the servants' quarters and Miss Drake's sewing-room.

Barbie and Ursula slept in the 'St Ursula' beds, and Mother had her original bedroom furniture, but there were some new additions to the furniture in the rest of the house, such as a polished mahogany table in the dining-room in place of the original oak refectory table, and two double-fronted bookcases which Father had designed for the front drawing-room.

This front drawing-room was decorated as the Bedford Square one had been – black walls, green painted floor, yellow curtains. The sofas and arm-chairs were still covered in black horse-hair. (From 1906 George Muntzer did all Father's upholstery work.) Father never lost certain prejudices – against loose covers, for instance, silk lampshades, fringes on anything, fitted or pile carpets, flowers indoors, fish knives, glasses with stems, and vacuum cleaners which he said ruined any carpet. Where we did have carpets, as on the front stairs (the back stairs were left to their cold stone), the landings and Mother's bedroom, they were always the same, designed by him – dark grey hair-cord with a narrow yellow and black border. Our glasses were also designed by him – of a tumbler type in three different sizes, for water, wine and port. There was never any pleasure in drinking wine from such tubby straight-sided glasses, but then wine, apart from port, was seldom served at home and when it was it would be a half bottle of tepid Graves or, rarely, a bottle of champagne. Father's favourite drink was port of which he was a connoisseur; he had it every day for the two main meals even when he was in India, and he would have a nightcap of whisky. When he went out he enjoyed anything that was offered to

194

him. I never saw him drunk but he often came home very merry from a dinner party.

I believe that some of Father's prejudices were dictated by economy: black horsehair never wore out and never had to be cleaned; it could be sponged when dirty; stemless glasses seldom broke; card lampshades were cheaper than silk. His aversion to cut flowers, however, seems to have had a very different origin. In a foreword to Francis Jekyll's Memoir of his aunt, Gertrude Jekyll, Father was to write, 'Once I had the misfortune unconsciously to pick a flower [in her garden] marked for seed. Her gentle reprimand could be likened to the story of Newton and his little dog. Such was the effect on me of her distress that I have never picked a flower since.' It is a fact that we never had flowers in the house and I can only imagine that it was for this reason.

Without any central heating this huge house was, of course, terribly cold, especially since we burnt peat instead of coal as an economy. The peat smelt nice but gave off far more smoke than flame. And then the large windows let in fierce draughts. One of the six smaller windows in the billiard-room-nursery had always to be kept open because the fire smoked continually. Nothing was ever done about it. One good thing at Mansfield Street was that family prayers were given up after we moved in there.

We had not been long installed before it was discovered that the servants' floor was infested with bugs. It turned out to be an infestation of very long standing so we wondered why the Bridgemans had never attended to it. The plaster as well as the paper had to be taken off the walls. Then Annie discovered that the cook – the best cook we had ever had who was also very pleasant and nice looking – washed every morning in her own urine, a practice to which she attributed her beautiful complexion. Another cook had to be sent away because she beat the kitchen-maid, and Annie was too frightened to go into the kitchen to get the nursery meals. Cooks came and went so fast on account of the 'wicked basement' that there was never a chance to get to know them. They were the curse of Mother's life. Father once asked her to stop apologising for the food; it made everyone uncomfortable and was not worthy of her. Barbie used to say that Mother chose her cooks because they had been cooks in a previous incarnation. Lady Sackville recorded in her diary that Vita had dined at Mansfield Street 'and saw that Emmie was a shocking hostess and had absurd little vegetarian dishes brought specially for her and looked so bored and McNed anxious and fussed'.

All servants were an endless trial to Mother except for the small nucleus who adored her and stayed for years. She had said that she could not run Bedford Square on less than seven; she could not run Mansfield Street on less than ten; yet we were never very comfortable. We could not so much as make ourselves a cup of tea and were not allowed to disturb the servants between meals. If we ever did ring the drawing-room bell we had to go and call over the banisters to say what we wanted. How much discomfort we had to put up with for the sake of Adam mantelpieces and ceilings and classical mouldings.

In the autumn of 1919 Robert returned to Cambridge, Elisabeth went back to her boarding school for one more term while Ursula and I went to Queen's College in Harley Street because it was so conveniently close. I remained there for four years whereas at the beginning of 1920 Ursula and Elisabeth went to Miss Wolff's, a smart finishing school in South Audley Street where Barbie had been for a time. Barbie was pursuing her glamorous social life and was rarely at home.

Father went to India again in November after two winters at home. His absence did not stop us from enjoying a happy first Christmas at Mansfield Street. The Baring family spent Christmas Day with us, as did Krishna and Nitya also, and we discovered what a wonderful house it was for hide-and-seek with its three staircases. The racquet court was fun too but

196

what we enjoyed most was playing on the service lift. We found that we could squat on the top and pull ourselves up and down with the ropes. This was forbidden which did not, of course, stop us from doing it.

Lady Sackville sent Mother £100 for Christmas to buy a new boiler for the house. When Mother wrote and told Father he replied, 'She is a kind old thing. She likes to warm you but oh goodness she is difficult to work for sometimes.'

Mother was very sad when in January 1920 Krishna went to live in Paris in order to learn French. She went over to see him as often as she could. Nitya meanwhile remained in London studying for the Bar.

* * *

Father had taken Herbert Ward with him to India that winter, and also a new assistant, Arthur Shoosmith, who was to remain in Delhi in charge of the office there until the official opening in 1931. The political climate of India had changed since Father was last there. Gandhi's campaign of passive resistance was in full swing. There had been a transfer of Government from the Viceroy's Executive Council to a Legislative Assembly, with Indian as well as British members, as a result of the Montagu-Chelmsford Declaration published in 1918 and promising drastic reforms. This necessitated redesigning the north side of Government House to make room for a circular Assembly building which it was decided that Baker should build. It was now known that Lord Hardinge's published estimate of four million pounds for the whole city had been wildly unrealistic. It would cost at least ten million.

Father's chief work that winter was the All India War Memorial. He also worked on the central dome of the palace. 'The work here is absorbing,' he wrote to Mother, 'but it is uphill. Money is master.' Although his and Baker's daily fee of five guineas had now been increased to ten, their subsistence allowance remained at 30/-, and the rupee had gone up so that there were now only nine rupees to the pound instead of twelve. For the first few weeks Father worked 'from bed to bed', hardly ever going out, which he liked. He was abusing his collaborator more than ever: 'Baker's work is to me horrible – slovenly, capricious, and then that odious pecksniff manner and sentimental attitude.' He wished that the Delhi Committee would get rid of Baker and let him, Lutyens, work as a member of the Public Works Department in control of all the young architects 'so that the whole thing would boil together instead of being on different hobs in different pots and pans'. All the young architects working for the Public Works Department went to him with their designs. 'I may have influence to help them as the younger men are charming to me and listen!! Do you despise me for this?'

One of these younger men, W. H. Nicholls, the Government architect on the Delhi Committee, averred that whatever he had 'learnt about design and the principles of design' he 'owed chiefly to Lutyens'. Nicholls, who had been in India for eight years before Lutyens first went there, was able to give the older man some hints about building in that climate. 'He never resented criticism,' Nicholls wrote, 'but he would never compromise in trying to comply with a criticism. If he thought one's criticism sound, he would immediately tear up a whole batch of drawings no matter how much care had been expended on them, and start the whole building design over again.' Nicholls liked Baker immensely as well as Lutyens and deplored their quarrel. He went so far as to say that 'Lutyens and Hardinge detested each other'.[1]

Herbert Ward remembers the long dining table in the architects' office at Raisina with Lutyens sitting at one end

[1]Unpublished reminiscences kindly lent to me by Mrs M. L. Boyce, daughter of Mr Nicholls.

and Baker at the other, scarcely speaking to each other. Their own assistants sat round them, not daring to fraternize. Another assistant on the other hand, Henry Medd, recalled that Lutyens's men were always encouraged to sit at Baker's end of the table and Baker's at Lutyens's. I do not know which version is true – probably both at different times. Herbie Ward loved Father; he also liked Baker very much and said he was a far better committee man, which I am sure is true. Ward remembers a meeting of the Delhi Committee one sweltering afternoon in a stifling room, discussing a name for the new city. Georgebad and Marypore were among the suggestions put forward as the sweat poured from them. At last Father, unable to bear the boredom any longer burst out with, 'Let's call it Ooziepore.' The meeting immediately broke up and no other name than New Delhi was ever suggested again.

In the middle of January 1920, to Father's joy, E. V. Lucas came to India in order to write a book. They went together to stay at Lucknow with Sir Harcourt Butler, Governor of the United Provinces. They were a large party and Father enjoyed himself hugely. They sang choruses in the evenings. 'We killed Tosti's good bye for ever,' Father wrote. In spite of telling Herbie Ward that he knew only two songs 'God Save the Weasel' and 'Pop Goes the Queen' – Father loved singing and had a good voice. He also loved dancing. Later on he would dance to Lady Sackville to the *Valse Mignon* on the pianola. She was astonished at his grace which she compared to Nijinsky. What he did not enjoy about this visit to the Harcourt Butlers was the tiger shoot that was organised for them.

Father had now been asked to design a Victory Column for Colombo and also houses in Delhi for the Maharajas of Bikaner and Nawanagar (Jam Sahib, better known as Ranjitsinhji, the cricketer). These Maharajas also wanted him to do some work for them in their own States, so he went first to Bikaner and then home in April via Jamnagar and Colombo. Before he left Delhi the gradient question was raised again: on returning to England he and Baker were to be allowed to re-state their views before the Advisory Committee in London which had been set up in May 1917. Apart from the cost of alterations Baker now made the point that it would be an insult to the new Government of India if the Viceroy's palace were to be given more prominence than the buildings for Government servants. Father threatened to resign if the decision went against him. 'Is it not a rather childish attitude to say that just because you can't always get your own way, you won't "play" any more?' Baker was to admonish him, '. . . Cannot you play "cricket"?' No argument was less likely to win Father round. To him it was not a game. It was a matter of vital principle – a fight against the sacrifice of art to expediency. The findings of the Advisory Committee would have to be passed on to the Delhi Committee whose final decision was not known for almost two years.

* * *

On the day Father sailed home from Colombo, 23 April, he received a cable to say that Barbie was engaged to be married to Euan Wallace. He sent back a warm message of congratulations, evidently not at all surprised or hurt that his approval had not been sought.

200

CHAPTER ELEVEN

Family Marriages and Bakerloo
1920–1922

Father arrived home just in time for Barbie's wedding on 10 May 1920. Euan Wallace, tall, dark and good-looking, was a Captain in the Life Guards with an outstanding war record. He was also very rich with a large estate in Scotland as well as being a most lovable and generous man. He had been married before and had two small sons whom Barbie brought up entirely because their mother had gone to live in Kenya. Father was so shy when he met his future son-in-law that he kissed him, much to Euan's delight.

Barbie and Euan were married at the Savoy Chapel whose incumbent was the only clergyman in London willing to marry divorced people. There were no settlements but Father said he would give Barbie £240 a year, the same as he was giving Robert. He had written to Mother the summer before, 'Barbie will have to marry a rich man and have a bigger world to march through, conquering.' When Euan left the army and became a Conservative member of Parliament two years after their marriage Barbie did find a bigger world and conquered it with ease. She never grew close to Father. Some of her friends were bored by his jokes and consequently she was embarrassed by him.

Father was delighted with her marriage, but a few months later came the greatest disappointment of his life where his children were concerned. He and Mother had been worried about Robert's extravagance, drinking and smoking ever since he went up to Cambridge. He was doing no work and had no career in mind. 'He seems like a boat at sea with his steering gear jammed,' Father had written about him to Mother from India in March; Father did not know how to help him. He had never been able to help him. Then that summer Robert fell in love with the sister of a Cambridge friend. Her name was Eva (with a short e) Lubryjinska. Her father had been Polish, with estates in Poland before the Revolution. Her widowed mother, who was Russian, was the sister of Dr Chaim Weizmann, who was to become the first President of Israel. Eva was seven years older than Robert, who had only just turned nineteen; she had taken a degree in chemistry at Manchester University and was now working as a research chemist.

We saw a great deal of Eva that summer when we were staying for the holidays at a rented rectory at Sparsholt in Berkshire. Mother loved her immediately and believed she had a very fine character and would be an excellent influence on Robert. Robert had now left Cambridge and, through Father's influence, had been given a job by Edward Hudson on *Country Life* at £2 a week, bringing his income up to £344. Without being at all pretty, Eva was seductive. She had a strong Polish accent, walked like a foreigner, slightly swaying her behind, and wore high-heeled black patent leather shoes in the country. Foreigners had always attracted me. Although she had no money beyond what she earned, she looked and smelt expensive and was always beautifully turned out. She had a great flair for clothes. (In the Thirties she became one of the best dressmakers in England.)

In August Mother had to break to Father the news that Robert wanted to marry Eva. Father protested that Robert was too young to marry anyone; he would not consent to his marrying until he was twenty-one. He had not met Eva but when he did he took an instant dislike to her; he shuddered at her long red nails which he said reminded him of vultures' claws dipped in blood. Up to the third week in September when we returned to London, Mother was pleading Robert's cause in almost daily letters to Father: Robert was really serious, she argued; she was so afraid that if consent was withheld Robert would marry without it and this would cause a breach which might never be healed. But Father refused even to allow them to become engaged. Dr Weizmann was also against the marriage on religious grounds, though he liked Robert personally.

On 27 September Robert left home after having high words with Father who was adamant in his refusal to allow the engagement. He returned after a while to plead again with Father, but when Hudson sacked him in the hope of bringing him to heel and he heard that Father was going to make him a Ward of Court so that he could not marry without consent before he was twenty-one, he eloped with Eva to Scotland on 15 November. Mother knew where they were but would not reveal their address. Father, therefore, engaged detectives through Sir George Lewis to trace them before it was too late. I naturally enjoyed the drama of all this immensely, especially when the detectives came to the house and questioned me. I wished I had known where Robert was so that I could have refused to tell them. I was all on the side of romance against stuffy authority.

During this crisis came the unveiling of the permanent Cenotaph on 11 November. This time Father had a prominent place in the ceremony and marched afterwards in procession to Westminster Abbey where the body of the Unknown Warrior was interred that day. Lady Sackville met McNed afterwards at lunch with Pamela McKenna and recorded that he was 'absolutely not self-conscious about his Cenotaph. He took us to see it, and behaved as if he had never had anything to do with it. We remembered how he designed it here [Hill Street] at dinner, alone with me.' And then on 17 November Father was elected a full Academician. Thereafter he taught regularly at the Academy Schools, something he always rather dreaded because it made him so nervous.

Robert was not traced and after three weeks residence in Edinburgh, where he and Eva lived respectably at separate addresses, they were married on 7 December by special licence. Two days later Father left for India without seeing or speaking to Robert. Father did not stop Robert's allowance but in his heart he was estranged from him for several years, and he never grew to like Eva.

Father must have felt angry with Mother for abetting Robert, and yet he was as gentle to her as ever, writing to her from the ship, 'I am so grieved darling at all the sorrow anguish it has brought to you but you have been supported by a conviction very different to mine and God grant I may be wrong.' He might never have said any more about it if Mother had not immediately after his departure written to him beseeching him 'to hold out the olive branch' to Robert. Father replied to this from Delhi on 7 January 1921:

I asked Hudson to take Robert back [which Hudson did] and to help him to rise above the (fatal) act. But men won't give Robert a job and pay him sufficient to live on and the world is full of war worn officers in search of livelihoods. He is forced into the arena and is at the mercy of sweaters. Give him my best love and tell him I will help him and he must not be discouraged. He has to go through a bad time. He would have had a bad time anyhow if he had waited but not such a bad time and for so long a period as he has to go through now. I do really hope darling that I am wrong and that he will pull through and come out of it with flying colours.

Ten days later he was writing in answer to another

204

letter from Mother that Robert had entered 'the world's arena naked and unarmed' without a career or even an apprenticeship:

It is not fair on him or on the woman he marries. I don't think you realise what a struggle for life is and means and what failure might entail. I saw Father's profession fail him and fortune vanish at the same time. A woman may weep but a man bleeds. It is too kindly that I feel. If I didn't care for Robert I wouldn't have fought for him as I did. But it is over now and he will have to stand the strain. With Ursula, Betty and Mary I hope we will pull together better and together be wiser.

His father's poverty never ceased to haunt him. On the same day, 17 January, in answer to Mother's entreaties, he brought himself to write to Eva — a very generous letter in the circumstances:

My dear Eva, I did all I could or thought I could, to stop Robert marrying at 19. Now he is married you are my daughter in law and I offer no apologies for what you may and must have thought brutal but which I did for love of the boy you love. I hope I may prove wrong and you can do more than anyone else to help to this end. We can have a common issue and a common interest which may unite us in affection and the romance will end by all living happily ever after for our allotted spans. Yrs. very E. Lutyens

Mother actually gave a dinner party in February to help Robert, something she had never done for Father. The guests were Sir Herbert and Lady Jekyll, the William Nicholsons (he had married again after Prydie's death), Edward Hudson, Ozzie Dickinson and Ursula because Hudson had said he would not come unless she was there. It went off very well. 'Hudson was greatly taken with Eva,' Mother reported, 'and talked to her all the evening and congratulated Robert most heartily when he left. He talked a lot about Robert – said how he had changed and improved and how well he worked. I know this will please you and help you to feel that Robert is really doing his best to make good.'

Father was having a hard time that year in Delhi. The work was behindhand and the Government was cutting down again:

The shortage of money will add two years – making seven years to finish this job. It will be black ruin. I hope the new Viceroy will be a man of business and understanding. Hailey [now Finance Minister] has blocked our appeal for more money. I now stand to lose on the whole thing £10-£14,000. It is so impossible a position that I should work for 15 years and lose all that money – so absurd I have no real fear yet. But money bores you as it does me and no one should know of our anxiety as it destroys credit and they think if a man wants money they can and will down him.

One can be sure that no one ever knew of his anxiety. He never wore a gloomy face in public. In this same letter in which he was bewailing his possible losses he was gleefully recounting two new jokes he had made: 'You know the pigeon English, specially accent Indians talk in, is called Chee Chee. So there is architecture and archi-cheecheetecture.' And then he had invented a motto for India: 'India expects every man to do his dhoti.'

On 19 January he was writing again to say that he and the Public Works Department were in anguish over a proposal to finish the central buildings in plaster because of the lack of money. 'It will all come to pieces and it is really a waste of a life time. I don't know what to do . . . I have written to Hailey but it is like talking to a fish. He is so offishial and is no use. If they decide on plaster buildings it means a year's work at least redrawing plans and re-estimating and all the work since 1913 wasted . . . Design is like weights in scales and you can't alter without one side coming down askew – balance is the essence of all good design – in colour and form. And Lor! the money their cold feet of political economy loses.'

The question of finance was now complicated by the fact that the Legislative Assembly had to be consulted. The Indian members, who had never been in favour of the new capital, protested at the expenditure that would have to come out of the pocket of the Indian tax payer, especially as the rupee had gone down again. Lutyens had always been in favour of paying for Delhi by floating a loan at 6% free of income tax, repayable with a fixed annual sum over forty years, thus freeing the work 'from the yearly political arena of the Budget'. He pressed again for this loan in 1921 but without avail. The new capital went on being financed by annual instalments which had to be fought for at every Budget. However, the absurdity of the architects actually losing money on their fifteen years work as the result of all the delays was recognised and it was decided that instead of being paid on a percentage basis they should receive payment in lump sums – £18,000 a year gross between them until 1924, £19,000 in 1925, £16,000 in 1926, and thereafter in decreasing sums until 1929 when it was hoped their services would no longer be needed. And money for continuing the buildings in stone was found.

This winter of 1920–1 Father had been given his own bungalow in New Delhi – No 1 Raisina, the first bungalow to be completed to his own design which was to become the Military Secretary's house. It had seven bedrooms, seven bathrooms, and three large sitting-rooms, one of which he used as an office. He complained that it was very badly furnished, with a scrap lot of furniture, and that the lights had been put in anyhow regardless of his plans. And as yet there was no plumbing. He was able to entertain his friends and staff which he enjoyed but he was also required by the Viceroy to give dinners almost every evening for members of the Legislative Assembly, English and Indians. This was very tiring and expensive and he felt it was hard that he was not given any entertainment allowance.

Mother had already started to pave the way to follow Krishna to India when Mrs Besant sent for him, as she might soon do, to start his life's work as the vehicle for the World Teacher, and now that Father had a house of his own in Delhi it would be easier for her to go. She evidently suggested it to him, for Father was writing to her on 16 February, 'I should love you to come out here, why not next year? but darling you would have for my work's sake to eschew all politics . . . If you come and play a wife's part – it might help *me* very much – but if the political element came in it would make my work HELL instead of ELL . . . Do think it over and see if you could work with me and for me – once! do.'

* * *

Some important new commissions awaited Father on his return home in March 1921 – the building of Gledstone Hall, Lancashire, for Amos Nelson, a rich cotton merchant; the little Piccadilly branch of the Midland Bank next to Wren's St James's Church (my favourite of Father's London buildings), and a far larger project for £1,000,000, Britannic House, Finsbury Circus, the Headquarters of the Anglo-Persian Oil Company. Reginald McKenna was now Chairman of the Midland Bank and was to give Father commissions to build several local branches of the bank as well as the main branch in Poultry in 1924.

On 20 June Father received the Gold Medal of the Royal Institute of British Architects which had been awarded him in

January. He had prepared a serious little speech for the occasion but only managed to utter the first and last sentences, for in the middle he broke down and cried from emotion.

A minor work in 1921 was the designing of Queen Mary's Dolls' House (now at Windsor Castle). The suggestion for this had come at a luncheon party the year before at which Princess Marie-Louise, a grand-daughter of Queen Victoria, and E. V. Lucas had been present as well as Father. The idea was to create for posterity a record of the way of life of a rich English gentleman in 1920 and to present it to Queen Mary as a tribute to her inspiring behaviour in the war. Father was immediately captivated by the idea, and Princess Marie-Louise, who became a great friend of his, undertook to see that the Queen accepted it – no very difficult task one would think. The scale decided on was one inch to a foot. It was Father who designed the house itself and most of the furniture. (There is an exact replica in one of the bedrooms of our St Ursula bed.) He also roped in all the best artists of the day to paint pictures for it and the best authors to write original manuscripts for the leather-bound books in its library. Firms were also approached to contribute such items as lifts, bathroom fittings, electric lights, china, glass, linen, wine, golf clubs, motor-cars and everything else imaginable needed in a gentleman's house down to a miniature packet of Bromo and a tiny fountain pen. The exquisite little frames for the pictures were hand-carved, and the curtains specially woven at great cost. Sixty artists and 250 craftsmen participated, as well as many donors of money for the furnishings; all the same, Father had to advance a great deal of money which he had some difficulty in recovering.

After the shell had been completed at Apple Tree Yard it was moved to our front drawing-room at Mansfield Street (a wall of Apple Tree Yard had to be taken down in order to get it out), putting that room out of use for almost two years. To me it was a joy because I was able to examine and play with every new object as it arrived. The Dolls' House eventually turned into a small palace for the King and Queen rather than a house for one of their subjects. The King's official red boxes were in his library.[1]

Queen Mary came several times to Mansfield Street to see how it was getting on, and once the King came with her. They asked to be left alone with it – 'to play with it', Father said. The Queen's favourite item was the miniature stamp album donated by Stanley Gibbons. On one embarrassing occasion she got her ear-ring caught in the beard of the engineer who was showing her that the lift and lavatory plugs really worked. Father had no hesitation in telling her some of his jokes which did not seem to shock her. Two tiny pillow cases had been made with MG embroidered on one and GM on the other. Father explained to her that these initials stood for 'May George?' and 'George may'. He also drew for her a picture of the King and Queen in bed with the caption 'Lazy Majesties', and another drawing showing a surprised hen looking over her shoulder to see a tiny King George just hatched from the egg she had laid. The caption to this was 'Lays Majesty'. One drawing he did not show her was of the King sitting on his crown as on a chamber-pot.

The first estimates for the Dolls' House furniture came in August. Father was having such fun with it that Lady Sackville scolded him for working harder on it than on the Persian Oil building. He was also making lots of pictures for Winston Churchill at this time to teach him how to draw, even though he had often declared that it was impossible to teach drawing to anyone. It was altogether a happy summer for him. On 2 September he was able to report to Mother that he had had £8,000 from Delhi and would soon be getting paid something

[1] *The Book of the Queen's Dolls' House* in 2 vols., edited by A.C. Benson and E.V. Lucas, with 92 plates, was published by Methuen in 1924 in a limited edition. The lavishly illustrated *Queen Mary's Dolls' House* by Mary Stewart-Wilson was published by the Bodley Head in 1988.

by 'the Anglo-Persian oil people' for whom he had just done 'a mighty fine tower'. This tower for Britannic House (now called Lutyens House) was one of a pair. They are large columns rather than towers, standing outside the main door.

I don't believe you realise [he continued in this letter] the aching anxiety of these past few years and I did not dare show it. My overdraft was over £6,000! I don't know yet if I am clear. I *do* now want to save for you and the children for whatever I pay away will leave you all the poorer. And you couldn't live on about £500 a year. *Really you couldn't* and I haven't as many years to come as have passed. So don't spend money needlessly on the strength of this, will you? Or else I shall be sorry I told you. Don't tell Robert and Eva because I really don't feel out of the wood yet.

Robert had now left *Country Life* where he felt there was no future for him and was working as a reporter on the *Daily Mail*. As well as giving him an allowance, Father was paying the rent of a charming little house for him in South Street, Mayfair.

At the end of September Father suffered a cruel blow. He heard that Baker had got the job of rebuilding the Bank of England above Soane's colonnade. This, apparently, was a job that had been promised to Father by Lord Cunliffe, the Governor of the Bank, who had died before the project was finally decided on. The new deputy Governor, Cecil Lubbock, was a friend of Baker's. Lady Sackville wrote in her diary on 18 September that McNed, who was dining with her, could eat no dinner after hearing the news. She felt so sorry for him. 'I have seldom seen McNed so upset and white, and yet he was very brave, and we hardly talked about it. It is such a pity that his genius is not recognised more.' If it had been any architect but Baker Father would not have minded so much. Baker had

211

now moved his practice to London so it was inevitable that the two men should become rivals.

*   *   *

Mother had been right in thinking that Krishna would soon be going to India. In May 1921 it was discovered that Nitya, who was still in London, had tuberculosis. Krishna sent for him to Paris to be treated by a French naturopath, Dr Paul Carton. In July he and Krishna went to Boissy St Leger, near Paris, where Carton had a house. At the end of the month Mother took Elisabeth and me to Boissy to be near them while Ursula went to stay with Barbie in Scotland. It had been decided that if Nitya was well enough, he and Krishna should go to India in the autumn. Consequently Mother was anxious to go there with Father that winter. Father wrote to her at Boissy on 11 August:

I do look forward to your coming – but have moments of misgiving – as it is a hard job to keep in touch with everybody and win confidence . . . If you suddenly think it might be comfortable to wear vegetarian sandals and your hair down – a collateral tide would sweep at right angles to my track and heaven knows where the drift would lead me, or should you do the things Mrs Besant has the credit of doing – or having done – I should have to leave India – so I want you by me to dispel my nervous nightmares and bring me loving morning light. We might have fun working together – I entertaining Indians and you the poor little conventional bureaucrats.

This was not at all Mother's idea of how she wanted to spend her time in India. Nevertheless, she must have reassured him for he agreed to take her with him. By November Nitya was pronounced cured and he and Krishna

212

set out for India together. Mother and Father were not far behind. After a visit to Balmoral where the King expressed his sympathy with Father over the gradient question and said that he expected the matter to be settled in his favour, they set out for India on 30 November. From Marseilles Father sent us a characteristic telegram: 'Pa and Marseilles.'

Krishna and Nitya were on the dock to meet them when they arrived in Bombay on 17 December. It was the first time Mother had seen them in Indian dress and they looked very strange to her. It was a wrench for her to have to go with Father to stay with Sir George and Lady Lloyd at Government House in Bombay instead of with the Theosophical friend Krishna and Nitya were staying with. 'My democratic soul revolts against all the pomp and glory – only it is more comic than anything else – a relic of a barbaric age,' she wrote to us about Government House life. She was depressed to find how out of touch all the officials were with Indian life and thought. She continued, 'I suppose there is nowhere else left now in the world where little nobodies can come and play at being kings and queens.'

After a few days in Bombay she was delighted to be off with Krishna and Nitya to join Mrs Besant at Benares for a Theosophical Convention while Father went to Delhi. She broke all precedents by insisting that her ayah should sleep with her in her compartment in the train, and on a later occasion, when travelling with an English friend and hearing that the train was going to be three hours late, they unrolled their bedding and slept on the platform. Her behaviour raised many an official eyebrow but was not as reprehensible as anti-British political activity would have been. For Father's sake she eschewed politics while she was there.

After a fortnight at Benares Mother joined Father in Delhi where Lord Reading was now Viceroy. As the daughter of a former Viceroy she was accepted in Anglo-Indian society in spite of her eccentricities. Father was enchanted to have her with him. She did her best to bring the English and Indians together in a social way, an effort he very much encouraged. She entertained more for him in one month in Delhi at No I Bungalow than she had done in the whole of the rest of their married life, but then entertaining was much easier there than in England; Pershotum ruled the servants and ordered the meals; besides, everything was cheaper. She gave one garden party for members of the Legislative Assembly, English and Indian, and was made extremely happy when, in her own words, 'an English member from Calcutta got up and told the assembled company that he had met more Indians on a social basis in that one afternoon than in the whole of his twenty years in India'. At the beginning of February 1922 she went off to Adyar, the TS Headquarters near Madras, which she described as the most beautiful place she had ever seen and where she was supremely happy living under the same roof as Krishna. Soon after Mother left Delhi the Prince of Wales arrived there on a visit. Father took him to the site of the new buildings and showed him through a periscope the model of Government House which had been made for the purpose of studying the gradient question. All the Prince said was 'Good God', Father told Mother. 'He spoke more to Baker in that he said Delhi should be stopped – money waste etc. He seemed nervous and bored, certainly self-conscious. But he has great attraction and is pleasant to look at. He hit a policeman on his legs with his cane who was shoving back a crowd of untidy masons. They, the masons, gleed at the rebuff to the hated policeman. I was sorry for the policeman too.' Father ended this letter of 21 February, 'Bless you darling and may peace and happiness beflower your path to your next incarnation which will probably be a passionate man linked to a cool woman!! Angel Emmie keep cool.'

At the end of February, after the Prince's departure, there

was a meeting on the site to discuss the gradient question with Lord and Lady Reading, Lord Willingdon (Governor of Madras) and Sir George Lloyd. 'I spoke to Reading about the inclined way – very calmly,' Father reported to Mother on 28 February. 'George Lloyd was very sympathetic about it; Willingdon charmingly neutral . . . I lunched with H.E. on Monday and spoke again, giving the King's message. There is a Committee meeting on Friday – 2.30 – pray for me.'

Lutyens and Baker were present at the meeting on 3 March, which went on for three hours. They all went to look at the model in which a cutting had been made to show Lutyens's plan for opening up the view of Government House. Hugh Keeling, the Chief Engineer, announced that the cutting would cost £166,650, whereas if it had been done when Lutyens first suggested it, it would have cost only £2,000. 'I cannot go on with Delhi if this is turned [down] now,' Father wrote to Mother next morning. 'My patience has been my undoing . . . but this large estimate makes the question so serious that I have – if Reading is against me – to resign. It will be a great relief getting away from Baker Rash . . . Baker played all his incidental music – and put his little summer houses [his Secretariats] up against my incline. I have few years left and must cut myself off from such a fiasco as this . . . I am afraid it will make a great difference to us all financially – But you have always been brave about money. I am up early and slept very little and feel happier and relieved at my decision if Reading turns me down. I wont *act* over quickly.'

Mother telegraphed to him when she received this letter at Adyar, begging him to do nothing until he heard from her. She then wrote him a very long letter saying that it would be *absolutely fatal* to his whole professional career if he resigned on that point. It would be the biggest triumph of Baker's life and 'give every enemy a handle to blaspheme'. He had made one big mistake and *must* pay for it. 'Be a man and stand up to your own mistake. If you resign you will be running away from a big

215

duty and you will regret it to your dying day. You know if it was only a question of money I should not care a bit. But you do trust my judgement *sometimes* and in this I feel a certainty.'

They met in Bombay before Father had had a chance to answer this letter. The voyage home with Baker and his wife was a very awkward one. Father would not speak to Baker while Mother did all she could to redress this rudeness. They arrived home to find Barbie with her first child, a son.

Father was to hear in June that the decision over the gradient had gone against him. He had met his 'Bakerloo' as he called it. He did not resign but he never forgave Baker. If this book were a biography instead of a memoir I should feel obliged to try to be just to Baker and put his point of view. I am sure he had a very good one. As it is, I feel no compulsion to do so. We were brought up to look on Baker as a villain who had ruined Father's life's work. It is only now, in going into the subject, that I realise what a small matter the gradient really was and how little the loss of the level way detracts from the glory of Father's achievement.

CHAPTER TWELVE

A Love Affair
1922–1923

Elisabeth went to Paris in March 1922 to study music at the
École Normal while Ursula came out that spring. She was
immensely attractive. One always knew when she was going
to a dance because the whole house reeked of rotten eggs
from a preparation called Veet for removing hair from under
the arms. It was, I believe, the first depilatory to come on the
market. Fortunately the smell did not linger on the user.

Mother was lucky in never having to do any entertaining
for her daughters or lift a finger to find them husbands.
Barbie had made her own way, helped by the war, and it was
Barbie who brought Ursula out. Ursula hunted with Barbie
in Leicestershire in the winter and spent the summer holidays
with her in Scotland.

Mother and Father had planned a new life together when
once they were settled in Mansfield Street. They had hoped
to introduce some kind of social life which they might both
enjoy – 'Dinners of eight,' Father had written – '3 of yours
and 3 of mine and then get some stunt. Not music as that
stops talk and makes memories and through them silences . . .
Of course, I am shy too and shyness reacts on me more than it
does on you, because I give offence by being loquacious. Your
silence is better. We might have rehearsals, because that side
of life has a great deal of play-acting in it.' The little dinner

parties never materialised. Chippy (Sir Arthur Chapman as he had become in 1916) continued to be the only regular guest for dinner until his death in 1925. When Mother's friends came to the house it was for lunch or tea when Father was not there. She never inflicted her friends on him in his own house, and he stipulated that no one except a member of the family was to use his room while he was away, an injunction Mother strictly adhered to.

A great addition to Father's well-being in 1922 was the advent of a new secretary, Miss Webb, who was to stay with him until his death. She helped us all and we all became devoted to her.

Father had reached the tableland of his social success by this time. His claim to be shy was true, but far from the loquaciousness, which hid his shyness, giving offence he was in great demand on social occasions on account of his exuberance and effervescent vitality. A hostess could rely on him never to let the ball drop and to talk vivaciously to even the dullest guest. Diana Cooper is reported as saying, 'Duff and I would give up anything if Ned Lutyens were free for lunch – he was such fun, oh, you can't think.'[1] Evelyn Waugh told me one day in the Thirties that he had met my father the evening before for the first time and had been flattered when he asked him to call him Ned – 'True he had his arm round my neck at the time—,' Evelyn added. That is so characteristic of Father – his instant friendliness, his love of the young. Osbert Sitwell was to write about him:

One had never seen before, and will never see again, anyone who resembled this singular and delightful man. An expression of mischievous benevolence was his distinguishing mark, as it was that of his work. He would sit, with his bald, dome-like head lowered at a particular

[1] *Lady Sackville* by Susan Mary Alsop, p. 219 (1978).

angle of reflection, as his very large, blue, reflective eyes contemplated a view, a work of art, or something particularly outrageous that he intended to say. Meanwhile he held in his mouth, rather than smoked, a small pipe – he smoked a number of small pipes during the course of the day – , and when he spoke, his speech tumbled from him quickly, like that of an impetuous schoolboy.[1]

When staying at Renishaw with Sir George and Lady Ida Sitwell Father relished asking the butler on Sunday morning, 'Is Lady Ida down?' My favourite witticism of his is his immediate answer to a question as to what should be done with the Crystal Palace: 'Put it under a glass case.' Another witticism he originated, though others have since claimed it, was made while eating some fish at the Garrick Club: 'This piece of cod passeth understanding.' The best likeness of him as I remember him is a sketch by Edmund Dulac, made during a train journey in 1922 – better than any photograph. The 1920 portrait by Augustus John, on the other hand, apart from the hands, bears little resemblance to him, nor is William Rothenstein's drawing in the National Portrait Gallery at all a good likeness, but the portrait by Meredith Frampton in the Art Workers Guild, of which Father was Master from 1933, and the bust by William Reid Dick in the RIBA are both good likenesses. More and more he came to wear two pairs of spectacles – one on his forehead and one low down on the bridge of his nose.

E. V. Lucas was to write about him in 1924 in *The Book of the Queen's Dolls' House*, 'His eyes grow merrier, his spectacles ever rounder, his head loses a hair here and there; but he is still undefeated, still an eternal child, an apostle of beauty and thoroughness, a minister of elfish nonsense. His friends were legion; his mind was electrically instant to respond to any

[1]*Great Morning*, p. 19 (1948).

sympathetic suggestion; he never broke his word; he never let you know if he was tired; and with it all he was out for fun.' But what I like best is the piece Harold Nicolson wrote about him after his death in *Friday Mornings*:

. . . It seemed strange to his clients that somebody so gentle should be so obstinate; that a man so considerate in the small affairs of life should be so relentless when it came to stones or staircases; that a man who regarded his own genius with such simple delight, and who viewed the solemnity of architecture with such awestruck veneration, should so frequently introduce into his buildings the jokes that he made in conversation. Never, however, since the days of Sheridan and Goldsmith has a man of genius been so widely beloved. Even the most sedate company, even the most imposing personages, would relax at the sight of that round figure, those round spectacles, that round and beaming face. He would intrude upon Kings and Cabinets with that bland certainty of proving delightful which one finds in a gay child . . . With eyes of unbelievable innocence he would gaze up to see whether he was being a success. He could be pleased so easily; sometimes, quite unexpectedly, he could be easily hurt.

Lutyens possessed the faculty of making everybody feel much younger. He adopted an identical attitude of bubbling friendliness whether he was talking to a Queen Dowager or a cigarette girl, a Cardinal or a schoolboy. He would on occasions disconcert the elderly by intruding with outrageous flippancy upon conversations which were intended to be sedate. When reproved for those excursions he would show the most disarming contrition and begin all over again . . .

These tributes make up a composite picture of a personality

as seen from outside – and what a contrast this picture is to the very private person with his anguish, anxieties and frustrations revealed in so many of his letters to Mother. Both images were true. But there was, I think, another and mysterious entity in him, untouched by either the social charisma or the pain and disappointment of his married life, whose only expression was in his creative work and to whom no one ever really penetrated.

He stayed four days with us in August 1922 at Hemel Hempstead in Hertfordshire where we were spending the holidays in another rented rectory. These days coincided with his silver wedding on 4 August. He gave Mother some pearls for the occasion which, according to Lady Sackville's rather jealous recording, cost him £300.

After another visit to Balmoral where he walked for five miles alone with the Queen talking Dolls' House, and talked Delhi to the King, he set out for India on 28 September, earlier than usual. He was more contented with his work in Delhi this year, getting on well with Lord Reading who was impressed with Government House which was now at last rising from the ground. 'My work is beginning to tell,' he wrote on 18 November. 'I have been designing very freely and easily just lately which puts me in good spirits and I feel there is more appreciative spirit about and Baker is irritating everyone. I know he does Keeling [the Chief Engineer] now by his soft talk and careless work.' And two days later, 'Keeling came in the morning and had a long outpouring of grievances about Baker. My comment was that God asked Adam to name the animals after he had created them. Baker names his animals first and then starts to create round a name and words.' This was Father's criticism of Ruskin too whom he intensely disliked, maintaining that he had done incalculable harm to English architecture by his theories of building: he had put words before design, words before creation. Father always had a deep distrust of all theorising about art. He was also a purist in words. Once when Mother wrote that she had had 'a lousy' Channel crossing he reproved her sharply. Had she really caught lice on the boat he asked her?

* * *

Father returned home on 15 January 1923. When he visited Lady Sackville at Brighton a few days later he told her, according to her diary, how grateful Emmie was to her for her friendship for them all, especially for him, and said that it had made all the difference to his life '. . . which,' she added, 'I know it has'. Poor McNed was so shamefully neglected at home. She had had lunch at Mansfield Street while McNed was in India and noted afterwards, 'Emmie expanded to me her view on the labour question and how they ought to be in power; and how to bring up children by letting them do all they like and trusting to their good instincts to do well. She is quite mad'; and after another occasion when she had dined there, 'Emmie shocked me greatly with her Bolshie views about everything, and was ridiculous about the New Birth of the World after the war. Her gestures were those of a mad woman.'

This year Lady Sackville decided to sell her houses at Brighton and buy a small house at Roedean, with seventeen acres of land which she rechristened White-Lodge-on-the-Cliff. (It is now number 40 The Cliff, and has been divided into seven flats.) She asked McNed to alter and enlarge it for her. She moved in in June while McNed was sending her, and continued to send her, different plans by every post. In 1920 she had left Hill Street, which was too expensive to run, and had moved into 184 Ebury Street, the Nicolsons' former London house where McNed had done some work for her. Hill Street had failed to sell for the price she was asking for it, and now she was unable to sell the Sussex Square houses either so she was feeling extremely poor and began to pay McNed in kind for the work he did for her for White Lodge. Pictures, rugs and furniture began to appear at Mansfield Street and in 1924 three large Mortlake tapestries. At the beginning of 1923 she had given him a little grey Rolls-Royce on the understanding that it was to be used for his work and not for family outings. (He repaid her for it by degrees.) Father called his young chauffeur James because he had always wanted to step into a vehicle of his own and say, 'Home, James.' We rarely went in it I am thankful to say since it made me terribly car sick. Father did not like going fast and James's neck would grow crimson every time a smaller car passed him.

I was very fond of Lady MacSack who was extremely kind to me. She gave me *The Oxford Book of English Verse* for my thirteenth birthday for which I shall always bless her. Barbie, however, has told me that she made a great deal of mischief between her and Father before her marriage. I know from Lady MacSack's diaries that she criticised us all to McNed and her other friends, abusing 'Emmie' and Robert in particular for their extravagance and complaining of the levity with which his children treated him. If we treated him with levity it was because that was how he treated us. She did reiterate, though, how loyal McNed was to Emmie and his children, refusing to say anything against them, which evidently annoyed her.

Passionate, demanding, dramatically possessive and emotionally unbalanced, she made more scenes with McNed over the rebuilding of White Lodge than she had ever done before. She was frequently sending him away in disgrace, certain that he would always come crawling back. She believed she had become indispensable to him. When she was not angry with him she petted, spoilt and flattered him. When he was in disgrace she would 'send him to his basket' – a distasteful metaphor which she frequently used. After they had made up some quarrel in 1922, she had written, 'Such a good little

McNed and so fluffy. Bless him to be so devoted after so many years – nearly 7 years – and he does not show the slightest sign of abatement.' And on another occasion, 'McNed feels very much being sent to his basket.' He had sent her 'doleful little pictures of his being in a basket with the lid tight down'. At other times she was writing: 'What a wonderful nature he has got, what patience and energy,' and again, 'He is never without a pencil, making new designs. His fertility of invention is too marvellous.' Everyone thought he was rich, she commented, but he was not; he was struggling 'to leave Emmie and the children £10,000 each'. He had told her that she was his 'bit of blue sky in the background when everything was black and stormy at home'. She loved his genius and the thought that she inspired him and provided conditions for him in which he did his best work, although after one bad quarrel she noted, 'One should never have anything to do with a genius as McNed is. A genius is always inhuman au fond. Everything is sacrificed on that altar.'

McNed was out of pocket on all the work he did for her. More than once when she complained of bad workmanship he paid the bill himself in order to pacify her. He even offered to sell Mansfield Street to help her, an offer she declined but which one feels she might have been quite willing to accept if he had pressed it. He tolerated the endless scenes she made because he needed so desperately to be needed by a woman.

From 1923 for the next three years their relationship was certainly close enough to be called a love affair, but whether they were physically lovers or not is uncertain. Mother did not think they were since Father, hating secrets, had said that he would tell her if he was ever unfaithful. But this would not have been his secret alone so he could not in honour have told. Mother hoped for his sake that they were lovers. There was not a trace of dog-in-the-manger in her make-up. It was MacSack who was jealous of her if anything. MacSack craved the exclusive devotion that Murray Scott had given to her, especially after discovering her husband's infidelity, and she must have known that McNed's heart was never wholly hers; Emmie always came first.

Mother was hugely amused by her. When MacSack took Father to lunch at the Savoy she would send her chauffeur round afterwards to Mansfield Street with the remains of the Brie cheese they had had. When Mother once sent her a calendar for Christmas she wrote back that she would rather have had the money. At one time she circulated a letter asking for money for tiles for the roof of her 'Home'. Her friends contributed, thinking it was for a charity, only to discover that it was for the roof of White Lodge. Another time she tried to market a sealed book entitled *What Every Young Man Knows About Sex*: it was to contain nothing but blank pages.

After the deaths of both MacSack and McNed, Ursula tried to discover whether they had been lovers. Ozzie Dickinson, a great friend of both, told me that he was convinced they had been, but then he was a tremendous gossip. More reliably, Vita believed they had been and sent Ursula thirty-nine of McNed's letters to her mother which she thought proved it, written in the years of their closest intimacy – 1923, '24 and '25. Couched for the most part in playful, lisping baby-talk they are an unpleasing contrast to his letters to Mother. In most of them he begins '*MBBM* Bleth you' and signs himself 'Your velly vellumy McNeddie'. One letter begins 'Oh my gorgeous MacSack'. Occasionally he called her his 'old fing' which she could hardly have appreciated seeing that she was eight years older than him.

The letters suggest that during these years they were writing to each other almost every day and that he often stayed at Ebury Street, looking on it as a second home. He told her rather superficially of his daily doings and of the people he met, but mostly he was soothing her over irritations with delays in building. The underlined M seems to have been a symbol; another symbol constantly used was a bow-tie which McNed would draw – two or three times in some letters. It apparently represented the tie between them. Once he elongated the tie into a propeller and wrote beneath it, 'A propeller that drives to heaven'; and below one tie he had written, 'A tie that adorns any neck that bears its burthen and above all a perfect blething. Bleth you.'

There are also a few earlier letters from him to her which Nigel Nicolson found in her diary. They are of no great interest except in revealing his deep concern for her when she was ill. In one there is a drawing showing him nursing her like a baby in his arms. The rest of his letters to her were destroyed by Vita.

I have found only three letters from her to him – one of 1927 after making up a quarrel, a short one of 1925 arranging a meeting, and the third, twenty-six pages long, also of 1925, written when he was in America. In it she recounts details of her health, her building projects, the entertaining she is doing and gossip about mutual friends. It is the letter of a woman happily and confidently in love, reiterating on almost every page her longing for his return. She uses a lot of 'bleth yous' and signs herself 'your velly well and happy MacSack'. But this letter was written after receiving from him a note on the eve of his departure for New York – the most lover-like of all his surviving letters to her. It began with a drawing of the tie symbol and ended with another in which the knot had disappeared so that the two bows were united. He had written under the first 'The Beginning' and under the second 'The End'. 'My own darling BM, I cannot bear even to say au revoir to you – supreme love brings supreme sorrows and it's supreme this love. *Your* velly vellumy, your McNedi'. Surely McNed could hardly have been more explicit than this in a letter. After all, he was a married man writing to a married woman, and he must have known that Lionel Sackville wanted a divorce which she would not give him. Among the letters

Vita gave to Ursula is one, undated, from Vita herself to her mother warning her lest McNed be cited as co-respondent.

One of McNed's and MacSack's mutual friends, George Plank, the American artist, wrote in 1961 in a letter to Vita, which she passed on to Ursula: 'Certainly B.M.'s hints about her relationship with McNed were more than broad.' Plank recalled that once when he and McNed were driving down to White Lodge, McNed had given his hand an affectionate squeeze and said, 'Dear Plankino, I have not one single secret kept from you, only I cannot talk.' Plank took this to be 'a confidence without words'. He continued, 'I cannot see the point of Ursula Ridley's raking up this matter, the two poor darlings are both dead, and I still love them with all my heart.'

Ursula's reason for raking up the matter was that she too loved Father with all her heart and longed to be sure that he had found physical fulfilment in those years of his association with Lady MacSack. I think it is safe to conclude that he had.

CHAPTER THIRTEEN

No 1 Bungalow
1923–1924

In the spring of 1922 Mother's brother, Victor Lytton, had been appointed Governor of Bengal, to Father's great delight, and it was arranged that in the winter of 1923 Ursula should go out to Calcutta to stay with the Lyttons. Their elder daughter, Hermione, had always been her friend. It also transpired that I too was to go to India that winter.

In August 1922 Krishna had undergone a spiritual experience that entirely changed his life and thereby Mother's life also, and, inevitably, Father's to some extent. At the time Mother had left Adyar in March 1922, Krishna and Nitya had gone to Sydney to see Leadbeater who had been living there since 1917. Nitya became very ill again in Sydney and it was thought essential that he should return immediately to Switzerland for another cure. They went by way of San Francisco intending to stay there only a couple of weeks, but a friend lent them a cottage in the Ojai Valley, about eighty miles north of Los Angeles, where Nitya felt so much better in the dry climate that they decided to remain there. It was at Ojai that Krishna's experience took place. After that he became quite certain of his mission as a religious teacher.[1]

[1]See my *Life and Death of Krishnamurti*, 1990.

Thereafter Mother found it easier to sublimate her love for him, and was happier in consequence. (It was at this time that Leadbeater announced that she had been accepted by the Master after nine years.) At the same time she became more ruthless in her efforts to follow Krishna along the spiritual path.

Krishna and Nitya remained at Ojai until June 1923 when they returned to England, Nitya having for the second time been pronounced cured. Krishna had always been particularly sweet to me but I had considered him merely as someone to laugh and joke with – and it was Nitya I had always loved best. I now became aware of Krishna's new spiritual stature; he had lost his vague, dreamy expression and become one of the most beautiful human beings I have ever seen, as well as developing a magnetic presence. A miserable thing had recently happened to me: I had lost the magic power to pretend and felt like an exile from Eden. The vacuum now became filled with a spell of religious fervour which brought me close to Mother. I decided that I too wanted to enter on the Path of Discipleship.

Mother was going to spend the summer holidays with Krishna and Nitya at a place in the Tyrol called Ehrwald and I was thrilled when she offered to take Elisabeth and me with her. Elisabeth had recently returned from Paris looking very pretty and grown up. She came with us more, I think, in order to be with Mother whom she adored than for any other reason. She had always been acutely jealous of Krishna. We were quite a large party, including three other girls whom Krishna had attached and for whom Mother acted as chaperone. We called the girls round Krishna *gopis* after the milkmaids Sri Krishna had danced with. I had been in love with Nitya on and off ever since I could remember. Now my feelings for him were greatly intensified, transcending my short-lived spiritual aspirations. My love was no less intense because he took very little notice of me.

When Krishna and Nitya returned to Ojai in the autumn, Mother decided that since she could not go with them, the next best thing would be to go to India to be with Mrs Besant. When she asked me whether I would like to go with her I jumped at the opportunity of being in Nitya's country even though it would mean leaving Queen's College where I was happy. I do not know whether Father made any objection to my going. If he did it would have been on the grounds of expense. He seemed to have very little interest in me. He had casually asked me one day that summer what school I was at although I had been at Queen's College since the autumn of 1919. If he thought I had been bitten by the bug of Theosophy he no doubt believed I would recover from it as quickly as Barbie and Robert had done.

Ursula travelled out ahead of us with her great friend Patricia Ward, a sister of Lord Dudley. Mother and I followed at the end of November, whereas Father did not leave London until much later, 3 January 1924. We were all to meet in Calcutta. When we arrived in Bombay on 15 December we were met by some of Mother's Indian friends and garlanded with wreaths of roses, jasmine and silver ribbon. We went straight to Benares for a TS Convention and then on to Adyar on 9 January, where we had the joy and privilege of staying in Krishna's own room at the top of the Headquarters building with a glorious view of the Adyar River where it runs into the sea. Everyone I met, Indian and European, was charming to me, treating me as an adult and an equal. The Indians were particularly affectionate and I made several close friends among them. I had been very nervous at the thought of meeting Mrs Besant but when she took my hand in both of hers and looked into my eyes with a loving concern that seemed to penetrate to all that was best in one, I was immediately conquered. As an advocate of higher education for women she was shocked that I had been taken away from school at fifteen. She recommended books for me to study which we bought in Madras. Among them was Wells's *Short History of the World* which became my bible for the next couple of years. I was as entranced with Adyar as Mother was. I felt perfectly in tune with her and thereafter until her death we had a very close and special relationship based not only on a natural affinity but on an understanding on my part of her aspirations and love of India and Indians.

I give these details of my own experience in order to point the contrast in arriving at Government House, Calcutta, on 22 January where we met not only the Lytton family, Father, Ursula and Patsy Ward but Cecil Baring and his two daughters, Daphne and Calypso. (Mrs Baring had died in 1922.) I understood that Daphne wanted to marry a man her father did not approve of because he was a Roman Catholic and that he had brought her to India 'to forget'. She was the object of my keen interest and admiration. I hoped with all my heart she would not forget. She didn't. She married her love and was extremely happy with him. I recorded our arrival in my diary:

Father isn't the tiniest bit pleased to see me – and I know he doesn't like me a scrap which makes me a little miserable as I am very fond of him indeed. The whole atmosphere here is unbearable. I miss Adyar – it is Paradise. And the people too. What a contrast! I miss Mummie dreadfully. True – I see her every day – but we have been so much together and so near to each other for the past month or so. I think I love her more than anybody else in the world. She is wonderful and beautiful inside. I am very proud of her, and, I think, everyone adores her – although they make fun of her. She certainly has the strength of her opinions which is a quality I admire immensely. She ought to be happy as her presence has the power of making so many people happy – and it is lovely to be loved. I feel very depressed, Ursie and I used to be such friends – but now we are oceans apart in everything.

The three Barings and Patsy Ward went with us to Delhi. Father and Cecil Baring shared a first class coupé, Mother and we five girls a second class compartment. There were no corridors on the Indian trains then. Each compartment had its own lavatory and wash basin. Father suffered more than anyone I have ever known from train fever. I remember that he would not take his socks off at night in a train in case there was an accident and he might have to walk along the railway lines in bare feet. In England, whenever he and Mother travelled by train together, he would go, professionally, first class and she third, and, of course, we children never went anything but third.

Our large party entirely filled Father's bungalow at Raisina. There was still no plumbing laid on. I shared a bedroom with Mother; our thunder boxes were placed side by side in the adjoining bathroom. The sweepers (the untouchables or Indian Christians) came in to empty them from an outside door. The bath had to be filled by our bearer. It was embarrassing to see the bearers squatting on the verandah sorting out the dirty laundry, including the linen sanitary towels of all the girls.

On the afternoon of our arrival we had tea with Father in his office and afterwards he took us to inspect his Government House. At that time it was not raised more than about three feet from ground-level and was still surrounded by desert. I helped to plant some trees while we were there. When I went back in 1957, Raisina had burgeoned and the trees I had planted might have been a hundred years old. Raisina was not an attractive place in 1924, especially when compared to the beauty of old Delhi. But the roses in our garden were wonderful; I have never seen such wonderful roses anywhere as in Delhi, though I described the white ones as looking blue with cold. The cold was intense except in the sun; an icy wind swept across the desert plain and the wood fire in the bungalow smoked in the best Lutyens tradition.

The next day we went round the stone-yard. The stone came from the same quarry as that used by Akbar and Shah Jehan. The base of Government House was of red sandstone, the rest of cream-coloured stone. A third of the stone needed had already been delivered. It was to become the largest stone-yard in the world, but then the palace was larger than Versailles. The only imported stone was Italian marble for the floor of the Durbar Hall. I described the yard as we saw it: 'There were little boys of 4 or 5 employed among the 12,000 men who worked there. It was rather a slow job as there are very few machines and great marble slabs are carved with little nail files. It looks too stupid for words.' No wonder Government House was not finished until 1929.

It was difficult for me to be fair to Raisina because the day after we arrived Mother broke the news that she would not be travelling home with us in March; she was returning to Adyar and would wait and travel back to England with Mrs Besant in April. 'That means going back alone with Ursie and Father,' I wailed in my diary, '– those two adoring each other, Father disliking me – Ursie interminably sarcastic.'

Now, in reading Father's letters to Mother, I realise that I was quite wrong in thinking he disliked me. They are full of loving messages to his 'sweet Mary'. These messages were never passed on and unfortunately he never showed his affection for me, and I, believing that he disliked me, must have behaved in a very surly manner towards him. I was not surprised that he adored Ursula. She was so attractive that winter in Delhi. She and Patsy used to dress up as pierrots and sing to their ukeleles. They had flirted outrageously with the ADCs in Calcutta and were thrilled when 'a particularly revolting specimen of that breed', as I called him, came to stay with us. Mother spent most of her time with Mrs Besant who was now in Delhi. The others crowded into two cars to go for expeditions and picnics while I stayed alone in the bungalow, feeling they did not want me. Why should they have wanted a sulky lump of a girl of an awkward age who no doubt clearly showed her disapproval of them? I was, however, taken to the Kutab Minar and to Agra.

Father must have heard me singing to myself some of the Victorian songs Nannie had taught us, and now he was always nagging me to sing them in public, especially one beginning 'Little Tottie went to Ma, Ma was very busy . . .'. This song had several verses and I was afraid of boring people with it, so I would only comply very grudgingly, whereas Ursula and Patsy hardly waited to be asked to sing. I realise now how easy it would have been to endear myself to Father.

Father had conceived the brilliant idea of having a black-board top made for the large round table in the dining-room. Each guest was provided with a piece of chalk. This was a huge help in entertaining, particularly Indian ladies who had only just come out of purdah and would cover their faces with their napkins when spoken to. They quite lost their self-consciousness when introduced to the exciting novelty of Noughts-and-Crosses.

I described in my diary a typical evening in Delhi:

Father is never happy if we have one evening alone. He thinks it waste of time if we don't have visitors to dinner. So every evening we have a boring couple from Government House or Raisina – and sometimes even two boring couples. Then the same regime is gone through after dinner. Ursy and Patsy sing the 'Armenians and the Greeks' and 'I'm weary of the ballroom said the girl' [verses they had composed, sung to the tune of 'I am weary of the garden said the rose']. Next I have to sing (without ukelele accompaniment) 'Little Tottie went to Ma' and 'Johnny Sands'. After that Mr Baring sings a long hunting song – and as a 'grande finale' Father gets up with 'Terrara Boom-dee-ai' and the 'Baboon's Sister'. This happens every single night.

Father would kick his legs in the air at 'Ta-ra-ra-Boom-dee-ay'. He was a very high kicker and very graceful. 'The Baboon's Sister' was a delightful song. I remember the beginning: 'The monkey married the *ba*boon's sister/Smacked his lips and then he kissed her/Kissed so hard he raised a blister . . .' Father had another song about a baboon which I loved: 'I went to the animals' fair/The birds and the beasts were there/The baby baboon/In the light of the moon/Was combing his bright blue hair/The monkey in a funk/Ran up the elephant's trunk/The elephant sneezed/And went down on his knees/And what became of the monkey, monkey, monk?'

Father was as happy that winter at Delhi as he had been at Folly Farm. He adored having Ursula and the Barings there. It was far the happiest time he ever spent in India. Each morning when he took his solar topee from the hall table he would say, 'Topee or not topee'. Old Pershotum would beam up lovingly at him as he saw him off at the front door. He was sensitive to his beloved master's every word, forestalling all his wants.

Mother did not often look amused, and it was painful when she sometimes snubbed him with, 'Oh, Nedi, *not* that one *again*.' She had a way of sitting on one leg at meals so that

235

her foot went to sleep and she was in danger of falling over when she stood up. This gave the impression that she was a little drunk, most unfairly since she never drank anything. She wished she could drink – it would have made social life easier for her – but even a sip of champagne sent her to sleep.

*   *   *

Father was as miserable at going back to England without Mother as I was. I find that he was concerned for me during the voyage because I had grown so thin and looked so unhappy. I wish I had known this; it would have made such a difference to me. He had great difficulty at first in getting my vegetarian food. Mother and I were the only vegetarians left now in the family. Father wrote to Mother on 27 March after getting home: 'It is horrid – widening waters between us all. I do want to be everything that is kind and generous to you – and it's no good expecting what's not to be had, if it is only a housekeeper – but I do want to be coddled and cuddled, cossetted and kreened – but perhaps in another incarnation – with 1/5,000,000th bit of me in it I'll get it – and won't want it.' He told her in this same letter that he had got back all he had spent on the Dolls' House which had now been removed from our drawing-room: 'I never told you to what I was committed – 11,000 [pounds] and have been paid back the 6300 I had spent: this is private and I was rather fearful of death before repayment as it would have hit you badly.' (The Dolls' House was put on show at the British Empire Exhibition at Wembley which opened in April. It was the chief draw and made thousands of pounds for charity.)

Mother answered this letter on 16 April in the train from Madras to Bombay on her way home:

Your last dear letter made me very sad. I do feel such inexpressible pity for you. Your sweetness and goodness to me is really beyond words. I don't know another man in the world who would have been as patient and kind and persistently loving as you have been to me – and I am such a *very* unsatisfactory wife – I give you no comfort, no home – nothing you want, but I do give you a very grateful love. It is a poor consolation and I am afraid no comfort to you to say I love you when I show it by always leaving you.

Mother had decided while she was in India that she wanted to abandon her bedroom and the great oak bed and make a bed-sitting-room for herself in the back drawing-room. She had asked Father to get a *chowki* made for her. This was a large, low square couch, covered in some plain material to hide its legs, on which the more well-to-do Indians slept at night and sat cross-legged on in the daytime, supported by bolsters. Father had the *chowki* and her new room ready for her by the time she returned in May. There was a door leading from the back drawing-room to Father's bedroom. The fact that he could now tolerate her next door to him while still maintaining their platonic relationship seems additional evidence that he and Lady Sackville were lovers. He and Mother had at last reached a *modus vivendi*. Thereafter they could chat through the communicating door which was always left open, and Mother made early morning tea for them both with an electric kettle, a new accomplishment she had learnt from Mrs Besant and was rather proud of.

CHAPTER FOURTEEN

America and Money
1924–1926

In June 1924 Ursula became engaged to be married to Matt Ridley. As well as being very rich with a family place, Blagdon, in Northumberland, he had a title. They were embarrassingly in love. What more could Father have wanted for his favourite child? They were engaged for three months. Most of this time Ursula spent at Blagdon with Matt and her future mother-in-law, a sister of Lord Wimborne and Lady Chelmsford.

Krishna and Nitya returned once more to England at the end of June, and Mother, with Elisabeth and me, was soon off to spend the summer holidays with them. First we went to Castle Eerde at Ommen in Holland which had just been given to Krishna with some 5,000 acres of woodland by Baron van Pallandt. (From this year onwards until the war, a camp was held at Ommen every summer, attended by several thousands of Krishna's followers from all over the world.) From Eerde we went to a castle hotel at Pergine near Trento in the Dolomites. We were the same party as the year before. Krishna started speaking to us every morning, trying to fire us with the desire to change ourselves radically so that we might become pupils of the Master. Mother must have written enthusiastically about our spiritual experiences

238

to Father who was as usual alone in London, for he replied on 8 August:

I so loved your letter and the truth of it all but it does make a cold life dont it, but I do want you to be happy. As one gets older one's vision becomes clearer and an occupation in material creation does crystallise thought and from experience one learns how dangerous and mis-leading ideas are until they are assayed in actuality by the senses we possess, and what happens with one sense must happen with others. If miracles happen then I know there is no God.

Most people, I think, will profoundly disagree with this last sentence, as I do myself, but to Father God was synonymous with order, and a miracle was disorder. At any rate this is how I interpret his statement.

Krishna and Nitya were going to India that winter and then on to Australia the following March to see Leadbeater again before returning to Ojai. Krishna wanted Mother, Elisabeth and me, and two other girls, to go with them to India and Sydney. Since Leadbeater was the only person qualified to give out Initiations, he was obviously the best man to train would-be aspirants for the occult Path. Mother must have written to him earlier in the summer suggesting that we should all go with Krishna and Nitya in March, for she received a reply from him at the end of August agreeing to receive us. It was all settled that we should travel out to India with Krishna and Nitya in November before Mother so much as mooted the plan to Father who, she must have known, would strongly disapprove of it. She mentioned vaguely that she wanted to go to Australia but said nothing about taking Elisabeth and me with her. I wanted to go simply because Nitya was going. He and I had made friends that summer

239

and I was more in love with him than ever. Elisabeth, I believe, wanted to go because she was at that time in a phase of genuine religious ardour.

Father's Indian office was moved this summer from Apple Tree Yard to 17 Bolton Street. He had plenty of work just now, his most important commission in 1924 being the head office of the Midland Bank in Poultry. Lady MacSack noted that he had '82 jobs on hand and never grumbles about any of them'. Most of his letters to Mother to Pergine were to do with money. Matt Ridley was still a minor and his trustees had asked for a marriage settlement. 'I am giving Ursy £250 a year,' Father wrote on 22 August. 'I ought to raise Barbie to that too.' Robert, he added, was getting more than his fair share – an allowance of £300 plus £400 for his rent. Father felt he ought to give Elisabeth and me £150 each. He had just made a new will. 'My will is to the children subject to your life for *you*.' It was his object, he wrote, to leave £10,000 each to his children after death duties. He reckoned he would have to save another £6000 before this could be achieved. He would sell Mansfield Street if he could get £16000 for it.[1] A week later he sent Mother his budget:

Assets	
Yours [from her father's settlement]	5000
Insurance [life]	11000
M Street	10000
Stocks	6000
With Barings	4000
In hand	2000
	49000

[1] Robert later sold Mansfield Street for £90,000, and today it is, of course, in depreciated pounds, worth far more than Father ever earned in his lifetime.

£5,000 would have to be deducted from this for death duties, he went on. He reckoned that his own expenses were £300 a year and that he ought to give Mother the same. 'I do want you to be happy and comfortable darling – money is all that is left for me to serve you with . . . If I get paralysed or ill I may have to live in a hovel on 1000 a year, that is 900 with taxes off and insurance another 200 which would leave £700. It would mean spending capital – my poor little savings.'

Mother replied that he had 'done marvels'; he really should stop worrying about money. Barbie and Ursula were not dependent on him. Robert could live without his help, though not so comfortably, and she herself could always earn dollars lecturing in America. She was all in favour of selling Mansfield Street which was very expensive to run. If he could not sell it she would take it over and run it as a Theosophical community. (This idea must have appalled him.) She reckoned they were spending £5,000 a year. She had a suggestion of her own to make: could he give her £200 a year; that, with her own £200, would be sufficient for all her personal expenses. Then if he would give Elisabeth £150, the same as Ursula had been having, and Mary £70, the same as Elisabeth had been having, she thought that £150 a month ought to cover all household expenses except wages.

This may sound awful [she went on] but it is only parcelling out what we are spending now but tying us all down to a definite sum. Then if we travel I will reduce household expenses so as to keep the same sum. While you are able to afford it it means a tremendous lot to me to travel – to go to India – Australia – I want to go this year. [This was the vague reference to the plan she had already decided upon.] After that if money fails I settle down or pay by my lecturing.

Then darling I want also to say that I know I am a rotten wife – and do not give you much comfort or happiness so if at any time you feel it would make you happier to bring another woman in to your life I shall never reproach you or feel you have wronged me.

Father replied jokingly: 'Another woman doubtless alluring but how can I afford it! and if I go blind or paralysed what then.' To this Mother answered with apparent seriousness: 'You say you cannot afford another woman – well, we must make every economy and see how we *can*, and we must think out how to do it.'

'How can I take another woman?' Father retorted, 'and give her a life with due protection etc. Oh Ems!! you are impracticable. I know you mean sweetly and well and I appreciate your conscience which prompts your thought – all I do and can do is to bless you – and help you to still your conscience but it is a rotten spoilt life and there let it rot! Your solution can only lead to a greater rot – license has a scourge at both ends. However bless you darling.' It does not seem from this that his relationship with Lady MacSack, whatever it was, was any real compensation for the 'rotten spoilt life'.

* * *

We did not get back to London until 29 September, only a fortnight before Ursula was married with all the panoply of a fashionable wedding at St Margaret's, Westminster. It must have been Barbie and Ursula between them who made all the arrangements. Mother certainly took no part in them. Father naturally opposed the India-Australia plan which Mother put to him during that fortnight, but he did not forbid it. I wonder what would have happened if he had ever put his foot down. In this case at any rate it would not have deterred Mother, for Miss Dodge (Father's hostess on the Baltic cruise whom Mother had converted to Theosophy in about 1912) offered to pay our return fares to Sydney and those of the other two girls as well.

According to Lady MacSack's diary she was at Mansfield Street on 22 October when Mother took her aside and asked her to be very kind to McNed – 'that she gave him to me to look after during her long absence – there was no better friend for him than myself. She was perfectly charming and so very friendly and wants me to be the one person to look after poor neglected McNed.' In a later entry she noted, 'How badly his children treat him but he accepts it serenely saying he is an old man (at fifty-five only) and says that young people hate old ones. He excuses everything in his children.'

We set off from London on 24 October. We were taking an Italian boat from Venice because it was cheaper. (Father told us that Venice reeked of Canal 5.) Father, as a Government servant, had to travel P & O; besides he did not leave London until 14 December. Towards the end of our voyage in the Red Sea, Nitya told me that he loved me. Until we reached Bombay I was in a state of ecstasy such as I have seldom reached again. Then on the last morning on board Nitya confessed to me that he had coughed up blood again. It was a return of his old illness.

From Bombay we went to Adyar and then, on 11 January 1925, to the Lyttons at Calcutta where we met Father. Nitya was now very ill and had gone up to the hill station of Ootacamund out of the damp heat of Madras while the other girls went on ahead of us to Sydney. The contrast between Adyar and Government House was as depressing to me as it had been the year before. 'Father is just the same,' I wrote in my diary, 'and I feel the same constraint towards him – and he appears as much bored with me as ever.' We went up to Delhi on 20 January. 'We are here again and it is just the same as last year,' I noted. But for Father it was not at all the same.

243

Mrs Besant and some of her retinue stayed with us which cast a blight over everything for him. We were told afterwards by Kim Cobbold,[1] one of our young guests passing through Delhi on a world tour, how terrified he was of being put at the vegetarian side of our round blackboard table instead of at Father's side with its jokes and drawings. Father made a drawing of Mrs Besant on a camel with the caption, 'Have you seen Mysore?'

While we were at Raisina this year I felt I ought to make some effort to get closer to Father. Fearfully, I took the opportunity when we happened to be alone one day in the drawing-room of asking him what qualifications were needed to become an architect. 'All you have to know is that water runs down hill,' he mumbled without taking his pipe out of his mouth or looking up from the patience he was doing. Then he added in the same mumble, 'Go and make boots.' I had often heard him say this before about boots. It was his advice to all young men at the start of a career, and I believed I knew what it meant: learn to do something really well, starting at the bottom. I have now seen in a letter to Mother his own definition of the remark: in talking to the Maharanee of Cooch Behar about her son he had preached the 'make boots theory' to her – 'that labour did not degrade a man but upraised him with his men, the people he worked with – by his work they would know him and he them and their needs and his good will and so forgive such weaknesses all men are heirs to more or less'.[2]

Of course I felt badly snubbed. I know now that all I need have done to make contact with him was to go up behind him and put my arms round his neck and my cheek against his. To this, I feel sure, he would have responded, though not with

[1] He was later to marry Hermione Lytton and become Governor of the Bank of England and Lord Chamberlain.
[2] 20 February 1929, from Delhi.

words. But can children (and I suppose I was still a child at sixteen) be expected to be wise with their parents? I had no idea then how much he craved love, even my love.

When Mother, Elisabeth and I left Delhi in the middle of February 1925 to return to Adyar en route for Australia, I recorded, 'Poor Father was so upset when Mummie went [he knew he was not going to see her again until the end of July]. I pity him and admire him from the bottom of my heart but I cannot love him. He works and slaves from dawn till dark and we spend his money like water on all the things he loathes.' There is a temptation to leave out that clause 'but I cannot love him'. Were it true now I think I would leave it out. I went on to say in my diary that to make matters worse for him Delhi, his life's work, was already crumbling. 'I firmly believe that the city will never be completed and certainly never inhabited – for directly the Indians get Swaraj they will abandon the scheme altogether – and the English officials care nothing as anyway their term of service will be up before it is finished, so there will be another ruin on the site of Delhi – but a ruin which has never been a glory in the past.'

It is wonderful to have been so wonderfully wrong. The city flourishes; the Indians are immensely proud of Rashtrapati Bhavan as they call what is now the President's Palace, and keep up the house and gardens beautifully. They have removed the portraits of the Viceroys and put stacking chairs in the Durbar Hall, but in other respects the palace is as it was when Lord Mountbatten, the last Viceroy, handed it over in 1947. When I went there ten years later, in 1957, the first time I had seen it since it was finished, I was moved to tears when suddenly, unexpectedly, I came across the bust of Father by Reid Dick in an alcove on the stairs. I could not help feeling a thrill of pride and triumph that the likenesses of all the British officials who had opposed him, particularly Lord Hardinge, had been removed while his alone had been retained by the Indians.

* * *

We went off to Sydney via Colombo on 13 March two days before Father's lonely arrival back in London. I was in a suicidal mood. I had had one letter from Nitya saying that he would always love me, but he was still desperately ill and I was not allowed to see him at Adyar, or on board ship or in Sydney. I was told that the slightest excitement sent up his temperature. He had very nearly died at Ootacamund. He was sent up to the Blue Mountains soon after we arrived in Sydney while we stayed in a suburban community of about fifty Theosophists of all ages and several nationalities with Leadbeater at its head.[1] We had not been there two months before Mother was said to have taken her first Initiation at the great occult festival of Wesak on the full moon of 8 May and Elisabeth and I our first step on the Path, that of Probation.

When Father got back to London on 15 March Lady MacSack was at first very cold to him. He had stopped in Paris on the way from Marseilles and it had been reported to her that he had met there Millie, Duchess of Sutherland, admired her greatly and flirted with her. It took him several days to convince MacSack that she was the only woman in his life apart from Emmie. After taking him back into her good graces she accepted his offer to pay for repairs to White Lodge, which she was grumbling about, and the residue of what she owed the builder. She paid him back, she noted in her diary, 'with surplus furniture I do not want – and 3 Bon Marché tapestries'. These tapestries were hung above Mother's *chowki* in the back drawing-room and were referred to as either Soho or Mortlake. Father himself said they were Mortlake. Lady MacSack afterwards claimed them

[1]For a description of our time in Sydney with Leadbeater see *To Be Young* (Corgi, 1989).

back. Father returned them to her, but they were given back to him again by Vita after her mother's death.

A week after getting back to London Father wrote to Mother in Sydney: 'I do want to be kind to you always – and on the other hand I do want you here always and for you to make much of me. Though never treated with hush hush as you treat Mrs Besant. I like humorous and human puja.' According to Lady MacSack's diary he feared at this time that Emmie might become President of the TS when Mrs Besant died. There was never the slightest chance of this any more than of her getting into Parliament although to Father's dismay she was offered a seat in a safe Labour constituency.

In April this year 1925 Father went to New York to receive during the Architectural Convention the Gold Medal which the Institute of American Architects had conferred on him the year before – their highest honour. He also wanted to talk to Sir Esmé Howard, the British Ambassador in Washington, about a scheme for a new Embassy which was now being considered by the Foreign Office and the Office of Works. It was on the eve of his departure for New York on 11 April that he had sent Lady MacSack that lover-like little note beginning 'My own darling BM, I cannot bear even to say au revoir to you . . .', and it was after receiving this note that she had sent him that happy twenty-six page letter written over the ten days he was away which he found awaiting him on his return. His note seems to have given her, perhaps for the first time, real confidence in his love.

He travelled to New York on the *Mauretania*, and back on the *Homeric*, getting home just in time for the Academy Banquet on 2 May after a week's absence. On the voyage home he wrote a forty-nine page letter to Mother about his adventures to reach her in India on her way home from Sydney. He had been met at the docks by several architects, including Harvey Corbett who took him in charge and put him up very luxuriously at the University Club. A great dinner of about forty architects was given that evening on the tenth floor of the Club. In spite of prohibition there was plenty of red wine and whisky and one architect brought him a bottle of champagne which he shared shyly with his neighbours. 'I think there were fifteen speeches and then me! I got out of it or rather into it lamely and out of it very lame. Lor! how I hate it.'

The next morning he went to Washington where he spent two nights at the Embassy, sight-seeing, talking to Sir Esmé Howard, going over the site for the new Embassy and preparing the speech he would have to make after the presentation of the gold medal. The site for the new Embassy on Massachusetts Avenue was impossibly narrow for an imposing building and the sum available ridiculously low considering the cost of building in America. No more was to be allocated for it than what the sale of the existing Embassy on Connecticut Avenue would fetch.

Back in New York he was entertained for every meal and not left a moment to himself. 'Lor! the American architects are rich,' he commented. 'The traffic is marvellous and perplexing with its one way roads only possible to a grid iron town plan whereby all the streets and avenues are parallel and at right angles.' He 'got deeper into the mire of despondency' when he was first presented at the Architectural Convention. 'I got out of a speech by saying that I had only been a few days in America and though I could speak a little English I could not speak American so Mr Corbett would answer for me.' The same thing happened on a subsequent occasion and he felt happier 'with this speech solution'.

But when the day of the presentation of the medal came – his last day in America – a speech had to be made. The occasion started with a 'dry' dinner at 6.30 at the Waldorf Hotel. He was given medicine bottles of whisky by friends which he did not have the courage to produce. Then they all had to go to the Metropolitan Museum where they were mustered on the top floor. 'They all put on robes and there was a standard bearer. We marshalled at the top of a great staircase going down straight into the great hall – packed with folk. The President [D. E. Waid] in robes and me in dinner shift with Davis who was our Ambassador,[1] followed by about 40 robed gentlemen.' They had to march round the hall, then stand by a dais shaking hands for an hour while the band 'brayed'. Not half the people had been presented when a halt was called.

We went up to the dais. Everybody standing and I, poor me, before a huge Union Jack. Then Waide [sic] spoke an eulogy and gosh! called to me and put a medal round my neck – a great very beautiful golden disc. Then up gets Mr Davis and he spoke a *most* moving eulogy on what I had done and on the Cenotaph. All very upsetting. And then I was all of a quake and more miserably moved than can be described. I asked Waide if I could read my speech [which had been typed out for him in Washington] to which he assented. Then I was committed! It took ten minutes to read. I had much better not have read it but just said thank you as best I could. But off I went and it got worse and I found myself trembling but could steady myself by pulling the paper I was reading hard. Then I was frightened that if I pulled as hard as I was pulling the paper would burst. I was thinking of every sort of terror as I read. At last it was over. No one could hear me which was something . . . Oh darling it was an ordeal and compliments can't be good for one. If they were I should be oh so good . . . But it is a wonderful place. Alive, keen, friendly. Great achievement and alive only to greater achievement. The scale they can adopt is

[1]John William Davis, American Ambassador in London 1918–21.

splendid – the sky scrapers growing from monstrosities to erections of real beauty and the general character of the work is of a very high standard indeed – far higher than anything on the continent or in England. They are all children with gigantic toys growing, I believe, to an equally gigantic manhood.

* * *

He returned to new financial worries, writing to Lady MacSack on 9 May, 'I feel velly poor as the shares bought years before the war Barings have sold and you can imagine what my savings look like!!'; and ten days later, 'Had the shock of my life yesterday – 3 years super tax in one lump. Gosh! I feel as if I had been modelled by Epstein.' As one does not know what his shares were it is impossible to say whether or not Baring's made a mistake in selling them at a loss. He would have avoided the shock over super tax if he had employed an accountant, but he never did and was to suffer a far greater shock three years later.

Mother did not return to England until 21 July. She had left Elisabeth and me in Sydney. Her excuse for doing so was that since we wanted to be at Adyar for the TS Jubilee Convention in December 1925 it was cheaper than bringing us back to England and then returning to India again. Father had written, 'I don't like them being left without you – yet I know it is expensive bringing them home – but need they go out again?' Nevertheless, he supplied the necessary funds for us to stay there. Mother left me in charge of our finances and I saw to my dismay from her cheque book that she had spent £194 between 6 April and 12 May. I was determined to cut down our expenses, and, indeed, when we left Sydney in November, I was able to take quite a large balance out of the bank.

250

Elisabeth was happy in Sydney. I was miserable but did not want to leave before I had seen Nitya who was still being kept away from me. He and Krishna sailed for San Francisco on 25 June, a fortnight after Mother left. I was allowed to see him for ten minutes in his cabin. He was dreadfully ill.

Mother had not been back in London three whole days after an absence of eight months before she was off again to Holland with Mrs Besant with whom she had travelled from India. Although Krishna was still at Ojai, a camp was held at Ommen that year, presided over by Mrs Besant. Mother returned to London on 27 July for the birth of Ursula's first baby, Matthew, born on the 29th, but went back again to Ommen on 3 August for another ten days. Father's letter to Ursula on the birth of her baby was that of a lover. He recalled her own birth in 1904:

My own darling

God blessed the day you was born – and oh that pink tipped darling showed herself when fate's curtains were drawn up – I often wonder why your arrow-shot clove my heart – perhaps in a previous incarnation I was your wife and the 'mother' in me begat the memory of a husband (you) in those days Mrs Besant was prancing in the battle front and everything was possible and now it is all so different. Instead of the flying dream when with some slight effort I rose beyond the reach of all and none could catch me, the flying dream comes again but it is I who cant – but only fail to reach the grail I want – and that darling is *you* always *you*, double U.

My darling Ursy God bless you. I cant
Your loving father
Father

Father went early that year 1925 to India – on 8 October. He found building going on apace in Delhi. Mother set off a month later with Mrs Besant and Krishna for Ceylon to meet Leadbeater and his party, including Elisabeth and me, coming from Sydney. Although Nitya was still very ill at Ojai he was thought to be out of danger so that Krishna had felt it was safe to leave him in order to attend the Jubilee Convention at Adyar. On 14 November, just past Port Said, a cable reached Krishna announcing Nitya's death. The shock was terrible for him, but after two days he recovered in a remarkable way. He felt that he and Nitya had become one and could never be parted again. Our ship was at Melbourne when I received a cable from Mother and Krishna telling me that Nitya was dead. When I saw Krishna at Colombo I too felt that he and Nitya were one. Gradually I transferred my love to Krishna, though in a much more sublimated form.

During a morning talk at the Adyar Convention on 28 December, a sudden change came over Krishna. He had been saying 'When He comes . . .', then his voice and appearance suddenly altered and his voice rang out 'I have come to build not to destroy . . .'. It was a thrilling moment for those of us who believed, as Mother and I certainly did, that the Lord Maitreya had made his first manifestation through Krishna.

We did not go to Delhi that year because Father was leaving earlier than usual. He went again to Jamnagar in the beginning of February 1926. Back in Delhi he wrote indignantly, 'I find that English foremen here are not allowed to work with their hands as they have to teach. How can one teach without a fellow working. I have very

252

nearly been near bursting point several times.' He now had the contract to decorate and furnish Government House and had found Indian craftsmen such as had worked in their villages from immemorial times. He wanted to use *khuddar*, Indian cotton, for all the soft furnishings. When he found it did not wear well he was reluctantly obliged to supplement it with materials from England and France.

On 12 February we met Father in Bombay where he presented Elisabeth and me with necklaces of seed pearls, a loving and generous gesture to daughters who had so displeased him by going to Australia. Mother had told him about my feelings for Nitya and he was sweet to me on the voyage home. When we got back to Mansfield Street Elisabeth moved into Barbie's room in the front of the house and I moved into Ursula's room at the back. We had inherited the St Ursula beds. We were each given an allowance of £8 a month. Sadly, we had lost Annie who had gone with Ursula as her personal maid. Nannie had the big night-nursery to herself as her bed-sitting-room. Now that we were all grown up she was rather unhappy except when she went to look after Barbie's children while their own nannie was on holiday. Far from becoming the old family retainer, she had grown very smart and looked years younger. The house was now much too large for us but it was not until 1929 that the big dining-room was given up and Father's bedroom made into a small dining-room. Father then moved upstairs while Mother continued to sleep in the back drawing-room. He did not want to occupy the main bedroom so I moved in there while he went into Ursula's room where he remained until his death. There were to be several other changes in the house before the end.

It was at about this time that a painted wooden bust of Father appeared which had been made in Delhi by one of his assistants. It showed him with a real pipe in his mouth and a solar topee on his head in the shape of one of his own Delhi domes. It was a wonderfully amusing likeness. Thereafter it lived in the hall at Mansfield Street on a ledge above the front door.

CHAPTER FIFTEEN

'Yet Another Continent Between Us'
1926–1927

That summer of 1926 Krishna held the first of many gatherings at Castle Eerde before the Ommen Camp. Mother, Elisabeth and I joined him there for three weeks early in July with about thirty other devotees of varying ages and many different nationalities. Father, returning from a happy visit to Ursula and Matt at Blagdon, found the house empty and a bill for ninety guineas from our family doctor, Sir Bruce Porter. 'Holland is the very worst place in the world for hot weather and canals out of order,' he wrote, 'so you will all come back from the Zuyder Zee ready for another ninety guinea touch of flu.' He sounded exasperated for once. 'The house is very empty. Have you gone away to make me sell? I do hope you are having a good time from all household worries that don't really bother you a bit!!' To this Mother replied: 'What an awful bill from Bruce Porter. I thought he charged £1.1.0 a time and cannot believe he came 90 times. I hate you to be all alone but what can I do? I have always had two months holiday with the children every year and I am only taking it a little earlier than usual.' We were back in London by the beginning of August. I had spent one of the happiest months of my life at Eerde.

In the autumn Lady MacSack had a violent quarrel with McNed over money. She had accused Thomas of stealing from her £1,500 which she maintained she had given him in cash several years before and had never had a receipt for in spite of repeated requests. She was furious with McNed for taking Thomas's side. After making up the quarrel to some extent McNed went to stay with her and reported to Mother on 5 October: 'I found MacSack very weak and tearful. I spent Sunday in bed reading her diaries. Very amusing. I marked everything where my name or Thomas's or any reference to building occurred for Mr Bull [her secretary] to copy out so as to get her side of the story over as accurately as possible.' He could find no evidence of dishonesty. Mother replied, ' I suppose I ought to be glad that Lady MacSack has made it up with you but I greatly fear you are only paving the way to fresh troubles as she is so unreliable.' Early in November MacSack discovered that in 1919 she had sold bonds for £1,500 and spent the money. This was the sum she had accused poor Thomas of stealing from her. She then magnanimously 'forgave' Thomas for McNed's sake.

Father had been asked to build another house for the Duke of Peñaranda. This would mean his going to Spain again before India, and he would also have to go to France for his war cemeteries. Just as I was settling down for the winter, embarking on my first novel and feeling despondent at the thought of not seeing Krishna again until the summer, a letter arrived from him on 22 October inviting Mother, Elisabeth and me to spend the winter with him and Mrs Besant at Ojai. It was an invitation Mother and I could not resist. Elisabeth did not want to go because she had just joined the Royal College of Music. Miss Dodge lent us the money for our fares which Mother was to pay back out of fees for lectures which Krishna had promised to arrange for her in California. We obtained our visas for America on 5 November, yet Mother waited until Father had left for India in the middle of November, via France and Spain, before breaking the news to him. At Gibraltar he caught his P & O

256

boat which put in at Marseilles. Mother sent him a letter dated 26 November to reach him at this latter port. 'I have got some news which will be something of a bombshell for you,' she began. Without actually saying so she made it appear that Krishna's invitation had arrived after he had left England. She gave the state of my health as one of her main reasons for going. By drastic and secret banting in the summer I had taken off two stone in weight, so Mother had some genuine grounds for worrying about me. She ended her letter, 'My darling, darling, darling Nedi. I love you very dearly and think of you so much. You won't be cross with me, will you?'

Father replied from Marseilles on 2 December:

My own darling, I feel there is yet another continent between us – another vast division of body and soul. I don't know if and when I go to America [for the Washington Embassy], if prices come out too high per-haps not at all, and you must have known [he realised that she had not had the courage to tell him before he left]. Anyway I hope you will be back in February when I get home. I am glad Betty did not go but she writes rather lonesome. Ought I not to pay Miss Dodge. You must tell me . . . I don't suppose I shall ever have a home – there and waiting for me to come back to. I am not feeling cross, only a little lost and a feeling of emptiness and lonesome but if you are happy, well I should not expect more. Bless you anyway. My love to Mary. Your very loving Nedi.

Mother answered from Ojai on 22 December that his letter had wrung her heart. 'It would be so easy if you were a brute or if you hated me. My only consolation for hurting you over this business of coming here is I believe it may be the saving of Mary's life.' She then went on tell him that she would not be home in February because a doctor in Los Angeles had diagnosed that I had latent TB; the perfect climate of Ojai would make a new person of me and she was sure he would not want her to leave me there alone. But she did not mention that the doctor was a pupil of Dr Albert Abrams, the inventor of a secret black box which was said to be able to diagnose and cure all diseases. It was this black box that had diagnosed my supposed condition and from which I was receiving treatment. I do not believe I really had TB which I was supposed to have contracted from Nitya, though I am sure Mother was sincere in thinking I had. However, I must say in fairness to Abrams's box that when I was X-rayed a few years ago for pleurisy the plate showed very pronounced TB scars.

Why should I hate you? [Father replied] I don't believe you will ever know or realise what I have suffered to bring you peace. I am worried about Mary – give her my love but why take her to the very place Nitya died in? Why not join a young party for winter sports in Switzerland – instead of to a beautiful 'grave' with old folk and unnatural for child occupation etc. . . . it is a dull twilighty life for the young. I remember the twilight in No 1 Bungalow when Mrs Besant stayed with us that winter – no fun allowed – a sort of church all day feeling, a solemnity of a Royal code.

I did not find it a 'twilighty life'. I was supremely happy during the five months we spent in that beautiful valley. And where did Father think I would have found the 'young party' to go winter sporting with? I had lost touch with all my conventional friends and relations. Before we left Ojai in April Mrs Besant announced to the Associated Press of America, 'The World Teacher is here.'

The double sadness of my parents' relationship was that Father's suffering had not brought peace to Mother. Her love for Krishna was still more often than not a torment to her, being parted from him an anguish; she longed for him to say, 'Leave all and follow me.' And she would have done so if he had asked her to – followed him barefoot with a begging bowl over the earth. In taking me with her to India, Australia and California she was giving me the most glorious thing she knew; it would have been much easier for her to leave me behind. Therefore I consider she was a mother to bless whatever her shortcomings may have been as a wife.

*　　*　　*

Father had spent a happy Christmas with the Lyttons in Calcutta and had met the new Viceroy, Lord Irwin (afterwards Lord Halifax) and his wife, a daughter of Lord Onslow, when they came to their official residence in Calcutta, Belvedere. This house had been occupied by the Governor of Bengal when Calcutta was still the capital and the Viceroy had lived at Government House. 'Christmas night we all went to Belvedere for dinner,' Father wrote. 'There were six tables – ten people at each table. Their Excellencies were not announced – they just came in separately and you found them there!! No ceremony at all, and after dinner Lord Irwin danced with his Controller, Colonel Muir!!' This was the fourth Viceroy Father had known and, from his point of view, far the best. On the way home, early in February 1927, he was able to report, 'The Irwins are so pleasant to work with. Such a difference. I feel happier than I have ever been with Delhi. I hope it lasts. They are simple, interested and deferential and one can say anything and one is – or seems to be – understood.'

In the weeks between Father's return to London in the middle of February and our return from Ojai in April, Father and Elisabeth made friends. She wrote about this time in her autobiography:

Alone with Father, for the first time, in spite of our

259

mutual shyness which in public we both covered with a spate of words, he was all gentleness, consideration and understanding. I grew to love and admire him beyond words and would turn to him for advice and help. After years of loneliness it was difficult for him to realise that it was possible for one of his family to need him and respect him as a great artist, but gradually he began to take me into his confidence . . . I now tentatively began to consult him about my own work . . . He was deeply moved by music, which always made him cry. Purcell was his great favourite because he was English . . . He became fascinated and excited at the realization that music was built on structural principles and relationships stemming, as did architecture, from the Greeks.[1]

He once said to her, 'When I was young and had not been perfectly trained I was very conscious of a lack of technique, but now I think I can say I have as good a technique as anyone.'

Elisabeth took charge of the household, and managed to improve the food to such an extent that Father began to ask his friends to meals. He and Elisabeth gave several little dinner parties. She mentions Orpen, Yeats, Seymour Hicks, E. V. Lucas, Freddie Lonsdale, Alfred Munnings and William Nicholson coming to the house. She said that Nicholson looked just like Mr Jeremy Fisher, a perfect simile. She also acted as Father's hostess at some private parties at the Garrick, and he took her on a weekend visit to Mr Koenig, a Silesian banker, and his wife for whom he had built a bathing pavilion and a Temple of Music at Tyringham Park in Buckinghamshire. Mrs Koenig was a great music lover and befriended Elisabeth thereafter in a number of ways.

[1] *A Goldfish Bowl.* p. 43 (Cassell 1972).

One evening Elisabeth returned home to find Father sitting in the morning-room playing patience by candlelight. She asked him if the lights had fused. 'No,' he replied, 'but electric light is vewy, vewy expensive.'

That this time alone with Elisabeth meant as much to him as it did to her is shown, I think, in this letter he wrote to her in July:

My own sweet darling Betty

Ever so many many blessings on your 21st birthday. I send you a little cheque of an amount convenable – and made of guineas in the hope of a happy golden future [21 guineas].

Bless you darling. I am not much of a father in a fathery way, but you make up by being a perfect daughter in a daughtery way as I think you aughterly should do.

Bless you darling,

V. very loving father

Father

*   *   *

Mother, still at Ojai in March, was now making the extraordinary suggestion that Father should open an American office and put Robert in charge of it. The country was 'fabulously rich' and she was sure that within a few years he would become a millionaire. Father wrote back with a patience he could hardly have felt:

Alas, my darling, it's no use conjuring up beautiful thought forms about Robert and architecture. It would take at least five years work to get into it – pass exams etc. My work is not like a shop walker who sells other folks stuff. I have to manufacture every idea I sell in the form of initialled plans . . . He had his chance in

1918 – 8 years ago and he might have been useful and helpful now.

Robert had left the *Daily Mail* in 1924 to work with Brendan Bracken as joint editor of *English Life*, an illustrated monthly magazine on the lines of *Country Life*. Robert persuaded Father to write five articles for the magazine in the course of the next three years – on *The Building of Imperial Delhi*, on *Art in Advertising*, on *Britannic House*, on *The Smaller English House* and on Gertrude Jekyll's book *Old English Household Life*, published in October 1925. Father did not like Bracken who often came to Mansfield Street and had the cheek to ruffle his hair. Bracken was always kind to me, however, and I became very fond of him. Robert insisted that he had once made a pass at him and we all believed that he was in love with Robert. Bracken had several paintings by Charles Lutyens hanging in his house in North Street. I do not know what became of them after his death. At the end of 1927 Robert joined the firm of R. W. Symonds, decorator and furniture designer. Robert had a real flair for interior decoration and made a great success of it.

When Mother and I got back from Ojai Elisabeth, rather resenting our intrusion on her new life with Father, went to live on her own in great squalor and discomfort in a furnished room near the Royal College of Music for £1 a week. She did not go with us when Mother and I went to Castle Eerde again in July for another of Krishna's gatherings, but moved back into Mansfield Street while we were away. We had only been there a few days when Mother received a disturbing letter from Father. He said that a telegram had come to the Central News Agency stating that a daughter of Sir E. and Lady E. Lutyens was engaged to be married to 'Km'. With the co-operation of his friend Lord Riddell, Chairman of the *News of the World*, he had managed to prevent the news being published on the grounds that it was a libel on a holy man and that he and the TS would take immediate action if it were. He wanted me to come home at once. It was a mild letter in the circumstances. Elisabeth sent Mother a more graphic account of his feelings: 'He was in a dead panic lest it be true. Swore that if it was he'd give up Delhi and all his work, turn us all out of the house and never see any of his family again, apart from giving you your £500. I told him he could sleep quietly as I could guarantee it was a lie but he never slept much and is miserable and afraid.'

How I longed for it to be true! Mother managed to pacify him and I did not return to London until after the Ommen camp.

*　　*　　*

Father went to stay with Lady MacSack at Brighton for a few days in October 1927. I imagine he must have been recuperating from some minor illness since he was not working. MacSack wrote pages in her diary about this visit. She wrote in French, a language she was apt to revert to when ill or agitated. She was very bored with McNed who, when he was not playing patience, was doing crossword puzzles or making rather risqué drawings. '. . . je trouve ses dessins trop indécents, quoique cela le laisse très froid. Il me dit que ces dessins viennent de son "mind" et nullement de ses sens. Quelle curieuse mentalité! Mais ces jeux continuels sont très dûrs pour moi, car il est impossible d'avoir la moindre conversation soutenue.' These indecent drawings were incomprehensible to her 'car c'est un homme d'une décence extrême. Il déteste la moindre conversation sur la question de Sexe. Et cependant, il peut parler si bien de tout, mais il ne parle jamais . . . Il dit que jouer ces cartes ou ses puzzles lui repose son mind fatigué. Mais comme il adore que je suis près de lui dans la même pièce, avec les fenêtres fermées, l'electricité illuminée, et les sept petites pipes allumées

263

sans cesse, tour à tour, – je trouve le temps long. Et c'est très fatiguant pour mes nerfs si faibles. Il ne comprend jamais que je sois fatiguée ou gênée, n'ayant pas le sympathie. Il me répête tout le temps, "You *must* be well" ou "You must not give way to your nerves", "You can control them if you want to". Oh God! . . . Emmie m'a dit qu'il n'arrêtait jamais to nag Robert. Alas! Alas! How long can my affection stand it?'

It is on this sour and exasperated note that her diary ends for good. Perhaps she had a little more sympathy now with Emmie.

* * *

Some time during that autumn of 1927 Father rang me up one day most unexpectedly to ask me to join him immediately for lunch at Claridge's. Nothing like this had ever happened before. The only times he had ever taken us to a restaurant was to the Berkeley Grill on two occasions for Mother's birthday, and he had never taken us to any form of entertainment. I had already had lunch but, greatly intrigued, I jumped into a taxi and was at Claridge's in a few minutes. I found Father at a table in the restaurant with a dapper little man who was introduced to me as Sir Roderick Jones, the Chairman of Reuter's, who turned out to be our host. Father was making a new drawing-room for him for the house he was soon to move into, 29 Hyde Park Gate, and was already discussing the possibility of a new Reuter building, which was not in fact commissioned until a few years later. I discovered afterwards that Father had told Roderick Jones about his worry over me and Krishna and that it was Roderick who had asked him to ring me up and invite me to lunch.

It was the beginning of a friendship that was to change my life radically and which I owe entirely to Father. Roderick was nearly fifty at this time and I was nineteen. Soon afterwards he invited me to Albemarle Street where he was then living and introduced me to his wife, Enid Bagnold, to whom I became deeply attached. Thereafter, I saw Roderick nearly every day and spent most weekends at Rottingdean where he had a house (he and Enid were great friends of Lady MacSack) and where I met many people well known in the literary world, including Arnold Bennett, Desmond MacCarthy, H. G. Wells and Logan Pearsall Smith. Enid was angelic to me and encouraged me in my writing. My stock went up at home when every morning Roderick's special Reuter messenger boy brought me a letter from him. For the next eighteen months Roderick and Enid were the centre of my existence, taking me to Paris and other places abroad. They were sympathetic to Krishna and I took them to Castle Eerde to stay with him for a few days in 1928. This strange three-cornered, and sometimes four-cornered, relationship is a story on its own that has no place here.

For all its peculiarity Father must have found this friendship preferable to my association with Krishna. Father really tried to do something for my social life now by inviting me occasionally to small private dinners he gave at the Garrick and introducing me to one or two eligible young men. I began to try to force myself to eat meat in order to conform, heaving at first over every mouthful, but this sacrifice did not make it any easier for me to fit into conventional English society.

CHAPTER SIXTEEN

Opening of Viceroy's House
1927–1930

Father did not leave for India until the very end of 1927. Charles Reilly, Professor of Architecture at Liverpool, travelled with him. From the ship at the beginning of January 1928 he told Mother that with the help of Reilly he had finished a review for the *Observer* of Le Corbusier's book, *Towards a New Architecture*, which had just appeared in an English translation. This review, which was published on 29 January, is as far as I know, Father's only pronouncement on the work of this architect, eighteen years his junior, who had so great an influence on his contemporaries and followers. (See Appendix.) From Delhi on 26 January he was writing:

I had two charming letters from Roberty Bobs. I do hope he makes a success of his work [as a decorator]. It is very hard and strenuous starting a new profession – an overcrowded one where competition is keen . . . For 5 or 6 years I went to no parties. I knew no one and worked till 12-2 in the morning. I bicycled a lot and walked a good bit but no sport and no other relaxation. Just work . . . It is great fun having Reilly. He is like a babe saying goo goo at every passing show and incident. The Irwins are charming and helpful

. . . The building is coming out well and is beginning to make its impression.

It was planned that the Viceroy should move into Government House at the end of 1929, though the official opening of the new city would not be until 1931. Father noted with amusement that the whole of Delhi had not cost the price of two battleships. The plant for drying the wood for the furniture, ordered two years before, had not arrived yet. It ought to have been ordered fifteen years ago, Father said. When it did come it would take a month to erect and then another eight months before the wood would be fit to use.

The Baker work looks distressing [he continued]. I do wish he had taken more trouble. I believe that no designer should ever read poetry etc. There is in the hearts of all men a natural desire for poetry. If read it is easily acquired and satisfied. If not read you have to get your eventual quota of it through and in your work and not be doped with other folks adjectives. *Do* work this idea out for me. I am sure there is a lot in it.

Father had read so little that his outlook was fresh, his ideas never second-hand. Where he was derivative it was from looking not reading. Baker, on the other hand, a great reader, never without a book of verse in his pocket, was inspired by the written ideas of others.

*   *   *

Father's work in England for 1928 included a commission from the Westminster City Council for a slum clearance and re-building scheme for the poor. The six-storey blocks of flats he built in a chequer-board pattern of grey brick and stone in

Vincent Street and Page Street, off Millbank, look as original and impressive today as when they were first put up. He also designed the lovely new bridge at Hampton Court in 1928. Some years later, after flying over London in his capacity of consultant to the Highway Development Survey of Greater London, he wrote to Mother:

I could hardly believe Hampton Court could be so small. My bridge from the air looks ever so much better than any others – why? I know but I shan't write it. But it was odd . . . One knew at once whether a good architect or a bad one had been at work. Very refreshing, knowing one was looking at things from what one might call God's point of view.

The importance of 'God's point of view' was something he had always tried to impress on his students and apprentices. I do not think he would have liked to know that in this he was following Ruskin who condemned the Renaissance architecture Father loved. Ruskin in *The Stones of Venice* had pointed out the ungodly spirit of the Renaissance as exemplified by the sarcophagus bearing the figure of the Doge Andrea Vendramin high up on the wall of the church of SS. Giovanni e Paolo in Venice. Only the visible side of the figure had been sculpted, whereas the figure on the monument of an earlier Gothic Doge in the same church had been as beautifully carved on the unseen side against the wall – the side God saw – as on the visible side.

In October 1928 Father went to New York and Washington again. In New York he met an American lady who told him that he ought to go and see 'the most beautiful cemetery that ever was at Etaples in France'. He enjoyed the sensation he created when he said that he knew it already because he had designed it. During this visit he designed a room in New York for Joseph Duveen, making no charge 'because Duveen has done so much for artists'. 'I think I am wise and feel it right,' he told Mother. Duveen became a friend.

Back in Delhi once more in January 1929, having left England in December and gone to Jamnagar on the way, Father was able to report that the Irwins were delighted with Viceroy's House, as the King had now decreed that the new palace should be called. 'It's all beginning to look mighty fine. I do think it's a gentleman's house.' The great dome was up to its springing. The gardens had blossomed since the year before. 'The tanks run and reflect and ripple, and my rainbow in the deep fountain has come off – a vivid rainbow and children *can* find its start.' A few days later the fountain gave, as he had hoped, a lunar rainbow. 'The roses wonderful, the mignonette perfume the whole place . . . I am making a butterfly garden.' He had made a butterfly garden for Lady Sackville ten years before. The idea was to make a garden of only those plants that attracted butterflies so that what appeared from a distance to be brilliant patches of flowers would turn out at close range to be a living shimmer of butterfly wings.

Father would have been very happy in Delhi that winter if it had not been for a further demand for £5,000 for super tax which, he said, would take all his profits on Delhi since 1912. This shows how little he made on Delhi – £5,000 in seventeen years. 'It's hard,' he commented. 'Damn democracy!' Baker's arrival in February was another 'cloud on his silver lining'.

Father concentrated during this visit on the furniture and furnishings for Viceroy's House. Apart from some antiques imported from England and some crystal chandeliers copied from old houses in Delhi and Calcutta, he designed everything himself, including the Viceroy's throne. No two mantelpieces were alike; he even designed the fenders, fire-irons and fire-backs. He had particular fun with his designs for the nursery chandeliers, all of brightly painted wood, one showing four angels praying to a starlit globe, another four prancing horses, and a third four hens, with their chicks, who had just laid eggs: hanging from the four arms of this wooden structure broken egg-shells spilt their joke (their yoke) in the form of light bulbs. All his gaiety, inventiveness, ingenuity and lightness of touch are revealed in these chandeliers. His nurseries had always been imaginative. The floor of the nursery in Viceroy's House was patterned in red and white stone checks for games of draughts and chess. The Delhi nurseries were built round a central open court protected by a high wooden screen. In order to break up the imprisoning effect of this screen he built a huge bird cage into each of its four sides. In two of his country houses in England there were windows at floor level in the nurseries so that children at the crawling stage could look out. On the nursery floor of his Washington Embassy he had inserted a small window in the main staircase to enable the children to peep down at the guests.

It was for Delhi that Father designed his most ingeniously imaginative clock of which only a few replicas were made. The case is of wood, gracefully shaped like an urn with two brass handles, painted pale blue and standing about 1½ feet high, the face of a horizontal oval, the hands expanding like lazy tongs to reach their fullest extent at the figures nine and three. The large brass key, in the form of a shamrock, fits into the top as an integral part of the design.

The extremes of humidity and temperature in Delhi were particularly hard on the English antiques which fell to pieces almost as soon as they arrived. Curtains were now being made, chiefly of French and English materials since *khuddar* had proved unsatisfactory, and carpets by Indian weavers to Persian designs. These were said to have taken 500 weavers two years to make. Father's desire to have some silver chandeliers he had designed made by Indian silversmiths had been overruled; they were manufactured in England.

Two inscriptions were now wanted – one for the Viceroy's throne, or State chair, and the other for the Jaipur column. Lord Irwin chose for the throne a line from *Proverbs*: 'Wisdom resteth in the heart of him that hath understanding.' For the column Father invented the lines:

> Endow your thought with faith
> Your deeds with courage
> Your life with sacrifice
> So all men will know of India's greatness

He would have preferred 'the greatness of India' but it made the line too long.

At the end of February he met Motilal Nehru for the first time who told him that Gandhi 'deplored the waste of money on architectural Piles'. 'I said it was all Indian work and much better to do than spin Kadda. That India where she once led in the fine arts is now deplorably behind times . . . He said he had not thought of the buildings as an education for the Indian mason, craftsman etc. . . . . He is a dear old man, drinks whisky, port, etc, mutton, everything. A black coat and Jodhpurs on which I drew buttons so that he looked exactly like an English Bishop. And that was all he was fit for if he didn't help India in her material world.'

For the first time Father was reluctant to leave Delhi although he longed to be home: 'I shall hate leaving the work for the finishing touches and the hands left are all thumbs and wits of dough . . . Everyone is careless, sloppy and unintelligent in the ways of good work and the Indian is hopeless. They smash 50% of what they do and have no more respect for their own work than anybody else's.'

He arrived home at the end of March to find more family trouble: I wanted to get married. Having reacted strongly against my abnormal upbringing – not against Krishna personally to whom I remained and still remain devoted – I

271

had fallen in love with a young man, Anthony Sewell, as unlike me as possible. He was ambitious, worldly, a gambler, high-spirited, extroverted, with a great zest for life and continually laughing eyes. One of his greatest attractions for me, though, was that he was bi-lingual in French and English having been born and brought up until the age of ten in Paris where his father had taken over the legal practice of Somerset Maugham's father. In spite of being educated at Eton and Cambridge, where he had taken a degree in economics, Anthony had no money apart from the £10 a week he was earning in a stock-jobber's office. His father had Parkinson's disease and the firm of Sewell and Maugham had gone into decline. I was under the impression, which persisted until I came to read Father's letters for the purpose of writing this book, that Father was giving Barbie and Ursula £500 a year each. I expected him to give me the same to enable me to marry; Anthony had stipulated that we could not get married on less than £1,000 a year. Father, though he liked Anthony personally, declined to do so, thus arousing my intense indignation: Barbie and Ursula did not need the money and I did.

Mother, who was extremely fond of Anthony, was on my side and we both nagged Father to let me become officially engaged. In April he gave into us on the understanding that we waited to get married until Anthony was earning enough to support me. Ironically, Father also made it a condition that Anthony should insure his life for £10,000.

I longed to get away from home as well as to get married. Life at Mansfield Street with Elisabeth living on her own had become excessively dull. When Father, Mother and I had meals alone together there was never any attempt at conversation. Father would take *The Times* crossword into the dining-room, throwing me an occasional anagram to decipher, while Mother read her novel all through the meal – usually a Wild Western. I was thankful to escape as soon as possible to the solitude of the nursery which had now become my writing room.

Mother also reached a critical stage in her life that summer of 1929. At the Ommen Camp in August, Krishna publicly dissolved the Order of the Star in the East of which he was Head, and shortly afterwards resigned from the Theosophical Society. He declared that he did not want disciples. (Subsequently he went his own way as a spiritual teacher, attached to no organisation but still attracting thousands of followers.)[1] The ground was cut from under Mother's feet. The World Teacher had arrived and was not saying any of the things expected of him. The following year she too resigned from the TS. Krishna had soared into an abstract realm of thought which seemed inhuman to her and where she could not follow him. She suffered greatly, her suffering being in some measure akin to what Father had gone through when she had disappeared into a mist of occultism. She still venerated Krishna as 'the perfect flower of humanity', as she called him, but was no longer a follower, physically or spiritually. When Mrs Besant died in 1934 her last link with Theosophy snapped.

Father on the other hand had just been offered a stupendous and thrilling new challenge – he had been asked in the summer of 1929 to design a new Roman Catholic Cathedral at Liverpool. This had come about through a chance meeting at the Garrick Club with Dr Downey, the Catholic Archbishop of Liverpool. Downey spoke of his intention to design a new cathedral. Father remarked, 'What fun for you', and they went on to discuss cathedrals in general. Later in the summer Dr Downey asked him to go and see him at Liverpool to discuss the new Cathedral. Since a Roman Catholic, Giles Scott, had designed the Anglican Cathedral at Liverpool, on an eminence looking out to sea,

[1]He died in February 1986, aged 90.

it seemed fitting to Dr Downey that a Protestant should design the Roman Catholic one; besides, he had probably divined that Father had a deeply religious nature. Downey had conceived his Cathedral of Christ the King as the greatest in Christendom, rivalling even St Peter's, with the largest dome in the world, and the site chosen for it would raise it above the Anglican Cathedral so that it would be visible to all shipping entering the Mersey. It was not until the site had been cleared and £100,000 raised towards the purchase of the land and digging the foundations that the project was to be made public. In the meantime Father kept it secret from all but Mother. He worked on his drawings in private in the racquet court at Mansfield Street. On the back of a letter to him from Mother from Ommen, dated 29 July, he made a first sketch of the Cathedral. 'The rain came in the Squash Court and stopped all my work there,' he reported on the 31st. The 31st was my twenty-first birthday and he added that he would give me £21 as he had given Elisabeth if he could, but that he was suddenly overwhelmed with an unexpected claim which had just come in for thousands of pounds of back taxes. 'I pay more to the country than I can spend or save . . . I shall want every penny I can lay my hands on for my work. It will come back in 5 or six years time but in the meantime I am fearfully cramped and the taxes take all my available capital.'

Taxes always came on him unexpectedly; no provision was ever made for them. It almost seems as if he was so frightened of money that he did not dare think about it. How much worry and how many thousands of pounds a good accountant could have saved him, but he would not have liked the expense of an accountant. This new claim was far more serious than any of the others, for it appears that he was now being fined for not declaring his full income. I have always understood that it was Mr Hall, the assistant in charge of the Indian office in London, who was responsible for making the tax returns for Delhi. He was a charming man, an excellent draughtsman and devoted to Father, but he was no businessman. Any false declaration would have been made inadvertently. One does not know how much liaison there was between the two offices but as far as my memory goes it was only the income on the Delhi work that had been wrongly declared.

Mother ignored this new financial worry. She wrote to him on their wedding day, 4 August:

32 years!! Isn't it wonderful. How happy we have been in spite of ups and downs. Do you know any other couple so happy and so loving and so *free* after 32 years . . . How wise I was to recognise your genius 32 years ago!! You see I can't praise you without praising myself! I may be covered with the mantle of your glory but I had the foresight to take shelter there.

Did she really believe they had been so happy? He did not deny it, writing on the 5th, 'Ever so much love for your sweet darling wedding letter . . . I work here in the Racquet Court and can't tear myself away'; and on the 29th, 'I work all night on my Cath., and hate to leave it – but in a week or so before I go to America I shall have completed the first of what may be a series of Cathedrals.' I do not think the first design was ever radically altered. It was to Washington that he had to go in September for the Embassy. By this time 'America bores me drefful' he was to confess.

Two months later he was off to India to prepare the Viceroy's House for the official reception of the Irwins on 23 December. (The official opening of the capital of New Delhi had now been scheduled for January 1931.) He did not arrive in Delhi until 18 December and then it was with a heavy cold. The next few days were chaotic. Many essential things he had ordered to be done ten months before had not been touched.

275

It's like an exhibition [he wrote] and it is impossible to conceive that they have been at it 17 years! And con-tretemps follow each other by the hour . . . Nothing is properly finished. It takes three hours or more to go round the house and round and round I go and oh I'm tired . . . The Indian not only smashes a lot of what he has done but a lot of other stuff in the operation. They have broken 3,000 panes of glass and 500 keys have been stolen besides door handles and window fastenings. The whole place is a-boil and I keep exploding and stopping to blow my nose. The English foremen work day and night and two of them have cracked up. If it had not been for the handful of trained craftsmen I can't imagine what would have happened . . . But on the other hand the house is fine and everyone seems to like it and to be bowled over which makes the large amount of sloppy hurried work the harder to condone.

W. R. Mustoe, the head of the Horticultural Department, told him that there were seventeen miles of hedges to cut. Father hung the pictures and arranged the furniture himself. There had been lots of terrible Viceroys, he said, but no good portraits of them.

Arthur Shoosmith has recalled that although his relations with Lutyens, whom he regarded as 'the most lovable of men', were exceedingly happy during all the years he was in India in charge of the Delhi office, Lutyens was on edge at this time and he, Shoosmith, was apt to get his 'ears boxed' for something which had nothing to do with him at all. 'One day, as we were inspecting the Mogul garden, the worm turned, and I said to him, "Sir Edwin, do you want me to go?" "Don't be a bloody fool," he replied. "What's the matter?" I told him and he said, "I don't mean it. I always say rude things to people I like; I dare not say them to the

276

others." And he put his arm round my shoulders, and so we walked down the garden.'[1]

All went well on the morning of Monday 23 December. Father had to get up at seven in a tail coat; the Irwins arrived about eight. 'The guard was inspected, then the city fathers presented an address to which H.E. replied. He then came up the great portico where I was presented to him and others of the work. At a given signal the doors were opened – no key as there was no lock – and they, Lady Irwin and H.E. went into the house and we left them alone and for the first time in 17 years the house closed to me.'

There were still endless things to be done in the house which he and Lady Irwin had to do themselves since everyone else took ten days holiday over Christmas to recover from the strain of the opening. Father was grumbling about this holiday to Mother in a letter of 31 December when a note was brought to him from Lord Irwin congratulating him on the KCIE which the King had conferred on him in the New Years Honours List of 1930 – a complete surprise.

Father received a letter from Mother on this same day (it was her first air-mail letter) which must have spoilt all his pleasure in his new honour. In it she pressed him to give me an allowance to enable me to marry at once. 'So long as I pay Robert's Rent I cannot give Mary more,' he replied (I was still getting only £8 a month), 'nor is it right and fair to me or anyone that I should pay out so much. The revenue people have made it more yet. I may be let in for a law suit. Even Francis Smith advises me to fight and anyhow I have to pay 14-15000 £ in taxes[2] . . . I must save – for you know darling I am getting on in years and I have not saved enough yet to

---

[1] *Architectural Association Journal*, March 1959.
[2] In August 1930 the Inland Revenue agreed on a settlement of £10,000 on condition that it was paid immediately.

pay allowances I have been cajoled into giving our children let alone a comfortable old age for myself which I should appreciate – I don't want to have to go back to Thursley days. When Roberty Bobs gives up his claim for Rent 400 £ a year I think I shall try and *allow* but *cannot settle* – to Mary 250.'

I was vaguely aware that Father had to pay a large sum in back taxes but I imagined, as did most people, that he was still a very rich man. He wanted the world to think this. In 1921 he had written to Mother, it may be remembered, that no one should know of their financial anxiety – 'it destroys credit and they think if a man wants money they can and will down him'. He still believed this. Not realising, therefore, the true state of his finances I went ahead with plans for my wedding which was fixed for 18 February 1930. This news was passed on to Father who expostulated, 'I have a most expensive family . . . However, I suppose Mary has sent out invitations and everything . . . I will get home if I can. If I can't I can't, that's all . . . However there it is. My love to darling Mary – and ever so much love and bless Anthony for me.' If only Father had told me himself of his money worries I might have been less selfishly impatient, although I had been engaged since April, three months longer than he had been engaged to Mother. As it was he no doubt believed that Mother had passed his worries on to me and that I was utterly callous.

Father arrived home just in time for my wedding at St Margaret's, Westminster. It was a bitterly cold day and he kept on his overcoat as he walked up the aisle with me. Just before we set off alone for the church he gave me a cheque for £100, telling me to cash it quickly in case he changed his mind. Both the generous gesture and the remark accompanying it were so characteristic of him that I laughed and hugged him gratefully.

As well as an expensive wedding he and Mother gave me a trousseau, my linen and a beautiful blue leather dressing-case. His rich friends and clients as well as my relations

278

had been wonderfully generous. We received over £700 in cheques, including £70 from Lady MacSack, as well as some really good furniture and Persian rugs. From then until the beginning of the war, when it stopped altogether, £40 was paid every month into my account. I believed this to be my due, no more than what Barbie and Ursula were getting. After reading Father's letters I cannot understand how Mother managed to 'cajole' so much out of him. Possibly she contributed part of it out of her own allowance. It certainly did not come from my siblings. It is a mystery that will never be solved now. If only we had fought our battles with Father ourselves instead of always through Mother. And yet I think he must share the blame for never talking openly to us or trying to win our confidence.

Anthony had insured his life for £10,000 as required; he was now earning about £700, so after paying the insurance premium we had £1,000 a year to live on. We managed very comfortably in a lovely little panelled flat, where Charles Lamb had once lived, in the Inner Temple, with one daily maid. How much happier Mother would have been if she could have started married life in such conditions – so much closer to the dream of the 'little white house'.

CHAPTER SEVENTEEN

The Cathedral and the Parthenon
1930–1932

Father was off to Washington again in the third week of May
1930. On the way to New York on the *Aquitania* he gave a
dinner party for twelve the evening before docking:

> . . . afterwards the climax was reached when the band
> was asked to play 'You should see me dance the Polka'
> and the deck cleared. A young man called Bingham, a
> beautiful dancer, as partner and off we went – 3rd off
> the floor and double time. I couldn't help laughing but
> we received a great ovation. I was blown empty and
> my partner was a rag. I am sure it did me a lot of
> good and I have been massaged every morning, so I
> have had six hours of massage. You won't know me. I
> am thin, long and dangerously vivacious. I do wish you
> were here.

He so loved to dance. His dancing to the pianola for Lady
MacSack had ceased by now; his relationship with her was not
what it had been. She was ill on and off with heart trouble;
her eyesight was very bad and she was becoming more and
more difficult to deal with. Vita suffered from her as much
as anyone else. She threw things at the servants and could

not understand why they minded, considering what a relief it was to her feelings. She had always suffered from the heat and now she insisted on having all her meals out of doors, even in winter, much to the discomfort of her guests whom she supplied with fur rugs and hot water bottles. In August Father was to tell Mother that he had not seen her for two months: '. . . alas she gives one no rest and the vague irregular meals bewilder the senses.'

In Washington Father had some of the same sort of trouble as he had had in Delhi. 'They are perfectly terrible at getting things finished,' he reported on 27 May, 'and the Office of Works official stringency as regards funds has led to a sort of mental paralysis . . . everyone is so tired of correspondence and estimating and reestimating that they are dog tired of the job. It is a pity to spoil a good building.' To my mind the Washington Embassy is one of his least successful buildings.

*　　*　　*

The commission for the Liverpool Cathedral was now secure. Estimated to cost £3,000,000 it would have been by far his most lucrative commission if it had been built. The drawings had to be in by the end of August 1930. He was even busier than usual that summer since he could not afford all the help he needed. Even so, he now had three assistants working with him on the Cathedral in the racquet court which 'spoilt the fun of being alone'. But he worked at it alone at night all through August. He felt hurried, '. . . and hurry generally means tripping and hence delay. And other jobs too press.'

In September the provisional plans were released to the press. From the beginning Father had conceived the idea of having a chapel dedicated to the Penitent Thief, a figure, he said, who had hitherto been totally neglected. But Dr Downey wanted the Lady Chapel built first. Father felt that he would never have been able to tackle the Cathedral if it

281

had not been for his early religious upbringing. Twenty years before he had confessed to a friend 'au fond I am horribly religious, but cannot speak of it and this saves my work'. From Gibraltar in 1926 he had told Mother how moved he had been by the singing of 'Greenland's Icy Mountains' by the garrison at an early morning service: 'All that Mother believed, felt and taught flooded back – the mysteries of a child's conception brain-waved again. So I am feeling very sentimental and want you here with me. But it is all beyond my reach – whether too high or too low – I only know it's a level I shall never reach again.' In his inspiration for the Cathedral it is just this level that he did seem to reach again: the simplicity of his early faith, his profound knowledge of architectural form and his technical experience joined in a last perfect creative flowering.

Father got on splendidly with Dr Downey. The priests of the Roman Catholic Church appealed to him in contrast to his shrinking from the sanctimoniousness of so many of the Protestant clergy. With Dr Downey, hugely fat and jolly, he could laugh and exchange jokes. Dr Downey told him about a telegram sent by an Irish priest who was withdrawing his donkey from a donkey race: 'Have scratched my ass.' In exchange Father asked him the riddle, 'What fun do monks have?' 'Nun.' And Father proposed a toast at one of the Archbishop's dinner parties: 'Here's to the happiest hours of our life spent in the arms of another man's wife – Gentlemen, our mothers!' When being shown round Westminster Cathedral by Cardinal Bourne and seeing, *Ave, Ave, Sancti* on a wall of the Lady Chapel, he asked, 'Tell me, Your Eminence, do two "aves" make an "oly"?'

When Mother heard that the Cathedral plans had been released to the press she wrote dampingly: 'I love to think of your great building, but I do wish it had been workmen's model dwellings and not a church! If you had been going to build a cathedral when we first married I should have been thrilled, but now I could weep. It saddens me that men should still be perpetuating superstition and priestcraft whereas I long to set them free from such things.' Nevertheless, this summer was to culminate in a new closeness between them. Mother had been at the camp at Ommen. (Krishna continued to hold these camps which were now open to the public up to the outbreak of war.) At one of his talks at the camp-fire he had said, 'The quality of true love knows no such distinction as wife and husband, son, father, mother.' This pronouncement was contrary to all that was most passionate in Mother's emotional nature.

There was a cold aridity, a dullness about the idea which repelled me [she was to write in her autobiography]. I could strive to make my love for the few purer, greater, nobler, less possessive, but I did not want to lose it altogether. The normal love of one human being for another seemed to me all at once so warm and precious that it was worth all the agony of pain and separation. My eyes were suddenly opened to the fact that my absorption in Theosophy and Krishna had largely separated me from a wonderful human love. If it had not been for my husband's extraordinary understanding and patience, and his great love, there would long ago have been a complete break up of my home. I now turned to him and found shelter and comfort in him as in no one else. He seemed to understand without words all I was going through and welcomed me back without a single reproach or reminder of how much of our lives together I had wasted.

This new intimacy between them was to be permanent. I am not suggesting that they resumed physical relations. Perhaps he no longer needed sex. Of two things I am convinced – that he was no longer Lady Sackville's lover, whatever their relationship may have been in the past, and that he had no other mistress.

Father and Mother went to India together that winter for the official opening of New Delhi in January 1931, and Mother made no attempt while she was there to see any of her old friends. Since they were together there is no account of the opening from Father. Mother, however, wrote us a full description of it. Edward Hudson was with them and they all stayed at Viceroy's House with the Irwins. 'All is so changed from the last years it is like a dream – the trees grown, the wonderful arch up [the All India War Memorial].' She found it thrilling to drive up the King's Way and see the palace appear, but Baker's 'great crime' was now so glaring that she understood at last 'Father's rage at the spoiling of his life's greatest work by the silly slope'. 'Yet,' she went on, 'this remains a colossal and most wonderful achievement and should make Father's name go down in history as one of the architects of all times. Hudson is so moved that he can hardly keep from tears. He said to me yesterday "Poor old Christopher Wren could never have done this!"'

Mother's understanding of Baker's 'great crime' must have been balm to Father. He had so seldom enjoyed her full sympathy. If he had had more understanding from her over it from the beginning he might perhaps have been less enraged by it. Useless to speculate on it any more than to speculate on how his life and work might have been different had he had a different kind of wife.

That evening there was a dinner party for ninety. The guests assembled in the Durbar Hall and dined in the State dining-room. 'The Viceroy is such a great gentleman,' Mother wrote, 'that all the pomp just slid off him. Even I felt happy and at my ease. Father was indeed lucky to have had such charming and appreciative people as his Viceroy and Vicereine for the inauguration of the House.' Father was afterwards to confess that when leaving the Viceroy's House

284

that year, for good as he thought, he 'had not the nerve to say goodbye to Irwin. I just walked out, and I kissed the walls of the House'.

Mother was rather ill most of the time they were away. On their return it was found that she was suffering from anaemia. The doctor insisted that she should eat meat; she did not protest (except at raw beef sandwiches) because in spite of all her years as a vegetarian she felt the need for it. She never went back to being a vegetarian.

* * *

That year of 1931 the lease of Queen Anne's Gate ran out. Now all the work was combined in a new office at 5 Eaton Gate, where the Cathedral occupied the largest space and the Indian work, consisting now only of buildings for Maharajas, the smallest. It was the beginning of the slump and expected work in England did not materialise. Father would have sold Mansfield Street, which was far too big with four of us married, and Elisabeth still living on her own, if it had not meant selling it at a loss. His new closeness to Mother did not prevent his going out on his own just as frequently; he had a great deal of social life at this time, enjoyed his clubs, and weekend visits, seeing old friends and meeting new ones.

In June, *Country Life* ran a series of four lavishly illustrated weekly articles on Viceroy's House by Robert Byron. A beautifully written editorial at the beginning of the series on 6 June (could it have been by Hudson?) praised the whole conception of New Delhi and particularly Viceroy's House: 'From the sphere of its dome to the filigree of its keys it bears the impress of a single genius and an unremitting care', and ended, 'The English public, intelligent or otherwise, have paid little heed to the birth either of the city or of the house. Even the more enlightened are curiously unaware that a *great*

285

architect, of the calibre of Bernini, Mansard and Wren, is working in their midst, engaged now upon the designs of the new Liverpool Cathedral.'

Robert Byron wrote in his first article: 'The coloured and theatrical façade of Islam has been annexed to a more intellectual three-dimensional tradition of solid form and exact proportion – in the tradition of Europe. The result has been to create one of the great palaces of the world, and the only one erected in the last hundred years.' These articles gave Father enormous pleasure – he referred to them as 'the great excitement of the summer'. The last one ended with an appraisal of the gradient question with diagrams and a photograph showing how 'the ramp' had all but obliterated Viceroy's House with a 'great sheet of asphalt hemmed in by a red sandstone trough'. Byron then made a plea for this great wrong to be righted.

The series finished with an article on 4 July, also by Robert Byron, on Baker's Secretariats, summing up: 'For its manipulation of great masses, his [Baker's] work at New Delhi may justly be celebrated. But, in the opinion of the writer, its detail and ornament, externally and internally, are, at best, commonplace, at worst as bad as anything produced during the last hundred years.' Father commented on this article to Mother who was staying with Ursula at Blagdon: 'It won't help Baker to amend his ways. In Africa when I was there he drew criticisms from me and appeared grateful and keen to learn. He came to Delhi and he was just obstinate and did everything I warned him not to do. I have never been able to fathom or connect the two faces.'

Baker in his memoirs, published in 1944, the year of Father's death, takes it for granted that the 1913 agreement, 'willingly entered into by Lutyens', to set the Secretariats on the same level as Viceroy's House, made it inevitable that the Palace should be obscured in the course of the approach to it; he is quite unrepentant about it. These bland, complacent memoirs, peppered with quotations from the poets, show that he and Father could never have collaborated successfully. The mystery is how they ever became friends in the first place.

On 20 June 1931, an article appeared in *Country Life* by Father himself on 'What I think of Modern Architecture'. He illustrated and discussed five modern buildings – the Water Works at Feltham, Olympia, the New Victoria Cinema, the Bechstein Hall and Yardley's, both in Bond Street. (The Bechstein Hall is now Russell and Bromley at the corner of Conduit Street.) He summed up that it was 'haphazardness, lack of grammar, inconsequence' that he found disturbing in much modern architecture. 'These adventurous young men thrill me tremendously and all my sympathies are with them. But good architecture needs more than bright ideas, and by my traditional standards most modern buildings seem to me to lack style and cohesion, besides being unfriendly and crude.' I think he hit on a good word there: it is the unfriendliness of modern architecture today even more than in the Thirties that makes it so hard to love.

* * *

In July Father told Mother that Francis Smith and Dr Downey's lawyer had drawn up a contract which 'secured the future more than the present as I don't want all my labours to go to Snowdon [Chancellor of the Exchequer] . . . Downey told the Pope that *I*! had put a crucifix up in my office where the Cathedral drawings are being made. The Holy Father's eyes filled with tears!' Mother replied that she was glad he had made a satisfactory arrangement with Downey but she would have thought that Snowdon would have got far more out of death duties than in income tax and 'you will continue to groan about money for the rest of your days'. Father, evidently rather hurt by this, assured her that in making the agreement he was thinking only of *her*.

'My arrangement with the Archbishop is wise I am sure. If I got a dollop of £30,000 or so I should pay on it and the three year average would burst me. Try and realise darling if we were not taxed for the dole I should be able to give Robert and Mary £1,500 a year or £2,000 each and save money too and wouldn't our children love me and you! for it!! Bless you anyway but do have a little patience with me.'

Mother quickly assured him in her turn that by criticising his agreement she had been thinking only of *him*. It seemed so hard that all the money for the Cathedral should go to his children and not to him. 'I want *you* to be free from anxiety and the worry of money.' His agreement with Dr Downey held; he received nothing for his work on the Cathedral until after his death and then it was £10,000.

The bogey of the tax man continued to haunt him. On 23 March of the following year 1932, the eve of 'the last day for tax gatherers', as he put it, he was in a panic because money he had expected to receive for Washington had not yet arrived. However, next day he was able to report, 'Money came in. Not enough but with an overdraft I paid my surtax – £5,800. The cheque was telegraphed from Montreal and I got it in time to satisfy the threat of the tax people. A great relief, but I feel as thin as a moulted sparrow in a snow storm. I have lost what might have been £2,000 a year for ever and ever – R.I.P. . . . The taxes I pay are again taxed as income so the bulk of my tax next year will be in the taxes I paid this year. Tax Vobiscum.'

Mother answered this from Blagdon where she was again staying with Ursula (she often stayed there in the Thirties): 'I don't know what you mean about Income Tax *threat*. Is it a joke or did you really imagine you were going to prison. You must realise why you have got into such a bad position financially in spite of the enormous jobs you have had.' She then went on to lecture him: he had never set money aside for tax or put it on deposit in the bank; if he had become a company it would have saved him thousands. Thomas was no business man; Francis Smith was old and not much use. Euan Wallace had offered to help him some years before but was still waiting for the necessary information. She was now going to take matters into her own hands: they must get rid of Mansfield Street immediately and move into a house they could run with two servants. She was going to give all the servants notice on 1 April and she advised him to pay no more rates after June by which time they ought to have vacated Mansfield Street. She thought he should dismiss James, his chauffeur, and send the car to Blagdon in order to save the expense of running and garaging it.

Father, still unwilling to sell Mansfield Street at a loss, obtained planning permission to make drastic alterations to the house. The racquet court was turned into a kitchen (his original bedroom next door having been the dining-room since 1929). A door was made in the nursery for a tradesmen's entrance from Mansfield Mews, and the rest of the nursery converted into a double garage so that as well as being able to garage his own car he could let the extra space. At the same time Mother moved up to her original bedroom, abandoned her *chowki* and slept once more in the great oak bed. Thus they were 'upstairs' together again at last, though in adjoining rooms. Apart from the front drawing-room and the ground floor morning-room, all the reception rooms were shut up, and to make the house more labour-saving now that the staff had been greatly reduced, gas fires were put in. (Father, at Elisabeth's suggestion, designed some really nice looking fires for the Gas Company, fitting flush with the wall and surrounded by grey marble panels.) Work on the alterations was begun in May.

Father offered the now empty basement with its huge kitchen to Elisabeth. She gave some very good parties there after she moved in. The summer before she had had a work publicly performed for the first time – a ballet called *The*

Birthday of the Infanta – to much critical acclaim and family jubilation.

* * *

In June 1932 Father attended an informal meeting of the Architectural Association at which he answered questions. The first question, of which he had had notice, was *Will you describe the construction and finish of the Dome of the new Liverpool Cathedral and its supports?* To this he gave a long, detailed technical answer. The impromptu questions were answered light-heartedly. *What do you think of the dirt of London?* 'The dirt of London is its glory. Have you ever looked at St Paul's Cathedral when the sun is shining? South-west it is seen to be white, and it becomes coal-black round the north-east side. It would not be half as beautiful if you white-washed the thing.' *What do you think of the future of women in the architectural profession?* 'The future of women in the architectural profession depends on what architect they marry.' This answer was not as flippant as it sounds. He was saying in fact that he did not approve of professional women. Another question was *Is it true that you suggested to a lady in Sussex for whom you designed a house that the nursery should be circular, and when she asked why, you replied, 'In order that the nurse may not put the children in a corner'?* 'It is partly true and partly wrong. It was not in Sussex.' *What do you think of steel furniture?* 'It is the kind of furniture I would not steal. With all due credit to the inventor, I do not see a home with it, there is no place for the cat to hide.' Father loved cats as did Gertrude Jekyll. A house was not a real home to him without a cat. He had one in his office and one in his bungalow at New Delhi but we had never been able to have one at home because Nannie was terrified of them.

I think Father must have had notice of the last question: *Do you enjoy having steel and concrete at your disposal as a medium of architectural expression?* 'I enjoy all construction, and the steel girder with its petticoat of concrete is a most useful ally in the ever recurring advent of difficulty. The thin walls are worth while, if only to watch your Client's face glow with joy at winning a few square feet of carpet. But I crave for the soft thick noiseless walls of hand-made brick and lime, the deep light-reflecting reveals, the double floors, easy stairways, and doorways never less than one foot six inches from a corner ... The time may come when we shall be able to choose girders to our taste, as we select the particular boughs of particular oaks for struts and braces. Then will girders become friendly and personal.'[1]

I am glad he did not live to see what has been perpetrated in London with steel and concrete, and even brick, in the last forty years, and the haphazard building which has resulted in the ridiculing and belittling of some of our most lovely old buildings.

* * *

Not long after this Father was to satisfy a life-long ambition – to see the Parthenon – something he had denied himself in obedience to his self-imposed rule not to go anywhere unless there was a job at the end of it. Now there was no job but an excellent excuse. Knowing that Ursula was going through an unhappy time he suggested that they should go on a Mediterranean cruise together. It would be his first holiday since the Baltic cruise with Miss Dodge in 1906. Father called this time with Ursula their 'Marvellous Marmalade Moon', though his over-developed critical faculty prevented him from enjoying much of what he saw. On 17 August they boarded at Marseilles a French ship of the Messagerie Maritime Line – small, squalid and dirty with 'no nonsense about women

[1] *Architectural Association Journal*, August 1932.

and children first'. Their cabins de luxe had bathrooms but
no water ran from the taps. Their first port of call was Naples
from where, of course, they went to Pompeii, touring the ruins
for three hours.

Oh! how tiring [Father wrote to Mother]; and each ruined
house was a bloody and near relation to the next and the
one before, while intermittent obscenities gave the glad eye
to the gentlemen of the party. Poor Ursie was not allowed to
share these voluptuous pleasures. The people of Pompeii
must have been a Ramsgate sort of Le Touquet. The whole
place has a horrible atmosphere of decadence, bad taste
and unintelligence. A pleasure seeking, rich and odious
people – though their pornographies were probably more
boring than the Guide would have us believe ... The Temple of Isis was particularly horrible, both its atmosphere
and in its hotch-potch of ill assorted pattern weaving.

Their next stop was Piraeus, the port of Athens. Father
was looking forward with intense excitement to seeing the
Parthenon:

We went ashore about 8.30 a.m. and drove through the
modern Athens – ugly, squalid, uninteresting, jerry-built,
Bungaloid growth. We got out at the foot of the Acropolis and walked up to the Parthenon – the Parthenon!!
The most tragic spot I have ever visited – bare, barren
and Waterloo of the waterless. Tourist ridden and the
Parthenon so knocked about as to become unpleasant
– heartbreaking to see, the utter valuelessness of all
human endeavour that one could acclaim an Austin 7
full of belching motorists as the one permanent symbol
we have left.
   The Parthenon was there – all I knew it to be was there
– but oh so little of it left. No one silhouette was perfect.

The restorations that are being attempted are woeful. It is a glorious remnant of what has never at its best been more than a unit. Perfect in itself and its ruin is by its achievement the more disastrous to its being. It has no relation to its site – no dramatic sense such as the Romans had. The site must have been chosen by extraneous causes – the settling of an eagle, a prophet's dream? I looked at it for long and got, the more I looked, the more depressed. The design is full of cunning and requires months of patient labour with accurate instruments to determine the method prompting its design . . . Destroyed for its beauty by man, as God surely destroyed Pompeii for its bestiality.

A day in Istanbul came next. The guide insisted on taking them to mosque after mosque when they declared that all they wanted to see was St Sophia. 'There was a particularly grotesque mosque – the "Blue Mosque" in that it was veneered with blue bathroom tiles and some blue paint. One of its proclaimed merits was that the dome was five metres higher than St Sophia and it had a wonderful echo. Also that the architect could neither read nor write. Oh! Shades of Tickner, the hedge carpenter of the Surrey bye-ways! He could neither read nor write – but this damned Turk couldn't build, and no amount or reading or writing could have helped him.'

At last to St Sophia which Father knew from its plans.

. . . and there she was – her marbles dulled by neglect and great Turkish escutcheons of Mahomed's relatives covering all salient points, and the skew-wiff carpets destroy all architectural presence. Lovely details – panelled marbles of too much variety, had all been polished.

Some extraordinarily childish, from a design point of view; the caps of the pilasters terminating the colonnades – just eked out to fit. Wren would have had a Roman fit. And the geometry of some of the vaulting in the angles of the main octagon was curiously uninventive. They had craftsmen, a patron, a great geometric idea – but in that, as the guides reported – it was built in seven years with three architects, it looks as though, in an intellectual way, it might have been built by seven architects in three years. Ursy remains my great and greatest solace – patient, cheerful, and translates the humanities with thoughtful humour.

They sat there for half an hour and 'looked and enjoyed the great "motif" in her Moslem weeds'. There was an American in their party who 'went about with a cinema kodak weighing 36lb' and irritated Father by keeping them waiting while he took 'a movie of a dilapidated Turkish Cemetery which nothing could have moved for centuries except slow decay . . . Anything particularly still, like an empty mosque, he at once, with the avidity of a mosquito, "movies" it.'

Rhodes, Cyprus, Beyrout, Baalbek, Damascus, Nazareth were all visited and described, and then a three hour drive took them to Jerusalem where they were delighted to spend the night in the luxury of the King David Hotel after the primitive plumbing of the ship. After lunch, to the Garden of Gethsemane – 'A backyard of a garden with a few very old olive trees said to be 2,000 years old. A hideous modern church built over the Rock of Agony. It was an appalling church with a bare rock railed in before the altar; and there were three terrible pictures of the Agony – one in each apse. The rest of the church was in mosaic. A would-be Byzantine affair.' The only 'good things' in Jerusalem, according to Father, were the Convent of the Ecco Homo and the War Cemetery designed by Sir John Burnet – beautifully kept –

'a relief after the slop and squalor that surged elsewhere around'. This shows that he could appreciate fine work by his contemporaries. Almost the worst building was the 'towered abortion' Kaiser William had built for himself which 'God had done his best to destroy by an earthquake'; the very worst, the Young Men's Christian Association building, nearing completion, with the tallest tower in the city 'and so lacking in a sense of humour that flanking the great phallic [sic] – obviously circumcised – are two round domed structures . . . Two thousand years hence its ruins will be unearthed and gentlemen will be shown it secretly, with hushed, indecent whispers; while women are kept away, and they will wonder what strange cult was practised in the YMCA.'

He found that the Church of the Holy Sepulchre revealed the Church of Christ as 'a fetish worshipping superstition mongering . . . savagely unintelligent institution'.

The church, in worshipping the Body of Christ in stones they think he touched (though no one discovered them for 500 years) have entirely lost sight of his spirit and neglected the message he had to give. How he would have hated and loathed and cried out against it all – the worship of idols with armed soldiers to keep the peace of God . . . How impressive would it have been had Calvary been a bare hillside, with no ornament or structure to hide his last vision of earth. Instead, another Church, with altars here and altars there. How convenient that the prison where Christ sat in the stocks waiting for his Cross, that the last few Stations of the Cross, Calvary, where he died, the Sepulchre, and the spot where the angel appeared to Mary Magdalene and the Stone of Anointing, are all so close together that one building covers the lot! It would be pathetic in its childishness if one's blood did not boil at the sacrilege of it; at the betrayal of all Christ tried to give.

How much Father must have thought about his own Cathedral while he was going round these holy places . . . And so to Jaffa, Port Said, and then Cairo by train. 'The Pyramids haven't changed since 1916 and the Sphinx has been marred by the uncovering of its base and paws. Its mystery flown! And mosques! After seeing half a dozen of them they become as tiresome as mosquitoes.'

At the end of the cruise, Father wrote this loving tribute in the joint diary he and Ursula had kept:

AVIS TO TRAVELLERS
Receipt against boredom and other ills:
Take, without dilution, large doses
of Ursie, and continue the process.
An intoxicant that has no evil effects
And stimulates the heart.

CHAPTER EIGHTEEN

Father and Son Together
1932–1938

It was not long after Father and Ursula got back from the cruise that Miss Jekyll's brother, Sir Herbert, died at the beginning of October 1932. Father went to the funeral and reported to Mother that it had been 'horribly moving'. Afterwards he saw 'Bumps, self-possessed and herself – very feeble she was in her bedroom with a delicious dark blue felt cap on her head [sketch] . . . She misses Herbert terribly as every day she had problems to set him and an hour's daily affairs.' This was Father's last meeting with Gertrude Jekyll. He had given her an invalid-chair a few years before which made a great difference to her comfort. She died on 8 December, shortly after her eighty-ninth birthday. She was buried beside Herbert in the churchyard of St John the Baptist at Busbridge near Munstead. Father designed their memorial. When he visited Munstead Wood eight months later he found it sad to see how soon the garden had 'collapsed – but it can't be helped. No Bumps and no longer the 11 essential gardeners'.

Lady Jekyll lent Munstead Wood to Elisabeth in the summer of 1933, and in the autumn she lent it to me as I have already related. Elisabeth had been married in February 1933 to Ian Glennie, a professional singer. They had very little money but no rent for the first few years because they lived in the basement at Mansfield Street. I believe Father was giving Elisabeth the same allowance as he was giving me. Father said that all she needed now in the basement was 'a little son and air'. This was vouchsafed to her in less than a year. Barbie now had three sons, Robert one and Ursula two. Father told me that if I did not have a baby soon I would be in a bathchair by the time I was forty. I replied with truth that I did not intend to have one until I could afford an old-fashioned nannie to look after it. This might be quite soon, for Anthony was beginning to do well. A loan of £1,000 from Euan Wallace had enabled him to buy a seat on the Stock Exchange; he had joined a very good firm and had been given accounts by the Midland Bank, Baring's and Reuter's through the kindness of Reginald McKenna, Cecil Baring and Roderick Jones. My first novel *Forthcoming Marriages* was published by Murray in August 1933 after three others had been turned down by various publishers. It was a success. I do not know whether Father actually read it but he was delighted with the praise it received which he was quick to pass on to me in Italy where I had gone, accompanied by Mother, to recover from a bad illness. It was very pleasant to bask in his approbation, to feel he was proud of me.

* * *

On 5 June 1933, the foundation stone of the Cathedral had been solemnly laid and building begun on the crypt, which was finished in 1941. In October 1933 Father went to Rome with Dr Downey to have the Cathedral plans approved and blessed by the Pope who was particularly pleased that the Lady Chapel was to be built first. After being received in audience, the plans were produced to be 'vetted ritualistically' and were pronounced by His Holiness to be 'wonderful and perfect'. 'I seem to have known all and every particular of the adoration of Our Lady,' Father told Mother. 'This comes from having a wife I love! So I know instinctively how to hail Mary.'

Shortly before this Father had written to Mother about Robert and the Cathedral:

> If he would take an interest in my Cathedral and my creed of building – and that would entail an absorbing study of the methods of great masters – I should dearly love to appoint him my successor as architect of the Cathedral. It would or may mean more in money to him than to me . . . Anyway I have a chance of influencing the coming generation – a torch to keep our 2000 year tradition – just alive.

Here were signs of the complete reconciliation that was to take place before long between Father and Robert to their mutual satisfaction. So far, Robert's only architectural work had been to make alterations in 1929 to Barbie's new house, 19 Hill Street, under Father's supervision – a project Father had considered 'great fun'. In 1933 he was to help Father with the building of the Drum Inn at Cockington near Torquay. It was not long after this that he set up in architectural practice with a qualified and experienced architect, Harold Greenwood, as his partner. He himself never passed an examination.

* * *

In 1934 a large model of the Cathedral was exhibited at the Academy and then housed for a time in the front drawing-room at Mansfield Street. H.S.G. Butler described how he once walked back with Lutyens to Mansfield Street after some dinner and Lutyens asked him in and explained the model to him. 'My meeting with him on that occasion, which took place at midnight was an extraordinarily moving experience,' Butler recalled, 'because for once at least he was deadly serious, and kept asking me whether I agreed and whether I liked this and that with an enchanting humility.'[1]

Father received an honorary degree of Doctor of Law at Oxford in 1934. His other association with Oxford was the building of Campion Hall for the Jesuits. This began in an unfortunate way. Plans for the building had already been prepared by a young architect, but they were not satisfactory. Father, on the advice of Lady Horner, was called in by Father D'Arcy to give an opinion of them. When he pronounced them 'Queen Anne in front and Mary Anne behind' he was asked to recommend another young architect. Instead, he offered to do the work himself. The first architect then accused him of unprofessional conduct and he was called up before the Disciplinary Committee of the RIBA. Although he was exonerated from the charge, it was felt by many of his fellow architects that he would poach commissions whenever he could. But as we know from what he wrote at the time of Robert's marriage, he looked upon the professional world as an arena in which a man had to fight for his livelihood. He would not have liked it if some other architect had seized work from under his nose but he would have regarded it as the victory of one gladiator over another – the triumph of professionalism.

In 1935 Father was appointed consultant and architectural adviser to Sir Charles Bressey in preparing the Highway Development Survey for the needs of Greater London for the next thirty years. This resulted in the publication three years later of the Bressey-Lutyens Report. On 3 September 1935, he flew over London in connection with this survey and wrote to Mother that evening. 'I have TODAY been up in the Air!! I flew and have flown. A fact. Gosh! how good to come

[1]*Architectural Association Journal*, March 1959.

home to earth – my own darling darling Emmie [crossed out] I mean Earth. I know and appreciate your heavenly quality – but you are mine in the humbler sphere: for in Heaven! God will claim you – and then I ask you? Where shall I be?'

So much of Father's work in the Thirties consisted of designing memorials. In 1933 there was the memorial in the church in the Park at Knebworth for Antony Knebworth who was killed in an aeroplane accident, and, in the same year, for Cimmie, Oswald Mosley's first wife, who had been Barbie's great friend at Thorpeness. In 1934 Cecil Revelstoke died and Father designed his memorial as he had done that of his wife at Lambay; in 1936 came the George V memorial at Windsor, and, later, the tomb of the King in conjunction with Reid Dick in St George's Chapel at Windsor. The fountains in Trafalgar Square which he designed in 1937 were memorials to Lord Beatty and Lord Jellicoe. In 1937 Lady Jekyll joined Herbert and Gertrude in the churchyard at Busbridge, the three of them resting side by side with Father's memorial behind their gravestones. He also designed a commemorative screen for them inside the church. And Lord Wimborne's memorial came this year – and many, many more in that decade.

But Father could bring wit even to gravestones. Lord Birkenhead, who died in 1930, once told him that if it had not been for the Washington Embassy, certain features of which he disliked, he would have asked him to design his memorial. 'That's a pity,' Father replied, 'because I've got a good idea for it.' 'What's that?' 'A rolling stone.' And when Lord Inchcape died in 1932 Father said that R.I.P. & O should be engraved on his headstone, and he made a drawing of it.

In January 1936 Lady MacSack's increasingly unhappy and eccentric life came to an end. In 1932 she had quarrelled bitterly with McNed. In May that year he told Mother that he had received 'a killing letter from MacSack' asking him for

£500, 'only 1% of the £50,000 she knows I have had for all the trouble I have given her'. He was probably not aware that at this time she was trying to make as much trouble for him as possible in letters to Sir Giles Scott, President of the RIBA. They are the letters of a woman scorned, hatefully vindictive; McNed had been neglecting her; he no longer tolerated being 'sent to his basket' and then running back to her wagging his tail when she condescended to let him out. Five of these letters have been preserved.[1] In the first, undated, she asked Sir Giles whether he would like to buy for the RIBA for only £500 the portrait of Lutyens by Augustus John which, she said, she had *had* to buy. (This was the unfinished portrait she had given £100 for because she liked it. The RIBA did not buy it. It was sold at auction after the war and acquired by our family.) 'I am sure you would like to have the portrait of your great artist however much I detest the man as you know for his dishonesty to me.' In the second letter, dated 3 June 1932, she wrote of 'the *arch*-extravagant Sir E. Lutyens'; and in a P.S., 'Beware of Sir E.L. No more false and dishonest man has ever existed. I have had a terrible awakening. He may go to prison someday – I can't tell you in a letter what a *Cad* he is—.' Evidently she was bombarding McNed with letters which he did not always answer. Still as vindictive in September, she was accusing him of stealing her furniture, even of snatching a mirror from the wall and dashing with it to his car, knowing that her heart was too weak to stop him. Then followed a list of things which she declared she had only *lent* to him, adding, 'I could go on forever, but you can judge how that clever man can be a horrid and dishonest CAD. I don't wonder that some of his colleagues hate him. I do.' In one of her three surviving letters to McNed, dated February 1927, she asked him to leave back in his will to Vita

[1]By Sir Giles's son, Richard Gilbert Scott, with whose kind permission the following passages are quoted.

all the things she had given him and to say that she had only lent them to him for life, in order to save death duties. How she thought this would save death duties I cannot imagine.

In October 1932, after selling at a loss yet another house she had bought on Streatham Common, which McNed had altered for her, she wrote to Sir Giles complaining that Sir Edwin had had 'the audacity to send her bills from the builder of £11,000 with his entire approval'. And in the last letter, dated 9 December 1932, she complained that the builder had sent her a writ 'approved by Sir Edwin for a perfectly unknown amount for £250' for the Streatham house. She would like 'to fight Sir Edwin in the witness box'. He was making her ill, she declared, increasing her blindness and reducing her blood pressure to 100 so that her heart was weaker than ever.

I have no idea how much credence Sir Giles gave to these accusations, nor how far he realised that the poor woman was mad. She took care to flatter him lavishly in every letter. They must have done McNed some harm, I feel, especially when she wrote in her letter of 9 December, 'There is not a good architect in England that I should have liked had I listened to the abuse that was heaped upon all of you.'

Father felt only deep compassion for her and would probably have continued to do so even if he had known of her letters to Sir Giles. He went on visiting her loyally if infrequently to the end. I hope her feelings had softened towards him before she died. She had no memorial. She was cremated and her ashes scattered out to sea at her own request. There was no memorial either for Granny Lytton when she died in 1936, aged ninety-five; she had chosen to be interred in the family mausoleum in the Park at Knebworth beside her husband.

Our beloved Nannie died of cancer of the liver in 1937. Happily she died at Mansfield Street and not in hospital, looked after by Mother and a nurse for some exhausting months. Afterwards Mother wrote to Father, 'So much of my life goes with her – intimacies with the children which she alone shared – details of my life which she alone knew' – and then as if she feared he might be jealous, she added, 'I mean silly little things.' Father designed for her in the churchyard at Knebworth what I consider to be his most beautiful and moving headstone depicting five angels – the five Lutyens children she had brought up.

In October 1935 when my baby was born it was Nannie who had found for me a treasure of a nannie of her own calibre in a grey coat and skirt who never wanted a day off. Anthony by this time had his own stockbroking firm and we had moved into an imposing five-storey house, 54 Rutland Gate, which we could not really afford and were able to furnish properly only up to drawing-room level. Anthony felt it was necessary to have such an establishment to impress clients. To me it was a nightmare. My baby, Amanda, was the first grand-daughter after seven grandsons. Father was enchanted with her. For a birthday present he gave her a large medicine bottle filled with silver threepenny bits, labelled 'Shake before Take'.

I took Amanda to Mansfield Street to see Father as often as I could. She loved him as much as he loved her. It gave me a vicarious thrill to see this growing bond between them – a relationship I had altogether missed with him. Later on he was to write for her one of his longest and most enchanting picture letters. In the war, in 1942, she sent him from the country a picture of some red dog-roses which inspired him to invent a pack of rose dogs to hunt the foxglove. As well as the pack and the fox with gloves on his feet, he made a drawing of himself on his 'peony', and of some of the other riders – Miss Lily Waters, Miss Tree on her chestnut 'Conqueror', an acrobatic lady riding on her mare's tail, Mr Lion – a dandy at hunt balls – Miss Primula

Primrose, the two Miss Whych Elms, Lords and Ladies and so on through most of the field for several pages of delicious coloured illustrations.

* * *

These years in the middle and late Thirties before the war were very active ones for Father. He went several times to Dublin in connection with the War Memorial he was building in Phoenix Park and to France for the opening of the war cemeteries as well as frequently visiting country houses to stay with old or new friends. He had gained confidence at last, writing to Mother on 8 August 1936, after attending the opening ceremony of Vimy Ridge, the Canadian War Memorial, designed by a Canadian sculptor – a grand occasion with the King and the French President there – that it was 'thrilling – various men I was frightened of are now beginning to grow into my best friends'. Before going to France for this ceremony Robert had told him that he must get his hair cut – 'so I got Miss Webb to do it with the office scissors'.

His letters at this time are brief and light-hearted. After a visit in August 1936, to Lord and Lady Palmer at Crowhurst Place he had written that when their 'wonderful gramophone' played *Sylphides* on Saturday evening he had got up and danced – '. . . you know my ballet? dancing for an hour. I did all the parts . . . it was a huge success which was in itself embarrassing and to day I am so stiff I can hardly move! You will feel relief no doubt of not having been there.'

* * *

In 1936 Father and Robert were to join forces. The year before Father had at last parted company with Thomas. Several people had been telling him for a long time that Thomas was taking advantage of the arrangement they had made from the beginning whereby in lieu of a proper salary Thomas might do work on his own account in his spare time, using Lutyens designs. Father was reluctant to believe it. Barbie remembers an occasion when Father, under pressure from Mother, decided to tackle him. He came home jubilant: 'I asked him straight out, "Thomas, are you cheating me?" He said, "No, Sir Edwin." What more can a man say?' But now at last Father was forced to believe that Thomas was spending too much time on his own work. Father did not attempt to fill his place. Instead, Robert and his partner came to fill the empty rooms at Eaton Gate.

Robert had now done work for the Rank family and for Marks and Spencer. In 1935 his firm had designed the Marks and Spencer headquarters in Baker Street – a most ambitious building which Father pronounced 'very good' – and also their shop, the Pantheon, in Oxford Street. On the strength of this work he was asked to build a new house for Lord Jersey, Middleton Park, near Bicester, Oxfordshire, in consultation with his father. Father had far the larger share in this collaboration, as Robert was quick to admit. It was the last of Father's great country houses and one of the largest – designed for a way of life that was soon to disappear – with dozens of bathrooms, rooms for visiting maids and valets and four separate little houses for staff. Father and Robert collaborated well, especially over the interior, for Robert had a far greater sense of comfort than Father had ever had. Their new association was a blessing to them both, especially at the beginning of the war when Eva went to Canada with her son. They drew very close then.[1]

[1]It was Robert who designed Father's simple memorial tablet in the crypt of St Paul's where his ashes were buried after a funeral service in Westminster Abbey.

CHAPTER NINETEEN

'Silence – Just Silence'
1938–1944

Father had never expected to go to India again after the official opening of New Delhi in 1931. But he was to go once more, his nineteenth voyage, in 1938. Lord Willingdon had succeeded Lord Irwin as Viceroy in 1931. At first Lady Willingdon had written to Father that she was delighted with everything in Viceroy's House; then rumours began to reach him that she was making alterations, structural as well as decorative. Her favourite colour was mauve which led Father to call her 'a *mauvais sujet*'. He was not afraid to protest to her by letter, telling her that if she owned the Parthenon she would add a bay window to it. Lord Linlithgow became Viceroy in 1936 and two years later asked Father to go to Delhi and restore the House to its 1931 condition.

In October Father travelled out with the Linlithgows who gave him details of Lady Willingdon's crimes. Before proceeding to Delhi he went to Jaipur to inspect the site for a processional arch which, the year before, Robert had been commissioned to build for the Maharaja of Jaipur. Robert had gone out there and asked whether his Father might collaborate with him in the work. (The plans for this arch, signed by their joint initials, were never executed.) Robert had been to Delhi and was afterwards to declare that

Viceroy's House was 'the most beautiful secular building ever built'.[1]

Bombay was extremely hot and humid when Father arrived there; in contrast it was bitterly cold in the train during the overnight journey to the station for Jaipur. He arrived feverish and by the time he had driven three hours to Jaipur itself he was delirious. He was put to bed in the excellent State hospital, and a telegram was sent to Mother from the Maharaja informing her that he had pneumonia. It was his first bad illness since his rheumatic fever as a boy. Barbie and Robert prepared to fly out to him, but by 1 November the crisis had passed and he was considered to be out of danger. Six cables were sent altogether on behalf of the Maharaja, reporting his progress. It was a weary time in the hospital for him, enlivened by visits from the Maharaja's children for whom he drew pictures of tigers and elephants.

By 10 November he was considered well enough to travel to Delhi accompanied by the two nurses who had attended him in his illness 'night and day, wet and dry'. He stayed at Viceroy's House. 'My thrill to be here gave me a choke,' he told Mother, 'and perhaps being a little on the weak side tears are very near the surface.' It was altogether a nostalgic visit during which he was thankful to be able to put right Lady Willingdon's 'vagarous vagaries'. 'It is amazing,' he wrote, 'her ingenuity to destroy tidiness . . . and to make riot and vulgarity . . . I start home to day week so in three weeks time I shall be HOMEMILY. Darling you did write me such a darling darling letter.' This must have been a letter Mother had written to him on hearing of his illness. Unfortunately it is missing. On his way to Bombay he was writing again, 'I have been asked to write the whole history of designing and building of New Delhi right from 1912. You will have to help me . . . until 1931 when I walked out and kissed a wall

[1] Address to the Arts Workers Guild, 1970.

of the House. I have since rubbed the place very gently with
my pocky-hanky—!' Alas, he never got far with writing this
account. It was something he and Mother could have done
together, something she could really have helped him with.

I doubt whether Father ever fully recovered from this illness. A few days after he arrived home in December 1938 he
was elected President of the Royal Academy. He was only the
third architect to hold that office. The honour, he said, was
as great a surprise to him as if he had been elected Pope.
Herbert Baker, with whom he had remained on frigid terms
since his Bakerloo, had generously written to him when his
name came up for election: 'I should like to vote for you for
the sake of our old friendship which I enjoyed so much; and
forget all the soreness and the harm – as one must in the
assurance and peace of old age.' Father accepted the olive
branch even if he did not seize it. In his reply he signed
himself 'ever as once was, Ned Lutyens'.

In the February after his election, a month before his sev-
entieth birthday, a dinner party was given for him and some
of his family at the Café Royal by present and past members of
his office staff and some old pupils and assistants. In thanking
them he said he would like to call them his children only that
would involve too many explanations to his wife. Instead, he
would call them his mothers, for one and all had given their
life blood to him and to his interests.

As P.R.A. Father relied greatly on Walter Lamb, the Secretary. At Council meetings he would whisper to him, 'Am I
doing all right?' In his speech at the Academy Banquet on 27
April 1939, he began by saying, 'The Lamb is my shepherd I
shall not want.' He went on to speak of the work by younger
artists exhibited that year: 'All great art is secret, and can only
speak through its own medium. So who am I to lay down
the law, beyond a prayer for sincerity? The most untutored
may hold honest convictions. Therein lies his strength: in the
fact that he *does* not know – that he does *not know*.' Much of

his speech was taken up with an appeal to the Government and to private benefactors 'to finance a School to promote a philosophy of real beauty'. He wished to reconstitute the Academy School of Architecture, at which he had begun to teach in 1914, and institute a Prize of London like the Prix de Rome to enable the winners to 'live the spacious life and research into those absolute values in which aesthetics and science could merge'.

This was the only Academy Banquet he presided over. The war came to put a stop to all public entertaining. Anticipating the war he gave up Eaton Gate in May 1939 and moved his and Robert's offices to Mansfield Street. At the same time he converted the main bedroom floor there into a flat for Mother and himself. Elisabeth now had a house of her own in Chelsea so the Tribes came to live in the basement as caretakers.

Euan Wallace, now Minister of Transport, was certain war was coming. He therefore put a country house at Mother's disposal early in 1939. He had sold his Scottish estate in 1936 and bought Lavington Park, near Petworth in Sussex. Lavington had been the parish of Henry Manning before he went over to Rome, and Beechwood, the house Euan lent Mother, close to the big house, had been Manning's rectory. Mother took her own servants to Beechwood, and for the first year of the war she made a home there for Amanda and her nannie and for Elisabeth's children and their nannie (Elisabeth now had twin daughters as well as a son). Lavington Park became a maternity home on the outbreak of war.

Father and Mother wrote to each other every day while she was at Beechwood. He spent an occasional weekend with her and she went up occasionally to London for a night. 'My darling,' she wrote after one such visit, 'it is such fun when I come up to you, like an improper adventure with a strange man in a strange flat.'

310

'War! it's come,' Father wrote on 3 September. Nearly all his office staff had already joined up. 'Miss Webb is staunch. I shall go on: something may turn up for me to do'; and next day, 'Money out-look bad – as nobody pays – all work stops – I feel rather stranded.' And on the 10th, 'My drawing board is a comfort to me and I can get lost in problems of my own initiative – all work has stopped, Cathedral goes on. Delhi Federal Council is absorbing.' These were the Delhi Federal Law Courts he was designing. Another project he could lose himself in at that time was the reconstruction of the Liria Palace in Madrid for the Duke of Alba which had been badly damaged in the Civil War. The Duke of Peñaranda had been killed in the Civil War.

On 18 October Father sent Mother a statement of his financial position. He had been having great trouble getting money in every month. 'Miss Webb harries people to pay up which is bad for ones credit in the bigger world.' In these circumstances he intended to ask Baring's to sell out his investments which brought in £900 a year (this shows that his savings had dwindled to about £18,000) and pay him so much a month so that he would be able to forget these monthly worries and anxieties, and then all the money that did come in he could save. Mother replied that he must do whatever would give him peace of mind. The little grey Rolls had now been tucked up in the garage never to be used by Father again and to be sold after the war. It was now that Elisabeth's allowance was reduced and mine stopped altogether. Barbie tells me that she never took anything from Father, and Ursula, the only one of us to have a settlement, now relinquished that income. I do not know about Robert.[1]

[1]After his death Father's assets for probate were £42,271. This included Mansfield Street and its contents and the £10,000 for the Liverpool Cathedral. Mother was his sole beneficiary and sole executrix.

311

The war brought my parents closer to each other than they had been since their engagement. Mother, who saw to it that Father had a letter from her every morning which was brought up by Tribe with his breakfast, hated to be parted from him at such a time but felt that she was doing a job by looking after the children and knew that he would be bored at Beechwood. She was as happy as she could be in the circumstances, sawing wood, weeding and reading to the children. He had written to her on 29 September:

> My own sweet darling, I have never loved you more or admired you so much for your calm generous bravery and patience. It is all terribly anxious and times will be hard and cruel – but oddly enough I have not for a long time been so happy in you and with you and your devotion to *our* children and grandchildren just blazes me with pride in you and devotion to you – darling how can I say how much I admire you and how great my love is for you.

And on 17 October after a visit to Beechwood he was writing:

> My own most darling. Your letter came like a halo and I feel blessed. Bless you greatly. I do not think I have ever loved you more than I do now or want you with me more, or to be with you more. I have always loved you – a rose bud perhaps in my button hole – but now you have opened to a glorious flower the best I have ever seen – your petals so gay and a scent of all that is heavenly withall. We may have great tribulations ahead of us but my love, your love, our love will transcend it

all. My thoughts are with you always. My darling, God! how I love you. I am ever your adoring Nedi my sweet heart Emmy.

And next day, the day on which he sent her his financial statement, confessing that he was going to ask Baring's to sell his shares, he continued, 'Another thing I have to confess to you! I have fallen in love again – it's a warming and exhilarating experience. She is such a darling if you knew what I know . . . I'll give you my darling – my own darling – one guess as to who she is!'

Mother had small vexations at Beechwood with quarrelling children and servants. Father begged her to tell him every anxiety and misery, however insignificant, because he wanted to share everything with her.

*　　*　　*

Robert had joined the Balloon Section of the Auxiliary Air Force at the beginning of the war when Eva went to Canada. He was stationed at a Group Headquarters in Cleveland Street, quite close to Mansfield Street, so he was able frequently to visit Father who now had his drawing-board in the front drawing-room which he used as his personal office. In the winter of 1939 the Royal Academy Planning Committee had been set up 'to study the architectural problems which would arise in the development of London after the war'. According to Austen Hall, the Hon. Secretary, this Committee had been formed because

all Lutyens's work had stopped and for the first time in his life he had nothing to do. He had only one hope, the cathedral at Liverpool, but the authorities there would not agree to the drawings going on, so here was this great man utterly unemployed and desperately unhappy. Some of his friends got together and said, 'This is impossible; let's start something.' We suggested to him, therefore, that he should continue to develop the Bressey-Lutyens plan of which he was joint author.[1]

The scheme won the co-operation of the London County Council, the King, the Minister of Transport (naturally, since he was Euan Wallace) and, above all, Lord Keynes. Reginald Blomfield, who was against the scheme, asked Keynes how it was to be paid for. Keynes replied, 'Sir Reginald, how are we paying for the war?' 'I don't know,' Blomfield replied; 'Exactly. Give us something worth paying for and we will find the money.'[2] Unfortunately very little of the Lutyens plan was used but Austen Hall maintained that the meetings at the Academy connected with it 'were the breath of life to him in his last years'.[3]

Although work on the Liverpool Cathedral was suspended during the war Father never stopped working on it, for luckily he did not know that nothing would ever be built of it except the crypt; therefore I do not think he was as unhappy as Austen Hall made out. Moreover, his closeness to Mother gave him great joy. The original estimate of £3,000,000 for the Cathedral had risen by 1953 to £17,000,000. The Lutyens plans had to be abandoned. A competition for a new Cathedral was held in 1959, one of the specifications being that the new building must be linked with the crypt. Out of three hundred entrants it was won by Frederick Gibberd, the architect of London Airport and Harlow New Town. There could hardly be a greater contrast than between the two architects.

[1] *Architectural Association Journal*, March 1959.
[2] Ibid.
[3] The first instalment of the plan, *London Replanned*, was published by *Country Life* in October 1942; the second, *Road, Rail and River*, in July 1945.

In April 1940 Father had another very bad attack of pneumonia and a thrombosis. He went to Beechwood in May to
convalesce. I have a happy snapshot of him taken during
this visit, reclining on the grass with Mother in a deck-chair
beside him. A wreath of artificial flowers which Amanda had
worn as a bridesmaid is placed askew on the top of his head.
When he returned to London he found it hard at first to get
back to work. His brain was tired for the first time in his
life. He was soon busy again, though, with drawings for the
Cathedral – work, he wrote, that could 'last the century'.

When the blitz started at the end of the summer of 1940
Robert and Mother were worried about his remaining at
Mansfield Street at night. Robert begged him to go and sleep
at the Langham Hotel where he himself was now sleeping.
But Father was fatalistic – 'You get it – or not! wherever you
are' – and he preferred to remain in his own house; indeed he
had a bet with Robert that the basement at Mansfield Street
was safer than the Langham. On the night of 16 September,
during a very bad raid which had forced Father down to the
basement, there was a long ringing at the front door. Tribe
answered it to find Robert on the doorstep with a friend. The
Langham had been hit by a bomb which had not exploded
but the hotel had been evacuated. Robert's friend was Joe
Links, who was with him in Balloons and afterwards at the
Air Ministry. I had not at this time so much as heard his name
but he was to become my second husband in 1945.

By the end of September Mother and Robert had persuaded Father that it was his duty to keep out of London
– he was not needed for the war effort and was in danger
of becoming an unnecessary casualty. He refused, however,
to go anywhere that was not within commuting distance of
London. Then he went to Knebworth for the day to see

the Lyttons and returned with the preposterous, though apparently serious, proposition that he and Mother should go and live in a caravan in the Knebworth grounds. Mother declared on 24 September that she was 'tickled to death' by the idea. Miss Webb went down to look at the caravan so that she could pass on to Mother all she would need to know about it. Presumably they were to have their meals at the big house since Mother knew no more about cooking than how to make tea. Father wrote touchingly to her on 26 September of his joy at the prospect of their being together again: 'I do so want to spoil you – smoking shall go if it in any way distresses you my darling, my darling. I must try and spoil you and be all to you that you could wish and ever pray for.' He then drew a sketch of where the caravan was situated.

I do not know what lucky chance prevented them from carrying out this crazy caravan escapade. Instead, Mother rented in October a small house near Ripley in Surrey – Ockham Mill belonging to Lady Stokes, mother of the artist Adrian Stokes, which was easily accessible from London by car or Green Line bus. Father stayed mostly in London but went to Ockham for the weekends and occasional nights in the week. He described the house as 'an architect's holiday – nothing fits – only hides itself in unexpected places. It reminds me of those old fashioned ladies who have great charm but are quite worthless.' The house was indeed charming which made up for any architectural defects, and the garden even more so with the mill stream wandering through it. The house was furnished in good taste and was nice and shabby with old chintzes and walls of that shade of green that only comes from years of fading. It was the nearest they ever came to the 'little white house' of the casket (it was white outside). Mother had always longed to live in the country and this was the first country house she had been mistress of. She had just two servants which had always been her ideal number. She too had now taken to playing patience as well as becoming a *Times* crossword addict. I like to remember them as I saw them on more than one occasion sitting opposite each other at Ockham Mill with the card table drawn up close to the warmth of a good log fire, laying out their respective patiences in silent and harmonious serenity.

* * *

In February of the following year, 1941, a family tragedy befell us in the death of Euan Wallace who had been a fairy godfather to us all. It was the first of a series of tragedies for Barbie who was to lose two sons of her own as well as her two stepsons before those ghastly war years were over. In 1945, though, she was married again happily to Herbert Agar, the American historian.

In the New Year Honours List of 1942 Father received the Order of Merit, the first time an architect had been accorded this honour. He never had occasion to wear it. I rather believe he had expected a peerage because I once heard him say that it was a pity that the title of Mansfield had already been taken. How he would have enjoyed designing his armorial bearings. In 1938 he had asked Sir Arthur Cochrane, Clarenceux King of Arms, to make out his father's pedigree. It was then that Bartholomew Lutyens's naturalisation papers had come to light.

By the spring of 1942 the raids had ceased; Mother gave up Ockham Mill and returned to London. By this time Father had developed a persistent cough which was to become increasingly troublesome. Once, when Robert was driving him down to Ockham, they had run into a stationary vehicle. No one had been injured but it was a great shock to Father. He tried to joke his cough away by attributing it to having swallowed his spectacles at the impact of the accident. He was always gallant, hiding in public his anxieties and increasing feeling of weakness. Christopher Hussey recalls an afternoon in the spring of 1942 looking in on him in his room at Burlington House where he was bent over plans for London: 'In the courtyard, the band of the American unit, recently arrived, was playing rousing music. Lutyens, with beaming face, seized me round the waist and waltzed me halfway round the room, with much the same *élan*, I suppose, that forty-five years before had astonished his future wife in Victorian drawing-rooms.' Yes, and it was with this same *élan* that he had kicked his legs to 'Ta-ra-ra-Boom-de-ay' in Delhi and danced the *Valse Mignon* to Lady Sackville and the polka on board ship on his way to New York ('thin, long and dangerously vivacious'), and *Les Sylphides* to the Palmers.

In the autumn of 1942 I went to stay at Mansfield Street for a few weeks. I had broken up my marriage and been in Dorset with Amanda nursing a desperately ill friend, earning my living by writing serial stories for the Amalgamated Press under a *nom de plume*. Soon after the friend died I was brought up to London in an ambulance with acute appendicitis which obliged me to send Amanda to a boarding school in Dorset before she was six. Since I had no home in London, Mother looked after me while I was recovering from this rather bad operation. I had heard how the bedroom floor at Mansfield Street had been turned into a flat; now I saw it for myself. Barbie's original bedroom in front had become the kitchen; the large night-nursery next door had been divided into three – a bathroom and two small bedrooms. Father's bedroom at the back had been enlarged by removing the partition which had formed a passage leading to the only bathroom, so that now that bathroom had become a private one opening out of the bedroom. Mother slept in the same room as Father in the other St Ursula bed. The two beds had been placed head to head along the wall which had been the back wall of the passage. Thus they slept in the same position as that in which they had sat on the beach at Scheveningen during their honeymoon, but now it was easier for them to communicate through the open wicker-work of the bed-heads than through the dense cane of the beach-chairs.[1]

The main bedroom had been turned into the living room of the flat. We had our meals in there on an antique oak, gate-legged table, the only piece of furniture from Father's first office in Gray's Inn Square. I occupied one of the new bedrooms while I was staying there, and the only maid, a tall, pleasant Scandinavian woman who happened to be a good cook, the other. Father was usually out to lunch, presumably at the Garrick. It was certainly warmer and cosier in this self-contained flat than it had ever been in the house before. Whether Father felt he had returned to the poverty of Thursley I do not know; it was not squalid. The fact that it was the war and not his own failure that had reduced him to such circumstances must, I feel, have made a difference to his apparently cheerful acceptance of them. And then it was a great happiness to him to find Mother so contented now that she had hardly any domestic responsibilities.

It was while I was staying at Mansfield Street that Father wrote his picture letter to Amanda about the Foxglove Hunt. I made suggestions for it and we had great fun with it together. During the few weeks I stayed there we became closer than we had ever been. When we happened to be alone one day he poured out to me all his bitterness against Mrs Besant. He put no blame at all on Krishna. Krishna once told me, 'Your father really liked me very much, and I liked him *tremendously*.' Father also revealed to me how much he had resented being made to insure his life at the time of his

[1] 13 Mansfield Street, which has a GLC plaque on the wall commemorating Lutyens's occupancy from 1919 to 1944, has belonged to the British Computer Society since 1978. The beautiful Adam mantelpiece in the front drawing-room, now the board-room, with a ram's head at each corner, was stolen in the course of redecoration. The bookcases Father designed have now been placed on either side of the fireplace.

marriage and what that extra £200 a year would have meant to him at the beginning. 'Then why did you make Anthony insure his?' I asked. 'Because *I* was made to,' he replied, perhaps reasonably.

Robert brought out a biographical monograph on Father in 1942.[1] I was still at Mansfield Street when the first copy arrived. There was one chapter entitled 'The Armature of Planes' which Father told me he could not understand a word of. All the same, I am sure he was touched by Robert's tribute to him, though perhaps even more embarrassed by it.

Father tried to give up smoking in the hope that it might relieve his cough; then in the spring of 1943 he began to cough up blood. His doctor (whose name I do not remember: Bruce Porter had retired by this time) insisted on an x-ray which revealed a slow-growing cancer of the bronchial tube. Father was not told of the diagnosis and never once asked what the result of the x-ray had been. Thankfully, no operation was suggested, nor any other form of drastic treatment.

He had less and less energy; the mechanism was slowly wearing down. His cough became very troublesome, especially at night, preventing him from sleeping. He attended the Hanging Committee at the RA in April 1943 and the RA Council meetings up till May that year. When he was too weak to stand at his drawing-board in his office at Mansfield Street he had a board made to go across his chair. He had never before sat down to work and did not like it.

Mother left him only once in 1943 to go in February to a nursing home in Newcastle for an abdominal operation which she feared might turn out to be cancer, but which proved benign. She had gone to Newcastle so as to be cared for by Ursula and in order not to worry Father. She did not tell him what she had suspected might be wrong with her until it was all safely over, a forebearance for which he expressed

[1] *Sir Edwin Lutyens. An Appreciation in Perspective* (Country Life).

320

his deep thankfulness. His last letters to her were written at this time. His writing, never very legible, was now almost indecipherable. Mother complained that she could read only one word in five. 'Can you hear my writing?' he asked with characteristic grace in one letter.

He could hardly speak above a whisper now. By November he was forced to take to his bed, his drawing-board on his lap. However, he insisted on getting up to attend a General Meeting and Assembly at the RA on 7 December. It was his last public appearance and a shock to those who had not seen him since May, so emaciated had he become. He told Ursula in a letter of 13 December, the last letter he ever wrote, how much he had enjoyed the occasion and seeing all his friends and colleagues again. 'It is an awful bore being in bed,' he continued. 'I am missing a great deal. I long for warmer weather, to give my cough a chance. If I was raised to the peerage I would call myself Lord Cough of Cough. I am tired of bed yet Mother will not let me get up.'

He had a day and night nurse now. He asked Miss Webb to bring up his Cathedral drawings and arrange them round the room so that he could study them. The detailed drawings had by this time been finished. His bed faced the door on to the landing whereas Mother's bed faced the bathroom door. He did not seem to know that the end was so near, although, according to Elisabeth, he told her, 'It is vewy, vewy hard to die.' Elisabeth, who was now living in Fitzroy Street with her second husband, Edward Clark, the conductor, saw a great deal of him. I, on the other hand, saw very little of him. I was working from ten in the morning till past midnight as barmaid-cum-librarian at the Churchill Club at Ashburnham House, Dean's Yard, Westminster, a club sponsored by Churchill for English-speaking members of the forces of all ranks of which Barbie was the chief organiser.

Just after Christmas Mother went down with a bad bout of influenza and was confined to bed in the small spare room.

Her last little note to him read, 'My darling, thanks to you I am having flu in great luxury with your nurses to attend to my wants. I have very little temperature – aches and pains better. Have a good night and meet me in dreamland.' Ursula had come down to see him which cheered him greatly, and Robert sat up with him the whole night of 31 December.

At the time of Barbara Webb's death he had written to Mother, '. . . when the time comes for us to part – silence – just silence – will be my medium of expression.' And so it was.

I had just arrived at the Churchill Club on the morning of 1 January 1944, when I had a telephone call to say that Father was dead. The news made little impact on me. The general horror of the war, the tragedies suffered by some of those very close to me and a bereavement of my own had left me numb at that time, but I wanted to get to Mother as quickly as possible. Since there were no taxis I took an 88 bus to Oxford Circus. Going up Whitehall, almost deserted, I quite unexpectedly found we were passing the Cenotaph. I was shattered. The aloof, lonely perfection of its beauty pierced me. I was brought back to sensation with an anguished regret that I had not loved Father enough, that I had so often gone against his wishes and done so little to bring him happiness. At the same time I felt a surge of enormous pride in him and in being his child and a kind of joy that the flood of love for him had come at last. Love is never too late. Since his death the love has grown. I know him now from his letters; I understand all he went through for us. I feel more and more my kinship with him.

The presence of the unanswerable mystery of death is always awe-inspiring and humbling. There is nothing the dead look like except dead. Father's familiar suits with their bulging pockets hanging in the cupboard had far more of him in them than the empty body in the St Ursula bed. I kissed the sleeve of one of his coats. It was warmer and more redolent of his essence than his forsaken forehead. I badly wanted something that had belonged to him. Going into the bathroom I took his razor – an ordinary old Gillette. It was a very personal memento and made me smile at the thought of how he had always shaved in the bath without a mirror.

Returning to the Churchill Club I passed the Cenotaph again. I can never pass it now without feeling he is there – it is his soul, the quintessence of his genius – as much a memorial to him as to the dead of two wars – but above all a triumphant affirmation of the spirit of harmony which makes order out of the chaos of materialism. Perfect order is perfect well-being.

The Observer, 29 January 1928

THE ROBOTISM OF ARCHITECTURE

'Towards a New Architecture.' By Le Corbusier. Translated from the Thirteenth French Edition by Frederick Etchells. (Rodkar, 25s. net.) (By Sir Edwin Lutyens, R.A.)

This book takes you down a new channel of architectural adventure – not without the risks and perils, that all adventure pre-supposes; and Mr Etchells, in his preface, plays the part of able pilot.

M. le Corbusier's theme is that architecture of our time should have the qualities of the machine. Efficiency and mass production are the watchwords. Houses are to be like the products of Mr Woolworth's shops – stamped out or cast in moulds and sold, I suppose, in ratios of 3d. and 6d. For such houses, Nature will provide a new humanity. Robots without eyes – for eyes that have no vision cannot be educated to see. Man may be small, but he has two eyes and can focus distance, and thereby measure things. He can raise or depress his vision by the movement of his head, up, down, right or left, and with little exertion can reverse all these aspects. Mass production would destroy in man the sense of three-dimensional habitations. He would lose the pleasure of thick soft walls, dumb to noise, when compelled to live in stark noisy little boxes, where skilled plumbers take the place of house-proud maids.

* * *

Architecture, certainly, must have geometric constituents, but lines and diagrams, in two dimensions, are not enough. Architecture is a three-dimensioned art. To be a home, the house cannot be a machine. It must be passive not active, bringing peace to the fluctuation of the human mind from generation to generation. For what charm can a home possess that can never bear a worn threshold, the charred hearth and the rubbed corner?

Humanity remains and will remain, I trust, humane. It is more likely that we shall return to the gorilla than become Robots, compelled to live in small enamelled cages. Emotion will never be controlled by sparking plugs. The logic of a French mind may make a Corbusier house, or even a Versailles, but never a Hampton Court.

* * *

M. le Corbusier makes great play with airplanes, automobiles, and Atlantic liners, finding in them affinity to the Parthenon. They are excellent, thrilling things in themselves and may well serve as tonics; for it is to be regretted that ugliness in a building does not kill as quickly as does a fault in their design. Physical efficiency, however, is not the sole test of a building. Phrases such as that cannot master design, or teach it; and, generally, the more discursive the literature in which they are used, the less the achievement. It is amazing to-day to see the works in brick and stone which the great writer on beauty, John Ruskin, was able to perpetrate.

M. le Corbusier tries to drive home his argument from the machine by delightful photographs of grain elevators, which thrill the imagination. In the spaciousness of the prairie they may stand out as magnificent objects; but take one and place it in an English valley, larded with traditional building and no formula about efficiency, and the machine would allay the horror of its aspect.

*　　*　　*

Again, 'Architecture has nothing to do with styles.' Styles, however, are no lie if looked at fairly, as the recorded and oft ill-recorded experience of men's endeavours. Among the most beautiful inhabitants of the world in which we live, you might place trees, and among trees the beech. How comes the beech to be? Created out of itself by the blind energy of its sap – no two trees are alike – yet all are akin and true to style. One may not appreciate style, but the experience of 3,000 years of man's work – creative work – cannot be disregarded unless we are prepared for disaster. Again the plan regarded as a generator sounds very plausible – easily said and easily accepted – but it contains only one of the three essential dimensions. All are equally important and without any one of them the other two are moribund. In all successful architectural design you can draw no hard line. Each part is mother to the others, and the whole one a family of sweet intercourse and gentle behaviour.

*　　*　　*

In discussing the Parthenon – a pure creation of mind, of fair and fine minds in great intellectual honesty – M. le Corbusier is profoundly emotional. Greek work is really beyond all modern conception. It is as deep in its use of light as are Einstein's problems. The ellipse to the Greeks was as the circle is to us. Every stone of the Parthenon was individual and essential to the whole. No more than four stones were identical, and no joint was horizontal. Such was their standard of reverence for a building that had to be created, – a perfect unity, an entity, stable and endurable for eternity.

The Parthenon cost three times, and the gold and ivory statue of Athene seven times, the National Revenue. How is it possible to compare such a building with an aeroplane, which one faulty stay or bolt may crash to the ground?

* * *

The appreciation of Rome comes as a relief. The assertion, however, that the Romans knew nothing of the use of marble, sweeps away one's breath. Give them credit, at least, for using it as a most precious pigment. A City of Towers is suggested, and it is a terrifying suggestion. How soothing later on is the view of Versailles – a work of real genius. For though you may criticise it with stiff immovable neck, still, luckily, the human head can walk round and look up the avenues as well as down them. Pleasant, too, is the thought of Le Roi Soleil, on whose pillow, when in bed alone, all the axes of all the avenues terminate. The men who laboured and, I hope, enjoyed the creation, could say, 'It is not we who have to bear that load.' In the City of Towers, on the other hand, with its bus-ridden elevator-tired Robots, what similar pleasure can they have?

As one reads this book one is always amused, sometimes excited, sometimes angry, at the boil of M. le Corbusier's emotions, but one never doubts his sincerity. His final prophecy is Architecture or Revolution; and we might welcome it, if by Architecture he did not mean mass-made cages suitable for machine-made men. To avoid Revolution, great patience and long-suffering must be endured. To produce Architecture, it is the same. Sacrifice is essential and the worship of the absolute directed towards an inconceivable and ever-growing perfection.

328

Index

329

330

333